"*Seven Pathways* will impact the world in a similar way as Henry Blackaby's *Experiencing God*. Spending time with Seven Pathways and in silence before the Lord will deepen your faith and draw you closer to the Lord. Readers will enjoy the journey through the Seven Pathways."

— **DR. BILL TAYLOR,** former director of Sunday School for Lifeway Christian Resources, president of Unlimited Partnerships Inc. author of *21 Truths, Traditions & Trends*

"Increased intimacy with God is a goal most Christians desire, but in the busyness of modern life, with a host of distractions and responsibilities, many people are unable to find the time to take the task seriously. After a debilitating injury, the author chose to respond to pain and uncertainty by pouring herself into pursuing a relationship with God using the ancient practices of seven pathways as a model. In Seven Pathways, she applies and integrates this approach to a modern world, providing practical and duplicatable applications, which can be helpful to anyone."

— **GLENN R. KREIDER,** editor in chief of *Bibliotheca Sacra*, Professor of Theological Studies at Dallas Theological Seminary

"In *Seven Pathways*, Mary Carmen dips her pen into the deep well of her own pain and suffering to write a book of authentic hope, healing, and love–a book that will lift you up, encourage your heart, ease your troubled soul, and provide a pathway (seven, in fact) to the throne of grace. Steeped in biblical, historical, and contemporary medical and psychological research, *Seven Pathways* offers reliable and practical guidelines to overcoming the oppressive effects of debilitating pain, be they physical, psychological, spiritual, or emotional."

— **REG GRANT,** ThD, chair and senior professor for Department of Media Arts and Worship at Dallas Theological Seminary

"This book offers an honest and refreshing account of trusting God through a difficult season."

– **MEGAN ALEXANDER,** *Inside Edition* and *Small Town Christmas* Host

"First, a WARNING! This book is way more than you think it is, and it will require way more of you than you may be willing to do. Now a PROMISE. If you walk the path Mary Carmen has laid out, your experience of and intimacy with God will deepen in ways you could not imagine. Her insights are hard earned and thoroughly biblical."

—**LLOYD SHADRACH,** teaching pastor and co-founder of Fellowship Bible Church in Brentwood, TN

"Out of her own pain-filled struggles, Mary Carmen Englert invites us on a journey to peace with God. She encourages us to walk with her to discover and rediscover through Scripture the healing grace of God the Father through Jesus Christ. Through simple spiritual disciplines, she beckons us to a deeper life of meaningfulness and joy."

—**DR. J. SCOTT HORRELL,** retired senior professor of Theological Studies at Dallas Theological Seminary

"Biblically anchored, historically reliable, refreshingly transparent, and deeply practical, Mary Carmen's *Seven Pathways* will introduce you to Jesus if you have never met Him or it will reheat your walk with Christ if your love for Him has grown cold. The pathways have a purpose: to help you know God and devote your life completely to Him. In a day filled with chatter and confusion, Mary Carmen is a reliable guide ready to lead you to a place of rest and clarity through the implementation of the Seven Pathways. She is a practitioner who has not just taught on the pathways but has also lived them. Now, thankfully, she has shared her insights with us all. Read it and be blessed!"

– **BARRY CHESNEY,** PhD, discipleship pastor at Valleydale Church in Birmingham, AL

"Indispensable! If you're seeking a book that will draw your heart to God through spiritual disciplines, look no further than *Seven Pathways*. Drawing from her own personal experiences with suffering, Mary Carmen offers a refreshingly simple yet profound approach to connecting with God. She provides readers with practical tools and theological insights to help them experience God's presence and truth, no matter what they are facing in life. I highly recommend it to anyone seeking to grow in their faith and develop a closer relationship with Christ."

– **CHAD KECK,** PhD, senior pastor at First Baptist Church Kettering, OH

"This book is life-changing! For those of us who are suffering and looking for answers, Mary Carmen Englert beautifully shares her personal journey and how she has come to a place of true healing. Whether you are going through trials or not, you will not be able to put this book down as you read and re-read through the pathways to make them a part of your life. Mary Carmen has not wasted her suffering but has chosen to rise above it by implementing these tested truths into her own life and allow the great Physician to begin healing her from within. She shares them with us in this wonderful book of wisdom and knowledge, history and theology, scripture and prayers, testimony and stories, practical advice and encouragement, and so much more. Be ready to be blessed and walk closer with the loving God who heals and restores."

– **MORROW LOTZ REITMEIER,** Baylor University friend, AnGeL Ministries volunteer, Bible study discipler, and marriage mentor

SEVEN PATHWAYS

ANCIENT PRACTICES FOR A DEEPER RELATIONSHIP WITH GOD

Mary Carmen Englert

Seven Pathways: Ancient Practices for a Deeper Relationship with God

Published by Forefront Books.
Distributed by Simon & Schuster.

Library of Congress Control Number: 2023906960

Print ISBN: 978-1-63763-158-4
E-book ISBN: 978-1-63763-159-1

Cover Design by Bruce Gore, Gore Studio, Inc.
Interior Design by Bill Kersey, KerseyGraphics

To my mom, Sandra Hutts

You continue to teach and amaze me with your selfless love, enduring strength, and wisdom. Thank you for your love and all the unseen sacrifice and faithful prayer covering me and for believing in me and Seven Pathways. *I received the best gift from God when He chose you as my mother, and I pray that I carry on your legacy of love, faithfulness, and strength.*

I love you.

Contents

Introduction

While the Bible has sold over five billion copies worldwide and over three-quarters of American households own one, many Christians, both those raised in the church and those new to the faith, don't understand what it says. Worse, many overlook the Bible's primary value as a means to developing a meaningful relationship with God. Our Bibles sit neatly stacked among other books or positioned as a decorative accent in our homes, more often treated as a piece of furniture than as a central pathway to the knowledge of God.

At the same time, a rising level of noise clutters our soundscape. We have become enculturated by the well-tuned societal message that there are no absolute truths or values, and we are free to determine right and wrong for ourselves.

The result is a basic inconsistency in our existence as human beings. On one hand, the culture says do what makes you happy, live how you want, and believe how you want. On the other hand, most people sense that there is right and wrong, and they experience the inconsistency of this philosophy in their everyday lives. For example, in a friendship, if you always do what is best for you, then you will often lose that friendship. There are certain values or beliefs that are foundational to a friendship. Yet the culture tells us that finding and practicing our own truths is the key to a fulfilled life.

I'm convinced that most people are aware of this disconnect at a deep, spiritual level. They sense that there is a God with His own values and worldview. In the calm of the night, when the noisy soundscape quells, we lie in our beds and reach out to the God we know is there. And when we go through a difficult time or someone whom we love is gravely ill, we instinctively pray. Even if they are not convinced the Bible is true, most people believe in God and desire to have a relationship with Him.

That was certainly true for me.

On a cold winter night in February 2018, I fell into the doorframe of my car, hitting the top of my head. Having lived in New York City for many years, I had bumped my forehead a few times getting in or out of a taxi and never gave it a second thought. This time was different.

Shortly after my injury, I developed pain throughout my head and neck, so much so that it was difficult to lie flat on my bed. I slept on an incline for months. My scalp became so sensitive to the lightest touch. Even washing my hair hurt. Then an allergic reaction set back my progress and exacerbated the pain in my head and neck. It was like having a bad sunburn that would not go away. The simplest of things, brushing my teeth and hair, blowing my nose, and touching my face hurt.

Unfortunately, the dosage of steroids prescribed to treat my allergic reaction over a short period of time left me with many side effects, including swelling of legs and ankles, stomach pain, rapid weight loss and related digestive issues, and an increased speed and sensation of running nerves in my head and in my back. All the steroids weakened my muscles to the degree that it hurt to bend, and I could no longer sit up straight on the floor. My clear skin was wrought with steroid acne for months. Previous to this injury, exercise was a part of my lifestyle for over twenty years, during which I had engaged in regular cardio workouts and weight training and did not suffer from any chronic form of pain. But the side effects of the steroids caused my heart to race daily for months, and then thankfully that ended. The steroids messed up my normal sleep patterns as I had always been a good sleeper throughout the night. Now, I was waking up about every hour and a half; I would get hot suddenly, start sweating, and then go back to sleep. After being awake for only four to five hours, I was still exhausted. Consequently, I struggled with chronic fatigue for months.

My skin became hypersensitive to heat and cold. One night I tried to remove a pan of baked potatoes from the oven. Though wearing an oven mitt, my fingers felt as if they were on fire. I threw the pan to the floor and searched the mitt for a hole, but there was none. Thankfully, that sensitivity to heat and cold has diminished completely over time.

By October of 2019, my pain was still increasing. And despite having seen over ten doctors, I still had no clear diagnosis or treatment plan. I was beyond discouraged with the local health care community and frustrated because I was doing everything that I knew to do to improve my health. In addition to consulting doctors, I was seeking God for help, filling my mind with His truth through the Bible, listening to biblical messages, and engaging in worship. I also sought natural healing by prioritizing sleep, eating healthful foods, lowering stress, exercising, and using holistic treatments such as craniosacral therapy and acupuncture.

It would have been easy to be mad at God for taking my "normal" life away, allowing this pain, for putting me in a situation of constant struggle to find a clear diagnosis while hitting one wall after another as doctors threw pills at me without result. I felt as if I were fighting for my life. It had been twenty-one months of feeling as if God was not hearing or answering my prayer for a clear diagnosis and healing. I felt as though my prayers never got past the ceiling, and I simply couldn't understand why God would allow things to get worse rather than better.

Yet instead of turning away from God, I chose to throw myself deeper into pursuing a relationship with him. My mom and I prayed together every night, including a specific request that God would be my primary care physician. I was convinced that God would not have allowed me to endure this trial for no purpose. After twenty-one long months, I finally started praying daily again, with a greater level of commitment, fervency, and honesty. I was now in a posture of humility and willingness to listen. I desired the presence and voice of God more than anything.

It was at this point that the Seven Pathways became a consistent part of my daily morning routine. God started waking me up each morning with songs in my head, such as hymns like "Great Is Thy Faithfulness," "Amazing Grace," and "Standing on the Promises." And He started speaking to me through dreams. Even after sleeping eight to ten hours, which was interrupted by nerve pain, I was still exhausted, and the medication I took for that pain made me groggy in the mornings.

Yet each morning, while the room was still dark, I slowly walked to the chair in my bedroom, eyes half closed, and nestled into a blanket to start my day with God. I began by focusing on five things that I was thankful for. There was so much that I could not do, and I knew I would soon be reminded of my limitations and pain, yet God was teaching me that there was still a lot that I could do. I just needed to alter my pace and priorities in this season.

I started improving during 2020, after a procedure to help my bilateral occipital neuralgia which was the diagnosis for the head and neck pain. Still, it was very slow progress as I had significant muscle weakness and a persistent frozenness in my shoulder and part of my back. I had also lost weight so that my clothes just hung on me. I have always been tall and boney, but not like that. I was still not wearing makeup in order to reduce facial pain, and I had quit highlighting my hair due to the sensitivity of my scalp. It was humbling to be unable to engage in the beauty routines I'd come to associate with looking "normal."

With each year I made significant progress and by 2022 I reached about 90% in my healing journey, with all the prior side effects resolved except for some head and neck pain. Thankfully, my head no longer was sensitive to washing it or touch nor my skin to heat, and I was sleeping normally. My mobility has been restored throughout my body, though I still have not gotten all my muscular strength back. I work really hard each week in the gym and in God's gymnasium. I desire so much as I work and pray that after this suffering, God will restore me and make me strong, firm, and steadfast again according to 1 Peter 5:10. During the research into my condition and the research for this book, after a CT, MRI, and biopsy, I was diagnosed with a lower-grade tumor in my right parotid gland. So, it appears that this tumor might be the culprit of a great deal of my pain, as the doctors have explained that many nerves run through the parotid. I am still on my healing journey and have entered another chapter as I will have surgery very soon and while working to bring this book into the world.

Prior to these health conditions, I had begun writing a book, which was about 75 percent complete. Now, having neither the energy nor the ability to complete the book, I felt like God was telling me to pray through that pain, loss, and sadness and practice thankfulness and contentment. That practice of gratitude uprooted the seeds of anger and bitterness that had begun taking root in my heart. I grew in contentment through my pain by focusing less on what I could not do, all the things that had been taken from me, and shifting my focus to the blessings that I still had. I concentrated on what I could do, then narrowed in on a few things that God helped me to see that I could do well, even during this time of limitation.

Two things that I could do well were to be silent and pray. Since I had a lot of pain around my ears, it was difficult to wear my glasses. So I started listening to a chapter of the Bible every day. I would pray for my needs, then I would quickly get busy praying for immediate family, extended family, friends, and other needs in the community and beyond. I experienced joy in praying for others and felt that I was accomplishing something by helping to move God's plans forward in their lives through prayer. Then I started walking outside every day unless the weather prohibited it. These walks soon became prayer walks on some days. As my list of people and needs grew, God nudged me to create a plan for praying for family, friends, and community and beyond and then to create a method of growing deeper in my relationship with Him through the seven pathways: thanksgiving, silence, confession, song, prayer, Bible study, and scripture meditation. Through this book you will understand the historical, theological, and spiritual significance and meaning of these pathways, so that you will be inspired to apply these practices in your spiritual life through our disciplined approach in our Seven Pathways Journeys through a book of the Bible.

This prayer journey began for me with listing five things that I am thankful for, even simple things, and for who He is and His goodness to me. Then I would celebrate the small steps I'd made and the difference I'd seen in myself, rather than focusing on how far I still had to go for a full recovery. Taking small steps in the right direction with the Lord will take you a long way toward where you want to go.

Second, instead of avoiding silence by staying busy or remaining distracted by the siren call of our consumer culture, I embraced the invitation to retreat with God through quieting my surroundings and self, then opening myself to listen for the voice of God and to focus on Him. While many of my nights remained restless, my weary soul found a place to sink into God's silent rest. I found soul rest in Him through this regular rhythm of spending time with God.

Third, I purposely shut out the noise in the inner chamber of my heart through confession. Through confession, I unpacked my sins before God. God did not use a judgmental tone with me. Instead, a compassionate and loving presence embraced me. Confession cast off the weight of my sin and freed me from guilt and its nagging reminders. This brought forgiveness and freedom. Also, confessing who God is and acknowledging His promises in a difficult time helped me to not stress out as much about my circumstances, uncertainty about my recovery journey, and the length of time it had taken. Confession grounded me in trusting that God was with me and that He would see me through and give me the endurance I needed.

Fourth, each morning, as I awoke to worship music then later listened to a song as the fourth pathway, music reset my mind, causing my first thoughts to focus on God's love, goodness, and forgiveness rather than on my circumstances and pain. This realigned my perspective so I could see my circumstances through a God lens. Other times, a song expressed what my heart longed to say or had experienced but couldn't find the right words to say.

I sang other songs as anthems of hope, infusing me with strength and joy.

Fifth, following the prayer pathway I mentioned increased my faith and joy, even in my very difficult situation, gave me endurance, and reordered my priorities. Prayer is where we develop the relationship with God that we are made for.

Sixth, after listening and meditating on a few books of the Bible, God nudged me to go back to a study on the book of John, using spiritual disciplines that I had started writing in 2005. I had taught the Pathways, as I was beginning to call them, as a weekend seminar at my church over fifteen years ago. But now, I was going to go through them for myself for each of the twenty-one chapters in John. I told God that this was not the right time, and I did not feel well enough to undertake this project. How could I begin such a large endeavor when I was still exhausted every day and experiencing a lot of pain? He reassured me that He would give me small steps and show me the way. He also made it clear that His plan was for me to write when I was not healthy, and He would bring me back to better health by doing so.

Following His guidance, I started each part of the Bible study experience of Seven Pathways by listening to a chapter of John, and then God would guide me to complete one of the seven sections for that chapter. The next day, I listened to the following chapter and completed the same section for that chapter. After cycling through all twenty-one chapters, I would listen to each chapter again and complete one more of its seven sections. Finally, I would meditate on and try to memorize a couple of Scriptures a week. God used those verses to encourage me and ground me with strength and give me hope. I wanted to become better at memorizing Scripture and build upon the practice I'd learned in college. I wrote Bible verses on index cards and worked on memorizing them during my morning routine. While in college,

I also mixed them in with French flash cards I was studying at the time. Through this practice of meditating on and memorizing Scripture, God began to bring to mind Scriptures, especially in the morning as I would awaken to a Scripture or song in my mind.

Starting my day with the Seven Pathways journey has helped me chart a course back to better health, has deepened my relationship with God, and has brought joy and peace during an arduous and exhausting recovery. My prayer is that God will use these Pathways in the same way in your life, restoring you both physically and spiritually. The Seven Pathways guided journey through Scripture is based on seven ancient biblical practices of thanksgiving, silence, confession, song, prayer, Scripture study, and Scripture meditation. Jesus is the way to God. These practices are not a substitute for Christ and His atoning work on our behalf. Instead, the Pathways are simple practices that will deepen your relationship with God, help you grow in faith, and enable you to experience God's presence. The Bible can be a difficult book to read and to understand. Think of Seven Pathways like a guide or mentor that is by your side, guiding your time with God as you journey through different books of the Bible.

Our goal is to help you create a rhythm or cadence in spending time with God through the Seven Pathways so that you will grow in your relationship with God and experience His presence, love, peace, and hope.

The Seven Pathways are not a checklist to complete. Think of each of the seven pathways as points on a journey. You can stay at each one for as long as you need to. Stop, rest, and feast in each one.

Life can become very busy, and the distractions and daily commitments can crowd out time with God. For me, it was not a deliberate decision to spend less time with God or skip my daily time with Him. I simply became so caught up in the busyness of life and felt like I had things under control that the most crucial relationship in my life began to slip away. That happens much easier and faster than we realize. That's why I'm here to help you, as a mentor, by giving you a plan that has been successful in restoring and deepening my own relationship with God.

As we spend time with God through Scripture, we learn more about Him and how He works in the world, and it teaches us how to live. This helps us become more deeply devoted followers of Jesus, helping us to discern His voice in our own lives.

The goal here is to start taking these little steps with God and stop focusing on where you have been or how far you have to go. I have learned to be patient with myself and see how the little steps with God have taken me far and to celebrate the small victories. Your past, shortcomings, insecurities, physical pain or limitations, or less-than-ideal circumstances are not an impediment to developing a relationship with God or God working through you. They are a platform for God to build upon. God did not give you someone else's story; He gave you your story. We don't want you to miss out on the most important relationship that you will ever have: a relationship with God. And we want you to experience the home that your heart has longed for, in God's hands, along with peace and joy in a relationship with Him, allowing Him to transform your days and nights.

Sometimes the most difficult circumstances can open your heart and unfold into a far greater experience of God's presence and restore vision and vigor into your God-given purpose in this world and restore your relationships. Though this journey I have been badly bruised and climbed mountains with cuts and then failing some spiritually speaking while developing spiritual muscles and endurance. Then I have enjoyed beautiful moments wrapped in His loving arms and covered like a Father who tucks His child into bed at night. I do all of this because I love God and have Him right by my side and His Spirit living in me. And because I want all of you to perhaps not have to go through some of the suffering that I have endured by looking for early warning signs of a tumor or suffering through many misdiagnoses like me. Jesus says that we will suffer in this world, so it cannot be avoided at times. But the good news is that suffering draws you near to God unlike other times if you will allow it because God is close to those in need and knows how to comfort, and He promises that He will work all things together for good. God never wastes a hurt. All the while during pain and working on my recovery, God has brought such peace, hope, and enjoyment through Seven Pathways. He slowed down my life to restore me both on the inside and out, and I want that for each one of you.

This book is for you to not give up because God has not given up on you. I want you to experience the same loving God and the nearness of God in which you will make life-changing memories with Him as I did. You are loved as you are. Be assured just as spring comes dancing across the landscapes after winter, spring will come for you too.

PATHWAY 1

Thankfulness

"Thankful heart is not only the greatest virtue, but the parent of all the other virtues."

—Cicero[1]

The greatest obstacles to thankfulness are the feelings of deprivation and envy fueling greed, resentment, and regret. With each scroll through our emails or social media, we are constantly bombarded with images, fueling the comparison culture and noisy siren call of consumerism saying that you are entitled to more, and more is better, which deaden our eyes and ears to thanksgiving. One year, after the new year, my pastor, Tim Keller, started a sermon series on the seven deadly sins. My first thought was I do not struggle with gluttony, and then after listening and chewing on his sermon on gluttony, I looked around my apartment, my closet, and then and at myself in the mirror with new eyes. I saw all the beautiful colors and styles of dresses in my closet and the beautiful bed draped in nice linens, and I decided during this season of lent that I would fast from shopping for myself for thirty days, unless it was for essential goods such as food or things necessary for daily life. Instead, when tempted to buy a new blouse or jeans staring at me as I walked down my neighborhood streets in NYC, I shopped in my closet. I had my best friend hold me accountable. We also scheduled a weekly call to pray. I was teaching second grade at that time, so there were many needs all around me. Instead of buying a new item, which I did not need, I focused more attention on buying resources to improve my students' experience in our classroom.

I so enjoyed the fast that I extended the time frame to one hundred-one days. I had never thought of myself as gluttonous before, but I realized through my fast that most people have an underlying condition of gluttony, and I was not exempt. Our culture is training us to feel deprived so that we will consume more, and then before we know it, we have developed the mindset of entitlement and a gluttonous and selfish lifestyle. This fast from shopping curated thankfulness and retrained my eyes to see bounty instead of lack. It also increased my thankfulness for

God's goodness and made me realize that what I have is a gift, and my job is to be a good steward of that gift. I am cultivating a more giving heart so I can share rather than consume. A giving heart is full, whereas a gluttonous heart is always running on empty.

In a culture that promotes entitlement and the idea that more is better, have we forgotten the gift of gratitude? From a young age, you can probably remember a time at Christmas when your mom nudged you to say thank you for an unwanted gift from a relative. For many, gratitude feels like a response of appreciation or an acknowledgement, an obligation, a tribute, or a kind, mannerly response, but not like a core attitude or attribute of Christians. According to modern, Western tradition, the dominant perception of thanksgiving is based on the emotional need to repay or acknowledge the gift or debt in order to maintain balance in a relationship. According to this model, thankfulness is reduced to a level of etiquette and removed from its prominence in Christian theology and social ethics. Christians might be described as faithful, loving, generous, hopeful, and obedient. But what if we gave thankfulness back its weightiness in Christianity? Could a hallmark of Christians be that they are thankful people? What if Christians were known for their gratitude?

Thankfulness is the first of our seven pathways to a deeper relationship with God. As you learn to practice this vital spiritual discipline, you will begin to let go of selfishness, which always manifests itself in ingratitude. You'll begin to see God's character more fully and love him more deeply. You'll be filled with gratitude, and you'll be happier.

In this chapter, you will learn what thankfulness is and why it matters so much to your spiritual life. You'll also see how Christians lost sight of this basic biblical virtue over time. Finally, you'll learn how to be thankful every day, even amid painful and unwanted circumstances.

What is Thankfulness?

Martin Luther considered thankfulness, or gratitude, as the most basic of Christian attitudes.[2] It is a right and natural response for a people who have been given so much by their gracious, loving God. While the term *gratitude* derives from the Latin *gratus*, which refers to a state of finding something pleasing, *thank* is a term whose first recorded usage was around AD 900. The word *thank* is originally rooted in *þancian* in Old English ("to recompense or reward") and is related to the modern word *think*.[3] To thank someone is to recognize thoughtfulness and reward it with recognition. In the Old Testament, *al-todah*,[4] "thankfulness," is not an equivalent of thanks between people for doing a favor or for helping them out with something, such as "Hey, thanks for doing that" or "Thanks a million." Instead, *al-todah*, thanksgiving, involves:

- Praise (from the root *yadah*,[5] which means "praise" in Hebrew) . . .
    - a. for the works of humans (Gen. 49:8; Ps. 45:17)
    - b. to God (Gen. 29:35; Ps. 7:17; 9:2;28:7; 30:12; Isa. 12:1)
- Expression of thankfulness for the actions of God (Lev. 22:29)
- Confession of sin (from the root, *yadah*, meaning "praise") (Lev. 5:5; 16:21; 26:40; Num. 5:7; Ps. 32:5; Prov. 28:13; Dan. 9:20)
- (Most often) a public declaration of the character and work of God (Ps. 107:22; 116:17)
- An act of remembering God's goodness and blessings (Deut. 8:11–17; Ps. 103:2)

When the verb, *todah*, "to thank," is used in the Old Testament, it is in reference to a sacrifice (2 Chron. 29:31; 33:16; Jer. 17:26;

33:11; Amos 4:5) or a sacrificial meal (Lev. 7:12–13; 22:29) or used in a musical context of praising God for who He is and what He has done (2 Chron. 29:31; Neh. 12:27; Ps. 42:5; 69:31; 95:2; 100:1, 4; 147:7; Isa. 51:3; Jer. 30:19; Jon. 2:10).

In the New Testament, the verb *eucharisteo*,[6] meaning to show thanksgiving for blessings to someone or God, is used thirty-eight times. For the Christian, in relation to God, the practice of thankfulness is the recognition of God's specific deeds, actions, and benevolence and the recompense with recognition, both in one's own private discourse as well as in public or one's written or spoken words in private as well as in public. In the New Testament, thanksgiving is often expressed before a meal (e.g., Matt. 15:36; 26:27; Mark 8:6; 14:23; Luke 22:17, 19; John 6:11, 23; Acts 27:35; Rom. 14:6; 1 Cor. 11:24, and many others) and particularly before the Lord's Supper (1 Cor. 10:16). "Thank you" is more than speaking the words. To say, "thank you," is an action of recalling, recognizing, or declaring God's goodness in your life in the past or present and a redirection of focus from self to God; it also cultivates humility. A general praise first awakens and prompts thankfulness. So the cliché, call-and-response phrase, "God is good all the time, and all the time God is good!" is not an act of thankfulness per se, though it may be one of praise. Instead, thankfulness is a core attitude or attribute prompted by recalling specific or ongoing action considered to be thoughtful and worthy of recognition. To briefly summarize, *praise* is a recognition of God's greatness, power, sovereignty, etc.; *thankfulness* is the condition produced by recalling how God's greatness, power, sovereignty, etc., has benefited us.

Benefits of Gratitude

Gratitude is a Christian virtue, first and foremost. It's also a key spiritual discipline, a pathway to experiencing a deeper relationship with God. Like most things that are good for you, gratitude provides a host of other benefits as well. In recent decades, positive psychologists have produced a mountain of research on the benefits of gratitude. Gratitude can make you happier and healthier, positively impacting emotional and psychological well-being, such as reducing envy, lessening depression, and offering greater life satisfaction. The following are just a few of the many scientifically valid studies proving the exceeding benefits of practicing gratitude for your health and overall well-being.

According to a Harvard Health article, two research studies, one of 8,000 people and another of 70,000 women, show that people who have a generally optimistic outlook on life have a 30% lower risk of developing heart disease, a 38% lower risk of heart attack, and a 39% lower risk of stroke. Additionally, among those who already possess cardiovascular disease, a thankful outlook is associated with lower risks of post-procedure hospitalizations.[7] Counting their blessings at least once decreased blood pressure and improved overall health. Two weeks of gratitude journaling before bed could make the difference between waking up exhausted and well-rested.[8] Gratitude journaling resulted in reduced depressive symptoms while continuing the practice of journaling.

Emmons and McCullough's groundbreaking research in 2003 was concerning gratitude theory and research and has inspired more work in this area.[9] Three research studies conducted to explore emotional and interpersonal benefits of gratitude resulted in the findings that practicing gratitude regularly has a significant impact on an individual's emotional, mental, and physical health. Celebrating the good in our lives instead of what is lacking or bad will expand our life satisfaction and enjoyment of life. Additionally, gratitude improves the quality of our relationships.[10] It also improves leadership skills and decision making.[11] Practicing gratitude regularly results in significant positives effects throughout every significant area of your life. With the positive benefits, practicing gratitude regularly is not merely something you should do, as your mother may have taught you. It's also a good life decision.

Given the obvious, proven benefits of having a grateful heart, it's surprising that we continue to cling to an attitude of entitlement, which produces precisely the opposite effect in our lives. The joy of gratitude and benefits of taking thankful actions are well known. So why do we continue to feel ungrateful? The answer has something to do with the development of the concept of gratitude over the last several centuries.

The Roots of Ingratitude

Based on all the overwhelming research of the positive effects of gratitude, you might be wondering how history has played a role in where we are today, with our culture of consumerism and our insatiable appetite for more. This chapter will explore the history of gratitude and will reveal significant theological and historical cultural views of gratitude and how those views normalized a flawed theory and practice of gratitude based on duty, which is still primarily practiced today.

Our research briefly traces the development of gratitude from the Greco-Roman culture, which was the cultural setting during the writing of the Bible, to the Renaissance, and then to the late modern history, from the mid-eighteenth century to contemporary culture. While many books prove how thankfulness is the right response to a gift or benefits received and the right response to the grace of God, I wholeheartedly agree and would encourage the reading of those works. The goal in this section is to give you a brief historical overview of the role of gratitude in social and political life during the first century and other subsequent periods.

Gratitude in the Ancient World

In the first century, the people of Rome and Greece were not without their flaws in their theory and practice of gratitude within their social and political lives. Regardless of the flaws, the role of gratitude as a foundation of society needs not be demoted to a social etiquette. Studying the erosion of gratitude in culture paints the picture of how we got to today's culture of entitlement and self-interest. For those of you who do not love history, stay with me, as I have tried to summarize a history of gratitude in socio-political life in the Greco-Roman era. This period is particularly important because it was the landscape culturally, intellectually, and politically in which Jesus taught, and His teachings were understood and applied within this cultural context. It also helps us see how distortions and erroneous teachings and applications of a biblical concept such as thankfulness create bad soil for other erroneous or incorrect teachings, which propagate in culture before eventually becoming a cultural norm.

Greco-Roman society was structured in hierarchical relationships that provided the foundation for social roles and identities. The Greek and Roman patron-client socioeconomic hierarchies shared many common elements, particularly how gratitude is at the center of sociopolitical ethics in both cultures. For our discussion, we will limit it to the common elements. The patron-client socioeconomic hierarchy was the basis of their societal structure. Reciprocity to patrons/benefactors was not merely a form of social etiquette but was an obligation. Within this patron/benefactor culture, when a patron acted generously toward a client, the client was expected to outwardly demonstrate thankfulness with an action not just with words. The failure to properly reciprocate was considered immoral and a sin, as it was a moral axiom for people in New Testament times. The Roman philosopher

Seneca (4 BC to AD 65) clearly illustrates this moral axiom as he denounces ingratitude with utmost severity:[12]

> There will always be killers, tyrants, thieves, adulterers, rapists, violators of religion, and traitors. But lower than all of these is the ungrateful man . . .
>
> Treat it as the greatest crime (De Beneficiis Ben1.10.4).
>
> Someone who fails to return a benefit makes a bigger mistake (Ben. 1.1.13).
>
> It is shameful, and everyone knows it, not to return the favor when benefits are conferred (Ben. 3.1.1).
>
> Ingratitude is something to be avoided in itself because there is nothing that so effectually disrupts and destroys the harmony of the human race as this vice (Ben. 4.18.1).

This economy of "gratitude" affected the fundamental existence of society transcending personal morality. Quite surprising is the absence of ethical focus in the Greco-Roman patronage system. The benefactor was concerned not about the sincerity of an individual's reciprocated gift but that the client fulfilled his duty with an appropriate gift based on the benefits received. In Peter J. Leithart's insightful book *Gratitude: An Intellectual History,* the author describes the image of gift giving as circular in ancient Greece and Rome with the exception of Athens's political system.[13] The proper response to receiving a gift was to reciprocate with a gift or favor. In this system, showing gratitude was not merely an expression of thankfulness for a gift or kindness. It was the repayment of a debt created by that benevolence. This foundational principle of "reciprocity" of the Greco-Roman patronage system is antithetical to the primary truths concerning God's grace in the Bible.

Jesus' Teachings on Gratitude

Jesus' teaching and Paul's heralding of Jesus' teaching contradicted the current sociopolitical ethics and cultural norms, shifting the focus from a balance of scales (or circular approach to gift giving) to a God-centered approach. They taught that God was the ultimate gift Giver and that His rightful place was at the center, and all thanks was owed to God. Choosing to follow Jesus' teaching collided with the current sociopolitical ethics and could afford consequences in the community.

In the culture of the New Testament world the words *charis* (grace) and *pistis* (faith) were not exclusively religious terms, as they are today, but they were socioeconomic terms referring to patron-client relationships. Patron-client relationships were the foundation of the economies of the ancient world. Patrons would bestow *charis* upon a client—providing him with the means by which to open a trade, establish the right social connections for his business, or be delivered from a dilemma. The natural response by the client to the *charis* of his patron was *pistis* (faith, or loyalty).[14]

Additionally, this system of indebtedness produced shame and an unhealthy relationship with humility. Feeling obligated to give a gift in return or grant special favors suppressed thankfulness and incited or provoked resentment. The client may be given the money to open a trade, such as a bakery, but he would need to provide the patron with baked goods upon his request. Also, he would not enter into a contract with another patron and honor this patron publicly for his acts of generosity. He was not to show ingratitude of any kind. This system of indebtedness influenced the inflated ego of patrons and was in some ways extraordinarily oppressive for clients who were funded by dishonest or greedy patrons.

In Ephesians 2, Paul uses the patron-client relationship to illustrate the relationship between God and humanity. This cultural analogy would be easily understood throughout the world at that time. Unlike the earthly patrons' gifts, God's grace was free: "For it is by grace you have been saved, through faith—and this is not from yourselves, it is the gift of God" (Eph. 2:8 NIV). For the Christian, joy, (*chara* in Greek) is a natural result of *charis*. Joy is the byproduct of grace. It is the response of the soul to the generosity of our patron—YHWH.

Christians were freed from owing favors or allegiances. This teaching collided with Roman society and business practices of giving gifts so that one might receive favors benefiting their business. Instead, Christians were to receive gifts and use those gifts for good, and they were also to give gifts freely without expecting anything in return. In 2 Corinthians 8:7, Paul reminds believers to excel in giving just as they are committed to loving, serving, and growing in the knowledge of the Lord and His will. Luke also exhorts this practice of generosity in chapter 8 of his gospel. The kind of giving that he is calling them to extend is to give to everyone without demanding or expecting any gifts or favors in return. And even if you were cheated out of something or it was deceitfully acquired, do not demand it back. Luke is highlighting the truth that everyone will give to someone who can pay them back, so according to the Bible giving goes beyond that to a requirement to give without expecting anything in return. Jesus' sacrificial death could only fulfill the requirements of a perfect and sinless sacrifice as payment for the sins of mankind. This same mercy we received, God calls us to give away. God will reward you for being merciful to the ungrateful (Luke 6:34–36).

Jesus paid the debt that you could never pay. This undeserved mercy merits a response of awe and wonder, but since our culture has hijacked our awe and wonder to scintillating entertainment through digital engagement, we need to redirect our attention toward God. His sacrificial death and resurrection for the payment of sin deserves our attention and infinite gratitude. This is incredible and fantastic! Thanksgiving will increase your experience of awe and wonder. Another way of saying it—your ability to experience the pleasure of knowing God, seeing how He works, and following His ways. Authentic gratitude cannot be legislated. Politically imposed, cultural gratitude is not the same as gospel-centered gratitude. Gratitude toward God's grace emits awe, wonder, and enjoyment. Grace will raise our internal thermometer of joy and lower the barometric pressure of guilt and shame and ego.

An overinflated ego creates a dungeon of selfishness darkened by ingratitude. "For ingratitude shuts the human spirit up in a world lightened only by the self, which is no light at all."[15] Whereas genuine gratitude naturally redirects focus from self and possesses a positive relationship with humility, the relationship between the two is likely reciprocal—humility cultivates a more grateful individual, while gratitude cultivates genuine and healthy humility.[16]

The Christian concept of thankfulness was a countercultural view in contrast to the cultural normative view of the Greco-Roman patronage system. Normalizing thankfulness as a dutiful response robs both parties, the patron and benefactor, of the power of gratitude to infuse joy to the giver and receiver and darkens the flame of Christian gratitude. Christianity teaches that Jesus paid a debt that you could never repay, thus freeing people from the obligations of duty imposed by this Greco-Roman system and other oppressive cultural systems throughout time. You can never do enough good things or pay Jesus back. The gift of grace frees all people from the oppressive burden of reciprocity imposed by culture and cultivates humility in both the giver and receiver. Thankfulness cultivates humility, and humility pries open the dungeon of selfishness darkened by ingratitude.

Gratitude through the Renaissance

The revolutionary changes in economic, social, and political life in the sixteenth and seventeenth centuries disrupted the Greco-Roman (classical antiquity or ancient) and medieval economies of gratitude, which taught that ingratitude was socially destructive. During the Renaissance, some writers renounced the uprising of a new system of the modern political economy and new modern theories of individualism. The politics of gratitude inspired William Shakespeare's plays in the wake of a new world order, or the feudal system. The political and cultural dimensions of gratitude and the monstrosity of ingratitude are central to his play *Coriolanus*, a tragedy set in ancient Roman times. Instead of remembering the prosperity due to the contributions of Martius (later called Coriolanus) as a military leader, the people call for his banishment from Rome and reject his campaign for the consulate. Rather than expressing thanks, they express hatred. Cornelius's outrage to their ingratitude leads to his demise as his ingratitude embitters him in revenge toward Rome. Accordingly, ingratitude is monstrous, and to exhibit ingratitude dehumanizes all participants.[17] Since gratitude was a central sociopolitical ethic, ingratitude was an abomination toward humanity and was considered inhuman. The character of Cornelius foreshadows the modern era's rise of individualism and the self-made man. Overall, the play depicts the evils of collective and individual ingratitude.

In the sixteenth and seventeenth centuries, the pillar of gratitude in European society, politics, and the church disrupted the rise of cities and a monetary economy based on social contracts. The culture no longer depended on the former terms of a gift economy to determine economic life but instead relied on social contracts. Michel de Montaigne, notable philosopher of the French Renaissance, Europe's first "individualist" and propagator of individualism, taught that men should "live by law and authority, not by reward and grace."[18] This individualism is not the sort characterizing modern society, as this individualism of the seventeenth century was based on the theology and teachings of the Bible, which show that duty and faith are owed to God alone. However, as society extrapolated or extricated the Bible and God from public life and relegated it to the private sphere, a new view of individualism emerged as the "autonomous self" during the Enlightenment and, with it, the shift from a collectivistic culture of Christianity toward an individualistic culture. The role of justice in society, without which a society could not continue, arises and distinguishes gratitude as adjunct and not primary to the foundations of society. Like the Reformation before, the English Civil War assaulted the pillars of social and political life, and Parliament and a group of egalitarian intellectuals questioned the foundational values of debt and gratitude and eliminated gratitude from the political order. The emergence of the distinctive "private" and "political" life fueled the advancement of the Enlightenment philosophy of individualism.

Gratitude in the Age of Reason

Due to the injustice and overreaching demands of the former patron-client economy, the people living during the next age were open to the new science of politics, proposed by English philosophers Thomas Hobbes and John Locke, which sharply deviated from past methodologies. Both Hobbes and Locke taught that individuals are autonomous and not dependent on anyone. Hobbes diverted most radically from classical and medieval thoughts in social and political theory with his beliefs that political order does not derive from God. According to Hobbes, natural laws govern human nature and political life, and his view of human nature was that people are chiefly driven by self-interest and a desire for power. For him, the greatest good was self-preservation.[19] This driving force of humanity's self-preservation influenced his view of his fourth law of nature. He explained that humans do not give freely but always expect something in return. If humans respond with ingratitude to the givers, then this sort of linear giving will have a negative effect on society, because the patrons might be reluctant with their generosity or will stop giving, which in turn, will hurt society. In this way, ingratitude is determinantal to the flourishing of society. The nuance in Hobbes's teaching is that gratitude is not owed to another person or to God, but that gratitude, according to natural laws, is the right response to political order based on the political hierarchy. Whereas Shakespeare viewed ingratitude as "inhuman," Hobbes viewed ingratitude as contrary to self-interest and destructive to the growth and prosperity of society. However, he did believe that men could act for the good of others and society at the same time, which meant that self-interest and multi-beneficial interests could be drivers in human nature.[20]

In his book *Elements of the Law*, Hobbes offers a biblical basis for gratitude, which is set on loving God and loving our neighbors as ourselves. Love is also equated with obedience. In his discourse on gratitude, Hobbes removes God as Creator and humans' response of gratitude to God as their Creator from his principals of human nature. Therefore, God's power is elevated above his other attributes, and man should relate to God first as a subject instead of the biblical view of man relating to God as the Creator and mankind His children, which evokes a response of love and gratitude. Humans love others and do good to others, not out of a response of gratitude for God's love and grace but based on duty as citizens of society and duty to the laws of nature.[21]

Like Hobbes, John Locke removed gratitude from political order, which is in contrast to his earlier writings that centered on the obligations and benefits of gratitude to public life and on gratitude being the duty of grateful citizens.[22] In his personal life, he acknowledged his gratitude to his benefactors, his debts to his patrons, and his gratitude toward his family. The obligations of gratitude in family relationships, which he based on contractual theory, operated outside the realm of political jurisdictions. The giving or receiving of gifts in friendship or among family was considered a private affair and outside of the market economy. Another way of saying the underlying faulty business principle still held today is, "It's not personal; it's strictly business." This popular mythology of the marketplace and political economy, which is free of the constraints and obligations of gratitude, still pervades liberal theory, that is, until another scandal breaks or undeserved favor is exposed. According to Locke, political authority is concerned with maintaining and upholding justice, not charity. As altruistic as his theory of charity and justice was, many wealthy people gave gifts for the purpose of receiving political loyalty and advancing their political power. His theory of social contracts leans toward benefiting the wealthy and has not proven beneficial to all segments of society. Locke's most notable accomplishment for the future of political theory was that he created a "private" social life distinct from the political sphere of "public" social life. A "gratitude-free politics" emerged as gratitude was no longer viewed a pillar of society but was becoming a moral sentiment or form of etiquette.

René Descartes, French philosopher and scientist, propagated the moralization of gratitude by categorizing it as a passion instead of a virtue. This was a departure from his predecessors Cicero and Aquinas and was revealed in his 1649 treatise "Les passions de l'ame."[23] In it he describes gratitude as a "kind of love," set in motion with the desire to reciprocate, and ingratitude as a vice. Descartes offers some helpful categories of three types of ungrateful people: the arrogant, the stupid (those not reflecting on the benefits they have received), and the vain. Descartes's most powerful and compelling contribution to the theory of gratitude was his concept of generosity. His conviction that one possesses nothing meant that people should use their resources for the good and flourishing of others and society.[24] The greatest soothing balm to anger is generosity, for a generous person finds satisfaction and enjoyment in giving, which in turn, curbs the arousal of jealousy or comparison.

Unlike Descartes, Jean Jacques Rousseau viewed reciprocating a gift or favors as a socially imposed duty that does not curb anger but incites it. For Rousseau, this emerging anger was not a result of human nature's corruption, an innate inner disposition, but came from social pressures and the conditioning of society. Rousseau believed that man was born good and had a natural disposition toward compassion that lessens love of self.[25] He also believed that giving gifts was a result of compassion, not duty. This empathy, or compassion, shaped self-love, which he believed made humans more moral and increased their empathy for those suffering pain; it also motivated generous actions. In part one of his Second Discourse, Rousseau defines self-love as it relates to self-preservation, stating that it is a desire to survive and live, and that self-worth inflames pride, envy, and greed, and encourages individuals toward self-centeredness. He explains that it is a result of rivalries, competition, and conflict within society and is not in one's inner being.[26] This view contrasts Hobbes's view of gratitude as one of the natural laws of society and Locke's filial bonds of gratitude. Rousseau believed that man was self-created and autonomous; therefore, the ethic of compassion is grounded in the conscience of all men where values or sentiments, his term employed, are formed. Quite different from the ethical subjectivism of our modern culture of anarchic emotive morality or moral relativism, his understanding of empathy or compassion was grounded in a universal belief that all humans possess a conscience. Unlike the view of Christianity that says that humans are born depraved with a propensity to corruption, self-centeredness, and greed, Rousseau's view says that humans are good with desires and thoughts to show compassion and give, but they are corrupted by their culture. His view of the abuse and burdensome weight of benevolence shut his heart to an intelligent and benevolent God, who is worthy of our grateful worship and who created the world and who set forth certain truths and values for mankind to follow for them to flourish.

Gratitude in Modern Times

Individualism rooted in Locke's philosophy continues to flourish as the modern era arises, and the role of gratitude becomes more individualistic and detached from all duty, even duty to God. Elevating the natural order and reason to the highest form of truth, from the influence of the Enlightenment, gave way to disillusionment, anger, and discontentment, eroding gratitude as a pillar of society. Our culture today is more self-absorbed than past generations were, and gratitude seems to have been lost along the way. Part of this is because of the affluence and abundance we enjoy compared to past generations. Today, a family doesn't have just one car, it often has one for each member of the family who is of driving age. Families often have separate bedrooms for each child, and each person has a closet full of clothes. Each of us has our own smart phone and possibly a TV in our room. It is difficult to be grateful when we are surrounded by an excess of things. This has fostered a sense of entitlement that past generations didn't have. The idea that one would have to work for these things is foreign to our thinking. Even the idea that respect must be earned seems foreign. Our culture tells us we are entitled, and it is not up to us to find our way.

Another significant factor is the increasing idea that there are no absolute values. In the past, it was taught that we should care about the needs of others and treat their needs as equal with our own. Today the focus is on us. Our needs and values trump the needs of others. Our own individual values and our desires replace any set of values passed down from past generations or even from the church. It is very hard to be grateful for anything when "it is all about us." However, in truth, we have much to be grateful for. We receive many significant gifts we don't even know about. Parents sacrifice and strive to give their kids things they did not have. They also protect their children from many of the harsh realities of life. Likewise, friends and even strangers often play important roles in our lives unbeknownst to us. And without question, Christ gave us the most important gift any of us could ever receive when He took our sins upon Himself and enabled us to have a relationship with God in this life and for all eternity. This continued erosion of gratitude has given way to our current cultural climate of entitlement and consumer culture of "more is better" and "buy now, pay later."

My Uninvited Friend

Lest it sounds as if I'm excluding myself from this culture of ingratitude and entitlement, let me say that I have experienced these same impulses. Learning thankfulness has been a journey for me, one that has sometimes been very painful. It began after I accidentally fell into the doorframe of my car with the top of my head, which triggered tenderness and pain in my head and a life-threatening allergic reaction, and then a diagnosis of low-grade tumor in my right parotid and surgery while editing this book, which you read about in the introduction.

In addition, I struggled with chronic pain in my head and neck. My upper back hurt to both the touch of a hand and the tufts of my mattress. I joke about it now, but I became a connoisseur of mattresses and toppers. I call that time "the year of the mattress." In my search for a diagnosis, during this dry, rocky plain of my life, several well-meaning doctors would say: "Just try this and see if it makes you feel better." It would have been easy to sink into the dry sands of disappointment, anger, and depression. I could see no paths in the desert. During this awful time, I turned to God, calling out to Him in prayer and reminding myself that God was my rock and deliverer: "I love you, LORD, my strength. The LORD is my rock, my fortress and my deliverer; my God is my rock, in whom I take refuge" (Ps. 18:1–2 NIV).

During this twenty-one-month medical nightmare, which included failed treatments by ten different doctors, I called out to God. I had been feeling drowned by the constant reminders of my limitations, my sadness, and my longings for the past, but He threw me a life preserver. I heard this gentle voice in my inner being saying, "Start your day focusing on five things that you are thankful for." Thankfulness saved my life.

Within the first few steps from my bed, I was reminded of my limitations. So I started each day before I even left my bedroom remembering things that I was thankful for. Once I started doing this, I realized that it was not hard to think of things. I started walking outside every day in the late afternoon, and I thanked God for the beautiful cloud formations, for the breezy days, and later for a couple of bunnies that I saw almost daily in the late spring through early summer of that year. The beauty and faithfulness of God's care over nature encouraged me during my daily walks and reminded me that my trust is not to be in the wisdom of man or any earthly means, but was to be in God. God's strength and power extended beyond chariots (see Ps. 20:7). Just as rain poured from heaven to preserve the health of trees, this same river from the waters of heaven, of God's faithfulness, would sustain my life and nourish me back to health.

> Your love, O LORD, reaches to the heavens, your faithfulness to the skies. Your righteousness is like the mighty mountains, your justice like the great deep. . . . Both high and low among men find refuge in the shadow of your wings. They feast on the abundance of your house; you give them drink from your river of delights. (Ps. 36:5–8 NIV 1984)

Life is given by God and is sustained by Him. For God is "the fountain of life; in your light we see" (Ps. 36:9 NIV). Jesus is the only one who could light my current path. By His light, I will see a path out, and by His light I will experience the enjoyment of His presence during this difficult season. God is also saying in verse 9 that both fullness and enjoyment of life are only found in Jesus. You can't have light without Jesus, who is the light.

I also thanked God for family and friends, who showed me love through delicious meals, cards, calls, and texts that came at just the right time. I spent many hours and days "holding up the chair" as my grandfather would have called it. The view from my chair inspired peace as I looked out upon the waters of the pool and at the patio that met up with a green lawn and cypress trees rising toward the open sky. My "peaceful" place served an advantageous environment for me to start hearing God's voice and spending quality time with Him the way that I had years before.

God started speaking to me in the daily things and offering advice, and I was now finally in a position to listen to Him, since I had stopped looking at social media, which was full of distractions and opportunities to see what I was missing. I had to get very real with God because I needed him in my real life. I still had far to go in my journey to healing, as I will describe in more detail. But in my journey to thankfulness, I had already taken great strides, even during this painful season.

Finding Gratitude in God's Nature

The first pathway to a deeper relationship with God is thanksgiving. This action of expressing five things of thanksgiving reset my mind each day focusing on gratitude for what I had instead of on what was lacking or my requests. Our default is to first focus on problems, limitations, and imperfections instead of seeing all the good things in our life and seeing God's goodness, even in the desert. Also, I simply needed the reminder that God is in the desert with me. Maybe you need that reminder today too. God is in the desert with you. God's waters of faithfulness and provision can make a river through the desert. Just as God parted the waters of the Red Sea, He can make a river flow in the desert season of your life. As I continued to practice thanksgiving first thing each morning, I started feeling stronger, and the desert did not seem so overwhelming because I remembered God was there with me. I felt grounded that God was with me in the desert and that He would lead me through. I received the hydration and strength that I needed through experiencing and recalling His goodness in creation and His provisions for my daily life.

Whatever season of life you may be in, or whatever circumstances you may face, you can find reasons to be thankful. The best place to start is where I did, with the character of God. Here are three attributes of God for which we can always be profoundly grateful. When you think there is no reason to be grateful, look here first.

His Abiding Presence

The first divine attribute for which we can always give thanks is God's abiding presence. Of His abiding presence in difficult times, Eugene Peterson speaks of God as the God "who stands, stoops, and stays."[27] Of this he notes,

> God stands—he is foundational and dependable; God stoops—he kneels to our level and meets us where we are; God stays—he sticks with us through hard times and good, sharing his life with us in grace and peace.[28]

Recalling how a compassionate, loving God stooped from heaven to take on human flesh and all the infirmities will steady the weight of the difficulties or pain and will lighten the load; it will also expand thankfulness in your heart. Since the distance between Jesus' life and our lives expands thousands of years, it can be helpful to connect with remembering an experience in your own life when someone stooped down beside you and stayed with you. You might recall a time when your mom or dad stooped down to pick you up after you fell or when they stooped down to clean your throw-up out of your hair as a child. Or it could be a more recent story when you were going through a hard time with your family or experiencing a health struggle, and this friend stood by you. Just as you find gratefulness in the embrace of a friend, Charles Spurgeon reminds us in an 1890 sermon entitled "The Tenderness of Jesus," we can find gratefulness in His arms:

> Jesus is touched, not with a feeling of your strength, but of your infirmity. Down here, poor, feeble nothings affect the heart of their great High Priest on high, who is crowned with glory and honor. As the mother feels with the weakness of her babe, so does Jesus feel with the poorest, saddest, and weakest of his chosen.[29]

Despite widespread success in a very effective public ministry, Spurgeon was quite open about his struggles with depression. In one sermon he was quoted as describing his depression accordingly:

> You may be surrounded with all the comforts of life and yet be in wretchedness more gloomy than death if the spirits are depressed. You may have no outward cause whatever for sorrow and yet if the mind is dejected, the brightest sunshine will not relieve your gloom. . . . There are times when all our evidences get clouded and all our joys are fled. Though we may still cling to the Cross, yet it is with a desperate grasp.[30]

Like many Christians today who struggle with depression, he was all too familiar with the cavalier dismissals of many other Christians that "good Christians" don't get depressed. Of this he stated that "God's people sometimes walk in darkness, and see no light. There are times when the best and brightest of saints have no joy."[31] When you can't see the light, remember that God stands by you.

His Covenantal Faithfulness

God's covenantal faithfulness is proof that God stands by you, and thanksgiving will flow from remembering God's covenantal faithfulness in your actions, such as expressions of thankfulness in your words or daily actions of following God's ways in your life or in the worship expression through participation in the Lord's Supper. An outward ritual for an offering required in the Old Testament for atonement is not what God requires when He speaks of a "thank offering" in Psalm 50:14 and Amos 4:5. Amos is perhaps rebuking the Israelites for their disobedience or generally rebuking their ritual offerings, which were inappropriate for a thank offering. The people in the Old Testament loved rituals in religion and often offered inappropriate gifts during their sacrificial rituals.

To thank God is to acknowledge your dependence on Him for everything in life, to pray to Him in times of need, and then to praise Him for who He is and His answer to your prayer. The premise of this covenantal relationship is that God is the Creator and Sustainer of all. Therefore, thanksgiving is expressed to God, and it is a declaration or confession of God's sovereignty and recounting of His goodness in the lives of men and the world. In thanksgiving, we also recount or recall His reign over all the earth in the past, present, and future. Psalm 96 says, "Ascribe to the LORD the glory due his name; . . . Say among the nations, 'The LORD reigns.' The world is firmly established, it cannot be moved; he will judge the people with equity" (vv. 8, 10 NIV).

When we acknowledge God's kingship and sovereignty as the Creator and Sustainer of the universe, then we understand He can only be faithful and good, and thanksgiving becomes a basis for trusting and obeying God in trials, suffering, pain, and uncertain times globally. So thanksgiving is a distinguishing mark of God's people and has theological, ethical, and social effects.

The most significant treatment of the relationship between thankfulness and remembrance in Scripture (apart from the institution of the Lord's Supper) is the warning of Moses to the people of Israel before they entered the promised land. The entire discourse throughout Deuteronomy provides valuable context. The setting of Deuteronomy covers Israel's preparation to cross over to the promised land. Moses leads the people through renewing their covenant with God, which encompasses the whole of the book.[32]

Unable to travel with them himself (see Num. 20), Moses charges the people to take extreme care to remember that it was YHWH who brought them into the promised land. He states,

> Take care lest you forget the LORD your God by not keeping his commandments and his rules and his statutes, which I command you today, lest, when you have eaten and are full and have built good houses and live in them, and when your herds and flocks multiply and your silver and gold is multiplied and all that you have is multiplied, then your heart be lifted up, and you forget the LORD your God . . . . Beware lest you say in your heart, "My power and the might of my hand have gotten me this wealth." (Deut. 8:11–14, 17 ESV)

Paul Barker points out that "remembrance is demonstrated in obedience."[33] Not only does a thankful heart remember good and exude joy, but a thankful heart is also prompted toward a devoted life of obedience to the Giver of blessings. Additionally in the ancient Near East, victory in conquest was thought to be a blessing of the gods conferred upon the conquering people for their righteousness. Moses warns Israel that nothing could be further from the truth and calls to their attention several examples of their sin. Instead, Israel's conquest and subsequent blessing of the land were signs of God's covenant faithfulness to His people and because of *His* righteousness.[34]

Thankfulness thus seems to be a key component in the economy of covenant faithfulness. It is the impetus that provokes us to remember (whether on no particular occasion or through rituals like Sunday worship, Sabbath, or the Eucharist) the blessing and faithfulness of God and to respond with the overflow of a devoted heart toward a life of discipline, obedience, and service by which we bless others because we have been blessed.

While the Lord's Supper celebrates the establishment of the new covenant, it also affirms God's commitment to His people. Paul's primary focus regarding thanksgiving is the redemptive work of Jesus. And Christ's redemptive act is the grounds for thanksgiving. Thankfulness is given to God for rescuing sinners "from the dominion of darkness" and bringing them "into the kingdom of the Son" (Col. 1:13–14 NIV). Paul instructs believers to offer thanks to God "in the name of our Lord Jesus Christ" (Eph. 5:2) or through Him (see Col. 3:17). Calling to remembrance Jesus' name when offering thanksgiving reminds us of our source of thanksgiving and of His sovereignty over all things. The ultimate agent of our deliverance is God. Additionally, for the power of God at work in believers through their work produced by faith and for their "partnership in the gospel" (Phil. 1:5), Paul gives thanks in prayer (see 1 Thess. 1:2-3).

Eugene Peterson speaks of the relationship of grace and gratitude and joy as the chief marks of a Christian:

> *Charis* [grace] demands the answer *eucharistia* [gratitude] . . . Grace and gratitude belong together like heaven and earth. Grace evokes gratitude like the voice [of] an echo. Gratitude follows grace like thunder follows lightning. God is a personal reality to be enjoyed. We are so created and so redeemed that we are capable of enjoying him. All the movements of discipleship arrive at a place where joy is experienced. Every step of assent toward God develops the capacity to enjoy.[35]

When you realize the enormity of God's grace toward you, you can't help but be grateful. Grateful people are joyful people. They taste and smell of the goodness of God, and they bring the fragrance of joy wherever they go.

"Let us be grateful to people who make us happy; they are the charming gardeners who make our souls blossom" (Marcel Proust).[36]

His Powerful Deliverance

When we confess or proclaim or sing aloud about who God is, this act of thanksgiving to Him is worship, and worship produces a fragrance of praise. And praise enlivens our heart with confidence that God is our only rock in the desert. Resist the pull to retreat into a den of anger, sadness, or depression, but instead get moving. "Shooting" and "throwing" up praise describe the Hebrew root of *yadah*. The Hebrew word occurs one hundred and fourteen times in the Old Testament (sixty-six in the psalter alone) and is used in the contexts of the act of praising, the confession of sin, or the inauguration of a time of praise.[37] In 2 Samuel 22, David, who loved God greatly yet was still greatly flawed (sounds like all of us), gives us an example of praising God after intense opposition, and he recalls how the Lord delivers those who love Him and follow His ways.

This is not about celebrating how faithful David was but celebrating how God is faithful. Filled with gratitude for God's deliverance, David burst into song. First, David praised God for being His rock and refuge in the desert as he sang these words: "The Lord is my rock, my fortress and my deliverer; my God is my rock, in whom I take refuge" (2 Sam. 22:2–3 NIV).

Next, David recalls God's pleasure and favor for those who desire to serve the Lord and to please Him in their lives. Celebrating how God delivered him, David recounts the Lord's "support" and help in bringing him into "a spacious place" (2 Sam. 22:19–20 NIV). David continues to sing, "He is a shield for all who take refuge in him. . . . He trains my hands for battle; my arms can bend a bow of bronze. You give me your shield of victory; . . . You have delivered me from the attacks of my people; you have preserved me as the head of the nations. . . . The Lord lives! Praise be to my Rock! Exalted be God, the Rock, my Savior!" (vv. 31, 35–36, 44, 47 NIV 1984).

It is important to not miss this: David attributed his victory not to his strength, but to God, who strengthened David physically and intervened in his situation. Look for God's hand when you are delivered from something or someone, and then celebrate! Take the time to praise God, because if you don't, you are the one missing out on experiencing the joy of God's faithfulness and the deepening of your relationship with Him. So speak of God's actions in your situation and tell Him the details. Thanking God will strengthen your faith as what you voice aloud will fan the flame of your love and devotion to Him. As you speak words about God's character out loud, those truths will work into your core beliefs about who God is and how He works in the lives of those who love Him. God designed thanksgiving as such a benefit to us so that we can experience His joy and its effects of grounding us in God's faithfulness.

Our deliverance may not always result in victory over our enemies in this life, but God will always deliver you through the situation. Deliverance might not always be a change in situation, but a change in your perspective. Other times, after a while, He will deliver you, or He may not fully deliver you until you go home to be with God. God never gives a time frame on His deliverance, but you can count on it. So keep calling out to the Lord for help, even when you do not see the victory yet.

While I was in the darkest time of my recovery, trying to get a diagnosis after fourteen months of pain in my head and face and then navigating the side effects of too many steroids that exacerbated my head pain and caused other health issues, I would continually call out to God these verses of deliverance. I would encourage you to pray some of these verses or other verses on deliverance:

- "Answer me when I call to you, O my righteous God. Give me relief from my distress; be merciful to me and hear my prayer" (Ps. 4:1 NIV 1984).

- "The LORD is good, a refuge in times of trouble. He cares for those who trust in him" (Nah. 1:7).
- "Heal me, O LORD, and I will be healed; save me and I will be saved, for you are the one I praise" (Jer. 17:14).
- "The LORD will sustain him on his sickbed and restore him from his bed of illness" (Ps. 41:3).

God hears your cry for help. Follow David's example and recall God as your rock where you find refuge from the heat of the desert. Speaking out or singing out for help and recalling that God is your refuge and rock in difficult times will remind you that God is the only security in the hardest of times.

My Continuing Recovery Journey

Continuing to knock on heaven's door during my recovery, as the weeks and months went by, gratitude to God helped me deal with the obstacles in my recovery. To combat my weariness from all the doctors, I continued to speak words of thanksgiving to God, the Great Physician. These repeated actions of thanks kept me moving and trusting that we would get a diagnosis. Though the ground beneath my feet was unsteady, God was my steady, my rock. All the rocks in the desert terrain were set as reminders of God's faithfulness. I would read Psalm 18:1–12, which starts with, "I love you, O Lord, my strength. The Lord is my rock, my fortress, and my deliverer; my God is my rock in whom I take refuge" (v. 1 NIV 1984). I needed God to adjust my vision with a lens of gratitude.

Navigating six months of rising nerve pain in my head and face after my allergic reaction, I finally received an MRI of my neck and was encouraged by yet another doctor's words that he could help. My hope deflated the next day. A physician's assistant at a reputable orthopedic group could not offer a clear diagnosis or and explanation of how her solution might help with the primary location of my pain. Instead, she sent me off with an order to go to a pain clinic to perform an injection in my spine. When I walked out of the patient room, my mother could see the disappointment in my eyes. After retelling the treatment recommendation in the waiting room, we remained motionless in shock for a while and both without words. We agreed that was not our next step, but we were still without another plan.

The next day we got together and decided that our next best step was to pray and start praying every day together for my healing and God's guidance in the healing journey. With each prayer thanking God for being the Ultimate Physician and asking that He would be my primary care physician, leading the diagnosis and treatment plan, we were grounding ourselves in the truth that God, who is the source of all wisdom and truth, knew my situation and knew how to turn it around. Thanksgiving grounds us in difficult times so that we can hear from God and keep moving instead of sinking into anger or depression.

Two days after the MRI on my neck and one day after mom's and my commitment to pray together every day, one of my cousins called and said that she had been thinking about me. Her husband had developed a neck issue and saw a doctor a few days ago who really helped him. She thought that he might be able to help me. I called that doctor on Monday and scheduled an appointment a few days later. The doctor knew what I had shortly after hearing my story, though looking back, the diagnosis was not based on imaging, as the MRI of my neck did not show any condition other than very mild arthritis, which is normal for my age. To make sure his diagnosis was correct, he explained how he would have to inject the right occipital to numb it to see if it removed the symptoms. As he injected it, I let out a short, sharp scream that my mom heard in the waiting room. But the next thirty minutes were heavenly because I was pain free. Even though it was for a short time, there was the seed of hope growing that I could again get to a life without this pain.

At last, the sixteenth doctor finally shared a clear diagnosis and treatment program in the twenty-first month of this medical journey, but I did not know at that time, the medical journey would be much longer. Unfortunately a few months later after a diagnosis and procedure in 2019, some pain returned, and I continued down the same path thinking this was a part of my recovery. Then as I struggled to make a full recovery for over two years, a new ENT discovered a mass in my right parotid gland. Since then I was diagnosed with a rare cancerous tumor in my right parotid and have had surgery and radiation during the editing of this book. I am overwhelmed with thankfulness for the best surgeon with such gifted hands, since he had to graft many nerves that the cancer had eaten going to my mouth and eyes. From the reports, it appears that the tumor had been there for some years. After five years of pain and fighting to recover, I am learning that thankfulness continues to flourish even with short term side effects.

Thankfulness also arises even in the "Why's." Why did a doctor not image the right gland where I started having pain and ear infections in 2018? Why did I struggle through so many misdiagnoses? Why did God allow this to happen to me? Did I have some occipital neuralgia or was the tumor the culprit to my pain the whole time? Lastly, gratitude rises in the unknowns of life, knowing the Lord's hand that is always holding mine. Each day, no matter the circumstances, I have the ability to see and fill up my heart with thankfulness that I have a God who stays and sticks with me during the hardest of times and shares His love, peace, and comfort.

Thankfulness rising on the inside caused the natural exhale of thanksgiving in my conversations as I shared the good news in many phone calls and texts to family and friends. Good news is meant to be shared. Not only is thanksgiving a confession or declaration of who God is but also an action of praising God for His actions in your life, in the lives of your family and friends, and throughout the world. You have some good news someone else needs to hear. Share it!

The Fragrance of Thanksgiving

Thanksgiving will produce a fragrance of contentment in you while you contend with suffering and trials. Contentment can be experienced while you are contending and fighting in prayer for yourself or for someone you love. Complaining is not the same as groaning or struggling to endure trials, suffering, pain, or difficult situations at home or work.

My mother hates whining. While my mom was driving my brother's children home from school one afternoon, one was whining about who got to sit in which seat in the car. My mother said to them, "Who hates whining?" In unison, they said, "Gaga hates whining."

Whiners look at a glass as half empty versus half full. They are quick to gripe or voice a criticism, as if they know better than others. When looking at a restaurant menu, they will complain about what is not offered on the menu, instead of being grateful for the abundant options and the ability to eat out. Sometimes whiners are more subtle with their frequent suggestions for improvements. They are so wanting to get somewhere else in life that they miss the contentment of their todays as being enough. Some of the "pro" whiners have more than enough money, status, clothing, and other possessions, yet they are the most discontent and least thankful. Implementing limits or guardrails in their lives will help them to appreciate the things and people they have taken for granted.

Other times, God allows financial hardships to encourage more responsible fiscal spending habits. Then He might allow forms of pain or suffering so that, through the curbing of indulgent or gluttonous habits, which are like a sickness, people might grow in gratitude, and this gratitude might heal the desire for those indulgences. God's imposed discipline might be one of His greatest invitations for you to develop a more thankful heart. Traveling through life on empty will make you a whiner or grinch, while traveling through life on full will make you a thankful giver or thankful singer.

Instead of making the limitations in my recovery seem so great, which complaining does, I decided to focus on the little steps that I was making in my recovery. Just like anybody, I sometimes struggled with complaining, because chronic pain weighs on you. Every night, even now, when I lie down on my pillow, I experience pain in parts of my head, and then it travels to my face sometimes. This has been going on for over four years now. Each day I have the opportunity to put off the whining or complaining to celebrate the progress by focusing on the lessening pain and the fact that I go to sleep so much more quickly—in about ten minutes or so compared to an hour and a half when this injury first started.

The Bible describes the "putting off" of our natural tendencies, such as greed, complaining, envy, and other evil desires, by using the analogy of taking off dirty clothes and putting on clean clothes (see Col. 3:5–10). I've had to learn to fight spiritually, while contending and not complaining and while looking to the Lord as my helper and the One who would give me advice, strength, and the steps toward progress. At times I felt pushed back and weighted down by my chronic pain, much like David's battle against his enemies in Psalm 118:12–13. But I would not be crushed or left without the strong arm of the Lord to guide me through. The Lord can lighten our load through whatever difficulty, illness, or battle we are experiencing as we enter each day with gratitude. (See Psalm 118:19.) I needed God to bring His light in my darkness so that I could see goodness too.

This is how gratitude realigned my heart from focusing on limitations or what I was missing in life to giving thanks for the good things and gifts in my current life. I started becoming good at just *being* and not doing. I still continued to pray for my healing every day, and I am fighting hard for it by walking outside every day (unless the weather is unfavorable). Then I started weight training three times a week to help my frozen shoulder and rotator cuff and to reverse the atrophy caused by the steroids and inactivity over a year. My morning daily time with God grew into a lot of listening and then praying for others. God helped me work around things. For example, when I would close my eyes during the day, I would start to fall asleep. So God encouraged me to pray with my eyes open. I developed a weekly prayer plan through my recovery, which I will share in the chapter on prayer.

Prayer is one my favorite gifts, which I enjoyed during my recovery. Another one of my favorite gifts was connecting more with one of my oldest best friends. My third favorite gift (though in no particular order) was the gift of this Seven Pathways plan, which helped me chart my way back to a deeper relationship with God and to better health. Words are not adequate to thank my mom and stepfather for going with me to all the doctor visits, bringing me home-cooked meals, giving me love and support, and celebrating the progress rather than focusing on the distance to a full recovery.

My old self would have never planned to write a book or start a business when I was recovering. God gave me very clear instructions on how to get started. He gave me the steps and an organized plan and said *this is the time.* I questioned Him, "Are you sure about that?" He told me that starting now will be an encouragement to others to get started even while they are facing negative circumstances. God gave me the gift of the daily cadence of engaging in the Seven Pathways, and I hope that this Seven Pathways plans will be a gift to you as well.

Gaining a Thankful Heart Posture

Breaking the habit of ingratitude will take some effort. But I have found some exercises that will strengthen your thankfulness muscles. Practice them until they become a habit and your default response to feelings of entitlement or self-pity. (I have adapted the following steps from an article I found at Harvard Health Publishing.[38])

1. *Remember God's past faithfulness*: Similar to the Old Testament calls to "recall and remember," calling to mind God's past faithfulness (in our own lives as well as those of our spiritual ancestors) helps us remember His track record in our lives and sets into proper perspective the unmet expectations in the present, which may be unmet because we're not fully aware of God's plans and how He is working all circumstances for our good.
2. *Pay attention to God's present work*: We tend to focus on what we need God to do or what He has yet to do. Especially for those of us from a Pentecostal/Charismatic background, we are often so concerned about witnessing God's work in the extraordinary that we miss what He is doing in the seemingly mundane and ordinary. I ask myself, Where is God presently at work in my life that I am overlooking?
3. *Remember that God loves you*: As Brennan Manning notes, at the end of the day we are simply beloved sons and

daughters of God.[39] This affords a contentment and peace as well as a thankfulness in our condition. We don't have to strive in response to God's goodness. We simply have to abide in Him and, in abiding in Him, the thankfulness will follow.

4. *Pay attention*: Similar to point 2, paying attention draws focus away from the hypothetical and cosmic and toward what is happening in the moment. In doing so, we can discern where the Spirit is at work around us and attune ourselves to joining Him in His work.
5. *Keep a thankfulness journal*: Start writing in a journal a few days a week, recording moments of your day that you are thankful for. In the morning, write about what you are thankful for and some thoughts that could make your day good, and then at night, revisit them. And then celebrate them by retuning for the next day.

PATHWAY 2

Silence

Every man who delights in a multitude of words, even though he says admirable things, is empty within. If you love truth, be a lover of silence. Silence, like the sunlight will illuminate you in God, and will deliver you from the phantoms of ignorance. Silence will unite you to God himself.

—St. Isaac of Ninevah[40]

We are pummeled by unwanted noise every day, and the increase of this noise takes a dramatic toll on our mental and physical health and especially our spiritual well-being. In a 2019 article from *The New Yorker*, David Owen details how researchers are growing increasingly concerned about the ever-increasing littering of the "soundscape." He cites Les Blomberg, executive director of the Noise Pollution Clearinghouse, who said, "What we're doing to our soundscape is littering it. It's aural litter—acoustical litter—and, if you could see what you hear, it would look like piles and piles of McDonald's wrappers, just thrown out the window as we go driving down the road."[41] This visual image powerfully typifies the degradation of our soundscape.

Owen goes on to say, "Bruitparif, a nonprofit organization that monitors noise pollution in the metropolitan Paris area," reported that the "average resident "of any of the loudest parts of the Île-de-France—which includes Paris and its surrounding suburbs—loses 'more than three healthy life-years,' in the course of a lifetime, to some combination of ailments caused or exacerbated by the din of cars, trucks, airplanes, and trains."[42] These physiological and physical factors include tinnitus, sleep disturbance, ischemic heart disease, high blood pressure, obesity, diabetes, adverse birth outcomes, and cognitive impairment in children. Another Western European study showed traffic noise can be a silent killer with cumulative effects for increased risk for stroke and a number of of other conditions, like high blood pressure.[43] Additionally, Owen's article elucidates the negative impact of noise pollution on marine life from sonar activity, marine craft, and other human aquatic activities. For instance, whales are sensitive to sonar activity and can bolt toward the surface in a panic reaction to the sound, and thus, die of decompression sickness. It's also believed to impact feeding and mating patterns, though scientists cannot be certain to what extent.[44]

The direct impact of noise pollution upon the human body is believed to be linked to the impact of sound waves vibrating against the bones of the ear. These vibrations transmit to the cochlea, which converts the vibrations into signals for the brain to receive. The brain, thereby, reacts to these signals, even in deep sleep. The first areas of the brain to be activated are the amygdalae, located in the temporal lobe and associated with memory formation and emotion. The amygdalae are also responsible for holding the flight-or-fight response of the brain, so the activation of the amygdalae releases stress hormones like cortisol.[45] People who live in a constant state of reception of sound pollution, therefore, have elevated levels of stress, and their bodies produce more cortisol, the primary stress hormone, leading to an increased risk of other physical problems, including heart disease, high blood pressure, sleep problems, weight gain, digestive problems, muscle tension and pain, anxiety, depression, and more.[46]

The consistent littering of the soundscape and the relentless virtual noise bombarding us every day is shaping a growing consensus that "silence is the new luxury."[47] Since silence is a commodity in short supply, the increasing demand for it has created new business opportunities for Finland's tourism to profit from sensory deprivation experiences. In the small Nordic nation known for its hospitable but stoic demeanor and preference for silence, marketing experts have deemed Finland's penchant for silence a marketable quality on which the country can be branded in order to boost tourism. Tourism boards show photographs of the wilderness with captions that read "Silence, please," and the Finnish watchmaker Rönkkö advertises with its new slogan "Handmade in Finnish silence."[48]

Given all of that, it should not be surprising that silence is our second pathway to a deeper relationship with God. To know God, we must learn to hear His voice. To do that, we need to shut down the clatter and learn to embrace silence. As you probably already know, that's easier said than done. In this chapter, you'll learn the difference between silence and solitude and find out why silence is vital for spiritual and psychological health. You'll also discover the true reason you find it so difficult to tolerate silence, and you'll gain simple strategies you can use to practice this pathway to the deeper life.

Silence vs. Solitude

In the most basic sense, silence is the absence of sound, yet in a spiritual sense, silence is much more. It is one of the mysteries of Christianity and an invitation to retreat with God. God commands us in Psalm 46:10, "Be still and know that I am God" (NIV). This is not a suggestion but a command from God. His commands are always for our good. It is a call to practice habitual stillness of the whole being—heart, mind, and body—before God.

So, as a pathway to deeper relationship with God, silence has three aspects: quiet surroundings, a quiet self, and an open heart. Solitude means being in a still place, keeping silent, and listening for the voice of God.

While closely connected in their practices, silence and solitude are slightly different. Dr. Charles Stone, lead pastor of West Park Church in London, Ontario, graduate in Mind, Brain, and Teaching from John Hopkins University and currently pursuing a PhD in researching stress in pastors, differentiates the two as follows:

- Solitude: "The practice of temporarily being absent from other people (in isolation or anonymity) and other things so that you can be present with God. It's not loneliness nor is it getting away from people . . . ." It's about positioning our bodies so that we can connect with God.

- Silence: "The practice of voluntarily and temporarily abstaining from speaking so that certain spiritual goals might be sought. It's about what we do with our tongues, what we say."[49]

Contrasted with solitude, practicing silence also necessitates active listening—of attuning our heart to the presence of God. Both Dietrich Bonhoeffer and Thomas Merton inextricably link the two, silence and solitude, as companions for spiritual discipline.[50]

In his book *Reaching Out: The Three Movements of the Spiritual Life*, Henri Nouwen speaks to the need to move "from loneliness to solitude."[51] He differentiates the two primarily in the internal disposition toward contentment. Loneliness is an aching—the most universal of human suffering[52]—that we seek to avoid at all costs.

Bonhoeffer's vivid portrait of human aversion to being alone is just as ubiquitous in our culture:

> We are so afraid of silence that we chase ourselves from one event to the next in order not to have to spend a moment alone with ourselves, in order not to have to look at ourselves in the mirror. . . . We are afraid of such lonely, awful encounters with God, and we avoid them, so that he may not suddenly come too near to us.[53]

Solitude is an aloneness coupled with the contentment to sit with oneself. Henri David Thoreau's insights, though written well before the ubiquitous influences of technology, are especially true of our social media, FOMO (Fear of Missing Out) culture.

In the excerpt below Henri Nouwen uses this quote of Thoreau's to portray our culture (swap "the post office" for "Twitter"):

> When our life ceases to be inward and private, conversation degenerates into mere gossip. We rarely meet a man who can tell us any news which he has not read in a newspaper, or been told by his neighbor; and, for the most part, the only difference between us and our fellow is that he has seen the newspaper, or been out to tea, and we have not. In proportion as our inward life fails, we go more constantly and desperately to the post office. You may depend on it, that the poor fellow who walks away with the greatest number of letters proud of his extensive correspondence has not heard from himself this long while.[54]

Yikes! The man (or woman) "who walks away with the greatest number of letters" (or likes, retweets, and shares) and feels gratified by them has failed in the inward cultivation that can only be developed in solitude and silence. Who is living from the inside out, and who is watching others live? Our culture is the most connected at all times but the loneliest.

Nouwen adds that "by attentive living, we can learn the difference between loneliness and solitude. When you are alone in an office, a house or an empty waiting room, you can suffer from restless loneliness but also enjoy a quiet solitude."[55] Through attentive and active listening in solitude to God, we cultivate the inner life that is grounded on the Rock, which is Jesus, and we drink from His life-giving waters as we commune with Him.

Psychological Benefits of Silence

As with thankfulness, silence offers a host of practical benefits in addition to spiritual growth. By reducing noise pollution in your life, you promote relaxation and lower stress. Relaxation activates the brain's hippocampus, which is crucial for building memories and fostering quality decision making and empathy. In growing children and teenagers, the space to reflect and think deeply actually contributes to greater brain growth as well as personal and interpersonal satisfaction.[56] Consequently, the overall benefits for practicing silence especially for child and adolescent development is far-reaching.

According to *Psychology Today*, there are ten reasons why silence produces psychological and physiological benefits. Silence—

1. Stimulates brain growth. At least two hours of silence has proven to yield the growth of new brain cells aiding in learning and memory.
2. Reduces the influx of stress hormones like cortisol and adrenaline.
3. De-stresses and calms your whole being.
4. Produces more enhanced sleep at night.
5. Reduces undesirable health issues like heart disease and tinnitus.
6. Produces greater self-awareness and reflection, leading to better decision making.
7. Produces better focus.
8. Enhances one's ability to be creative, to fantasize, and to daydream.
9. Allows a person to be able to prioritize better.
10. Causes us to know when to speak and when to remain silent (allowing us to avoid more foolish "foot in mouth" moments).[57]

The practice of silence is a vital pathway for cultivating your relationship with God. It's also a great way to improve your physical and psychological health, not to mention your work and social relationships.

Our Aversion to Silence

While the benefits of practicing silence are staggering, a strong aversion to silence still prevails. For many people, silence creates restlessness and anxiety. A study published by a team of researchers at the University of Virginia and Harvard University found that college students would rather administer a mild electric shock (that earlier they stated they would pay to avoid) to themselves than sit in silence, with their own thoughts, for fifteen minutes.[58] Another research study at the University of Gronigen, Netherlands found that Anglophones tend to be the most uncomfortable with periods of silence. After a four-second silent lull in a conversation, English speakers became unsettled. In contrast, a separate study revealed that Japanese people were content with silent periods in conversations more than twice that long—8.2 seconds. These contrasting comfort levels of silence are reflected in the difference between the American proverb, "the squeaky wheel gets the grease," and the Japanese proverb, "a silent man is the best one to listen to."[59]

One study suggests that people are likely more uncomfortable with the idea of sitting and thinking than actually doing it. In this study, students were requested to sit in a room alone with their own thoughts for six minutes and thirty seconds. The students were not told how long they were going to be sitting in the study beforehand. The participants demonstrated, during the period of silent reflection, a greater degree of reflection upon the present moment (53.1% reflection on the present; 19.6% reflection on the past; 27.3% reflection on the future). During this study individuals were also more aware of themselves than they were the time. The study also showed little support for the suggestion that students found the period of "just thinking" to be aversive. Perhaps the perception needs to be adjusted culturally, promoting silence rather than noise. Once people experience silence, they experience the benefits, and the benefits resonate with them measurably.

Our aversion to silence stems from the fear of being alone with ourselves. Once still and alone, we are afraid of the thoughts and memories that might surface, such as past failures, mistakes, regrets, and a list of things that we would rather remain buried and forgotten. We often associate engaging in periods of silence with a replay of past mistakes, so we would rather stay busy than be alone with our own thoughts. The growing perception of the lack of silence as a public health crisis because silence is essential to personal health draws our attention to our acute need for silence. Yet we are unclear how to silence our inner voices and actively listen to hear the voice of God.

How I Learned to Pause

In order to attentively and actively listen to God, we must build times of peace into our day, times in which we pause. Just as we might hit the pause button while watching a movie as not to miss anything during a bathroom break, we need to hit the pause button in our personal lives too. Our hectic calendars can run us rather than us running them. We need those moments in our day to be still and silent to connect with God so that we are refreshed and strengthened for our day. Scheduling peaceful margins in your day for your time to connect with God will ensure that you are not running on empty. I speak from experience.

There have been times in my spiritual life when I felt like I was coasting on the last fumes before the car stopped. In my late twenties, I was going strong at work, the gym, spiritual life, church, Bible studies, time with friends, and a busy social life.

But my life was too hurried and didn't have the peaceful margin with God that I had regularly scheduled with Him for many years before then. I told one of my best friends that I do not get tired, and she looked at me like I was strange.

Not too long after that, I got mono, and I have never been so tired in my whole life. I was so tired that it was hard to sleep. This was one of the turning points in my life (and there would be many others) when God created circumstances to make me be still and silent so that I could hear from Him and take the turns He wanted me to take on my life path.

God got my attention enduring those sleepless nights when I was so tired that it made it hard to sleep. The Bible says to "be still and know that I am God" (Psalm 46:10 NIV). The Hebrew word for "be still"[60] is often translated "to sink, relax, or to stop or cease." Relax. Stop, that's enough for the day. According to the *Theological Workbook of the Old Testament*, it is most widely used to mean "to let drop" (Deut. 4:31; Josh. 10:6) or "to let alone" or "refrain" (Judg. 11:37; Ps. 37:8).[61] It draws a connection to a cessation of activity, similar to a builder who puts down his tools at the end of a day or a bird who closes its wings when it is done flying. It also can imply the figurative loss of heart or energy.

Another way of expressing God's call to be still is, "Rest in Me and pay attention to Me." God allowed me to experience much stillness during those nights and days—since being still and resting was about all I felt like doing for a few weeks—that I might learn to rest in Him. Sinking into my bed, which normally was so comforting, did not produce the same results. So, instead of sinking my heart into my work or relationships, I started again sinking into a regular rhythm or cadence of spending time with Him and just listening more because I was out of the Lord-help-me mode. Now, I need just one thing: His presence to encourage and strengthen me each day. What I am saying is that I needed Him.

We are all looking for something to sink our hearts into, whether it be a relationship, children and family, a job, an activity, a hobby, alcohol, shopping, tennis, drugs, or travel. Our hearts are made to sink into God first because He designed us for relationship with Him, and no other relationships can fill that God hole. We need to schedule some time to sink into the couch with God. He is saying that I am your safe person, the one whom you can relax with. Through this experience of being still and silent with God, I found much comfort and looked forward to the time with Him because it was so refreshingly peaceful and restorative to my relationship with Him. I started to hear from Him again for wisdom and guidance in my life, and it was so good to have that time to be comforted by His love and to have Him affirm that He would bring good from this tough time.

During that time, God swung a door wide open when the seminary that I had applied to for their Master of Theology program mailed me a scholarship that would pay for almost two years of my program that I had not applied for. So I transitioned from teaching seventh grade to entering a seminary program at Dallas Theological Seminary.

Through this most recent and current experience of God allowing my normal life to come to a standstill and giving me the space for much silence in my life, I am learning the importance of building a peaceful margin in my days, in both the hard and the good times. It just took me about fifty years to learn that I will not get where God wants to take me when running on empty. I can't run on the gas from last year or from my relationship with God from two, five, or ten years ago. Just as you can't run your car on old fuel, you can't run on your old relationship with God. Yes, remembering God's faithfulness from the past will encourage you today, and God can use that to carry you through hard times.

All that you have learned and your experiences with God, He will use to encourage you and your faith as He is lovingly shaping you to be more like Him and in the unique way that He made you to impact the world. Just as any friendship or romantic relationship requires regular and consistent time, so does your relationship with God. Stop running on empty. Fuel up each day by connecting with God.

In a culture that chooses many idols to satisfy or repress its restless hunger, the church stands as an alternative society, incarnating—though imperfectly—the kingdom of God for which everyone deeply yearns. The church's role is to help us grow and form spiritually, to be people whose deepest thirst is quenched by the satisfying Water of Life. We need to restore the metanarrative of the creating/saving/empowering Triune God. As churches cultivate a lifelong spiritual formation, worshipers will discover that spiritual growth and godly wisdom will genuinely satisfy them in ways that consumerism never could, because consumerism only left them deprived of the true joy of being the beloved of God and caused a looming anxiety and discontentment of the soul.

The Practice of Silence

For many people silence creates restlessness and anxiety. Once we enter through the doorway of prayer into silence, a noisy crowd of thoughts, feeling, fears, and disappointments assail or assault us such that we have difficulty quietening. Our inner life is weighted down with this noisy, stubborn crowd, convention, or caucus of thoughts and allows them to ruin our moments of silence. The inner noise of our soul can make silence seem impossible, and many have given up fighting to get inner silence back. Instead of allowing a stubborn crowd of thoughts to drown us, we must humble ourselves before God and invite Him into our crowd of thoughts, for He knows how to silence them. Silence for the purpose of connecting with God is the landscape in which God's voice can be clearly discerned.

Remove Noise

At face value it seems obvious that noise and silence are opposite. And from a purely scientific perspective, that is true. The absence of noise is silence in the same way that the absence of light is darkness. However, anthropologically (and perhaps theologically) speaking, this is a matter of greater debate. In speaking of interpersonal and cross-cultural communication,[62] noise and silence are not simply opposites but can also be distinct constructs. Put differently, silence cannot only be a passive absence of something else but also an active phenomenon all on its own. This is a common proactive tactic employed by mental health professionals—who are often intentional—to observe five seconds of silence after their patient stops talking to encourage reflection and/or further dialogue.

Theologically, silence is both the opposite of noise and a distinct phenomenon. To illustrate this, the apostle John uses the material reality—that darkness is the absence of light—to also draw a theological metaphor between the holiness of God and its incompatibility with the darkness of sin and the forces of evil (an active phenomenon) in 1 John 1:5. In the same manner, the removal of noise for the pursuit of silence as a spiritual discipline to connect with God is a material reality. We must actually remove noise from our lives to pursue silence.

Focus on God

We live in a noisy and distracting world, which bombards us every day with virtual noise as we scroll through social media or explore Netflix or other media services or channels. The development of the post-modern spirit, created by the rise of science and technology, economics and communications, has led to the decentering of both self (incoherence) and society (fragmentation) in contemporary culture. This modern myth built on the faulty enlightenment idolatry of progress gave way to hopelessness and grave anxiety as the twentieth century unfolded into world wars, the Great Depression, Hiroshima, the Cold War, Chernobyl, 9/11, terrorism, the internet, the Great Recession, the rise of China, and the pandemic.

As a result, people have no overarching story or metanarrative and do not know who they are. They lack a nucleus of identity, a personality shaped by moral authority and mentoring models. In *The Consuming Passion: Christianity & the Consumer Culture*, Rodney Clapp focuses upon "the idealization and constant encouragement of insatiability—the deification of dissatisfaction"[63] propagated in modern consumerism. This sacralized consumption has devoured classical Christian theology and practice. People are trained in the school of insatiability. The highest value is freedom, defined as a vast array of choices to meet a felt need. The shift of a technological-media center usurping the role of the church to shape our system of values, embody our faith, and express our cultural essence is ominous in its effects on identity of self and of a group, culture, and psyche. It represents the shift from dealing with human questions to dealing instead with utilitarian questions, from asking, "How will this affect people?" to asking, "How will this make a profit?"

The bombarding of an endless spiral of images in media for the purpose of entertainment is eroding our culture's deep symbols. Without these symbols representing our values, beliefs, traditions, and institutions, a society has little connection with sources of humanization, and it instigates styles of everyday life whose primary function is ephemeral entertainment and trivial comforts. A diminished connection to the past and its powerful symbols shaping traditions and values contributes to cultural malaise and a lack of basic personhood, which is a major reason young adults and a growing number of older adults cannot make commitments to a job, marriage, or a family.

Listen

Many people perform outward rituals of worship and do good work for God but have failed to invite Christ to make His home in their heart. They have not welcomed Him into their interior heart chambers, thought life, or daily affairs. The need for welcoming Him in is clearly illustrated in the story of Jesus' entrance on Palm Sunday as recorded in Matthew 21:10, where we see how intense passion or sterile enthusiasm may not be genuine but may be religious pomp and varnish. When festivities of Palm Sunday concluded in Matthew 21, no one extended Jesus' hospitality, so Jesus returned to Bethany to stay with His disciples. This is critical! Worship is not merely a matter of expressing praise for Jesus in public. It goes much further to include a call to all people to examine their hearts.

A person is first a Christian by allowing Jesus to make His home in his or her heart. When a person believes that Jesus died for his or her sins, he or she receives forgiveness of sin and the Holy Spirit. In John 14:16–17, Jesus speaks of how once someone believes in Him, then His presence will be with them through the indwelling of the Holy Spirit, who will make a home in their heart. In his letter to believers in Ephesus, Paul prays that they will invite Jesus to be at home in their hearts (Eph. 3:17). The invitation is to let all your thoughts come to rest at the cross and to let Him reframe, realign, and direct all of them, and then to soak in the light and warmth of His love. The answer to this call is to practice active silence, meaning not just be quiet but actively listen to God.

In our culture, we suffer from a glut of information while experiencing an insatiable connectivity that erodes our essential need for silence. We must silence the noise in our lives to experience the restorative peace of the quieting of our soul in the presence of God. Silence is a proactive, spiritual discipline, an active phenomenon, wherein we can attune our hearts to hear God and experience His presence as He makes a home in our hearts.

Silencing the Inner Voices

When beginning to walk the pathway of silence, you'll notice that the quiet space you have created almost immediately fills up with a tangle of inner thoughts. Eager to hear the voice of God, you may be frustrated by the onslaught of internal noise. You find yourself flooded with anxious thoughts about the day ahead, or the one just passed. You recall old sins and mistakes, which bring feelings of shame and regret. You remember wounds caused by others and cannot shut out the painful recollections. It's as if the inner chambers of our being are full of many old tapes playing of past fears, failures, losses and gains, hopes fulfilled, hopes crushed, loves lost, and loves won. With our multitudes of tapes, the noise of our inner chambers can make it hard to hear the voice of God. You may find that you have successfully blocked out the exterior noise pollution only to be assaulted by a jumbled array of inner voices that worry, threaten, or accuse you.

Whether a Christian or non-Christian, everyone has their old tapes; these tapes can create inner anxiety or static that influences one's current life choices. Some of the tapes get stuck on repeat, meaning we return to the same patterns of thought or become caught in a cycle of unhealthy or sinful patterns. The good news here is that the same outer calm that allows these voices to emerge within you also creates an opportunity to silence them. As long as we bathe ourselves in the constant wash of exterior noise, we cannot permit the Lord access to these chambers of our heart. So our default will be to try to maintain our sense of security, happiness, and well-being apart from Christ. Stilling your heart through the pathway of silence is vital for opening every area of your heart to the Lord's voice. Only when you silence the world and confront these inner demons can you quiet them in the presence of God. All the hurts, mistakes, regrets, and shame of the past must be surrendered to Jesus. This is the pathway to a deeper relationship with God.

Relationship vs. Accomplishment

Many people view the Christian life as a series of tasks to be accomplished. The first is to accept the Lordship of Jesus Christ, symbolized by baptism. After that, many believe, there comes a series of rules to be obeyed and good deeds to be done. Their thinking is that, as we follow this false pathway of achievement, we will experience more of God's presence and love. Yes, God has set guidelines for living, but experiencing the Christian life is so much more. C. S. Lewis used the German term *sehnsucht* to describe the pressing, restless longing for fulfillment that nothing can satisfy. St. Augustine describes our longing for God best in this statement: "Oh, Lord, thou hast made us for thyself, and our hearts are restless until they rest in Thee."[64]

Fulfilling a to-do list does not satisfy the need for a real relationship and genuine connection with God. Think back to the first picture we have of God relating to humans in the Bible. God did not hand Adam and Eve a to-do list of how to relate to Him and tasks to please Him. Instead, He talked with them as they walked throughout the garden and shared instructions throughout the day. Other times in the Bible, God gave clear instructions on living, which He wanted recorded, such as the Ten Commandments, so that all people throughout the centuries would have these instructions since He was not physically with them. Adam and Eve had the physical presence of the living God every day. Adam and Eve's sin separated them from the fellowship that they had enjoyed with God, and from their sin grew seeds of fear and doubt in God's goodness.

Until Jesus' birth, people offered sacrifices according to the Old Testament's standards to atone for their sins, and all of these sacrifices foreshadowed the ultimate sacrifice of Jesus' life for the forgiveness of sin. With the arrival of Jesus, the eternal Son of God makes visible all the transcendent characteristics of the Father, so that we might grasp who God is in human flesh, as He would otherwise be indescribable and ineffable. We need both outer and inner silence in order to move from an achievement-based religion to a deep, relational faith.

Finding God in Silence

In their work *Silence and the Word*, Oliver Davies and Denys Turner speak of the relationship between silence or the "hiddenness of God" in relationship to the incarnation of Christ as described in the opening of John's Gospel. What was hidden to man concerning God's infinite wisdom, character, and power is made known in the person of Jesus. Citing Origen's *De Principiis* (1.2.8), the authors state, "He [Jesus] takes the illustration of a statue, which is so large that it fills the whole universe, and which we cannot 'see' because its immensity blocks our view; we could only see the characteristics of the statue if they were manifested in a smaller copy, precisely reproducing all the detail. So the Son is the 'exact image' of the Father."[65] Through experiencing God in the hidden space of silence, the incarnation of God as the perfect image of Himself in Jesus can be reasonably known. Meaning that our finite minds can't grasp all the fullness of God, as we only see in a mirror dimly—currently—but then we will see face-to-face (1 Cor. 13:12).

For all who believe that Jesus paid the full debt for their sins—past, present, and future—through His sacrificial death and resurrection, they are no longer declared guilty but are credited with Christ's righteousness. Paul emphasizes that no one is righteous (Rom. 3:10), and Christ's record of righteousness (His obedience to God's law and His sacrificial death) is transferred to a believer's account. When you receive Christ, your account for your sins is marked "Paid in Full." God's Spirit brings about this change in our being, freeing us "from the law of sin and death" (Rom. 8:2 NIV). For just as all people who are "in Adam" (his descendants) will die, so all who are "in Christ" (who are "children of God through faith," Gal. 3:26) will live and receive God's gift of grace and righteousness, which exceedingly triumphs over sin and death (see Rom. 5:15–17). Through faith in Christ, our separation from God because of sin has been bridged by the death and resurrection of Jesus. Therefore, Jesus unites believers to God through His death and resurrection.

The Bible describes this union with God through faith in Christ, using the words "in Christ" (2 Cor. 5:17 NIV). The controlling effects of the sinful nature have now been put to death by Christ, and now believers, through the Holy Spirit, have the ability to yield to and be empowered by the Holy Spirit to live in freedom, breaking sinful or self-centered habits and living as children of God, not burdened by the demands of the law, striving to earn God's favor (Gal. 4:31—5:1; Rom. 8:4–8).

God has sent the Holy Spirit, the Helper, to live within believers to guide them, give them wisdom, and convict them. The job of the Holy Spirit is to reveal truth and give us counsel on all matters. The Holy Spirit lives within us to help us experience God in our real world. Seeking to know and understand, through silence, the greatness of God, made known in Jesus' indescribable gift of salvation, opens us to the Spirit so He can reveal Him to us through means of silence. (See Rom. 8:26–27.) If you want Him to help clean out your heart tapes, then you need to invite Him to that part of your heart. There can be no real silence of the heart and mind without the confession of sin and receiving of God's forgiveness. Confession and forgiveness quiet the replay of past failures. If you are exhausted from trying to perform for a God who seems absent, if you're tired of going to church and not experiencing God in your life, and you're wearied from the constant replay of your mistakes and failures, then silence and confession are pathways to experience what your soul has longed for—embracing God's presence and hearing His voice in your daily life.

Through times of silence, we experience the mystery of a loving God speaking and listening to us. Shutting out noise and busy distractions opens the door of communication with God. Perhaps Mother Teresa said it best in her interview with former CBS anchor Dan Rather, as described by Ron Mehl:

> "When you pray," asked Rather, "what do you say to God?"
>
> "I don't say anything," she replied, "I listen."
>
> Rather tried another tack. "Well, okay . . . when God speaks to you, then, what does He say?"
>
> "He doesn't say anything. He listens."
>
> Rather looked bewildered. For an instant he didn't know what to say.
>
> "And if you don't understand that," Mother Teresa added, "I can't explain it to you."[66]

What I think Mother Teresa is saying is that the focus is on listening and not speaking. God's way of speaking is beyond words. It's a deep revelation of truth or insight, a kind of knowing that comes from being present in quietness for the purpose of listening to God.

Confronting the Old Tapes

Some of my friends would speak about God working in their lives and how a Bible verse impacted their lives, so I wanted to know God the way that they did. I knew that God speaks through times of prayer and through the Bible, since the Bible is an inspired and true account that reveals who God is, how He works in people's lives, and the affairs of the world. Each morning I carved out time for a peace margin in my days for the purpose of connecting with God and hearing from Him on matters in my real life, through studying the Bible in small groups, at church, and alone, and then through numerous digital resources and events. As I opened my heart in silence during prayer and through studying the Bible, God started speaking to me. He revealed how to process this tape, and then helped to start the process of reforming my thoughts and reactions. And He led me to verses in the Bible that could help my situation.

For me, I have found it most helpful to bring one tape at a time, one that continues to replay in my mind, along with its effects, to God in a time of silence. When you do this, there is no rush. Practice self-compassion and allow yourself permission to slow down and resist the urge to go through your tapes like you might scroll through social media. You can't rush God or turn Him on or off with a click or swipe. Choose a quiet place to be alone with Jesus and ask God to speak to you, and ask Him to help you listen.

One of the first tapes I chose was on a frequent, unwanted replay that, unfortunately, had some new additions. In solitude and silence, I examined my insecurities and self-will shaping my identity underneath the thoughts and actions on this tape. I asked God to make sense of this tape—what past experiences shaped these patterns, what these patterns said about what I believed about God or myself, and how I could change these thought patterns. I needed a change from the inside out. So I got serious about spending more of my time finding ways to listen to God through silence in prayer and reading the Bible. I had been praying for some things for a long time, so I really wanted to hear from God. I figured that since we were in a relationship, I should give Him time to speak, so I needed to posture myself to listen. I needed to hush now. Silence helps us control our tongue and teaches us to listen. Listening is a high-value asset in God's economy. Connecting with God in silence is a pathway to know, love, and experience His presence in your real world. God is not going to break into your tape room. He is waiting for your invitation.

When God makes His home in your tape room, you will notice that your old tapes are triggered less. Your overly emotional reactions to circumstances or a person are less frequent. You will notice that you are more patient in a circumstance that could have easily triggered a reaction of anger or frustration. What you are experiencing is a shift or rewiring of your reactions, a shift the Bible would call "the renewing of your mind" (Rom. 12:2 NIV). The good thing about old tapes is that you can always record over them. You are not limited by your old soundtracks. Your final story is not your old soundtracks, so get to work on the new tracks.

Our identities can be shaped by the ways those old tapes have attacked our self-worth or identity. The need for love or self-esteem is part of being human, and it is not a sin to have those needs. Our overreaction or how we seek to gratify those needs can be sinful. Our natural human reaction is self-preservation. The cure for replaying patterns that have shaped a false identity based on those tapes is nurturing a close relationship with God. This will restore our sense of our true identity in God and regain a spiritual perspective. Thomas Merton says, "Since our inmost 'I' is the perfect image of God, when that 'I' awakens, he finds within himself the Presence of Him Whose image he is."[67]

Through silence, God realigns our identity in Him, from whom flows endless resources of love, affection, purpose, security, worth, power, and strength. Our true identity grounded in God does not need constant affirmation nor is it demanding or easily agitated by another's disapproval or lack of understanding. Our true self finds our identity in God. Merton expresses with artful language man's identity in God: "The secret of my identity is hidden in Him, He alone can make me who I am, or rather who I will be when at last I fully begin to be. But, unless I desire this identity and work to find it with him and in him, the work will never be done."[68]

Walking Myself to Health

During my recovery, I greatly needed the health benefits of sunlight, but I also needed the time to experience the light of His presence and its effects, which would increase my spiritual strength, give me wisdom, and comfort me with peace during a very difficult time in my life. Since I was ghastly pale from the steroids for treating my allergic reaction, had developed inflammation in my neck and back, and had decreased muscular strength, especially in my back, hips, and feet, along with a frozen shoulder, I decided the benefits to walking outside were advantageous to improve my health. Also, since I was more alone during the early stages of my recovery because of my need for rest and quiet time (even the motion of talking would send pain up the sides of my head), and with the pandemic altering the way we socialized, walking became a great way to fellowship with family and friends.

A wellness expert from the Cleveland Clinic, Dr. Michael Roizen, noted the health and psychological benefits of a daily walk, citing how the increase in heart rate while walking reduces the risks of a heart attack and stroke, lowers blood pressure and LDL (bad cholesterol), and releases endorphins, which increases one's mood, self-esteem, and energy and reduces stress.[69] In addition to increasing vitamin D in our bodies, which is also essential for healthy brain function and reduces inflammation, taking in fresh air while walking outside improves overall brain health and healing, as the brain needs oxygen for healthy neuron function.[70]

Jesus draws the analogy of Himself to being a "light" or "the light of the world" (1 John 1:5; John 8:12 NIV). So the more time we spend with Jesus the more we increase our overall health and spiritual benefits from His light. The more that we receive His love and forgiveness into our hurts and bruises, the more we experience healing. His light dispels the darkness of guilt and shame. Also, the closer we get to the One who never exhausts His patience, the more we absorb His qualities of patience into our own lives and then reflect that to others.

So, in the spring of 2019, I laced up my tennis shoes and started taking silent walks outside at least five days a week. I was weak physically, so I started with ten minutes of walking for a month and then increased my time incrementally until I maxed out at around forty-five minutes a day. The beauty of the cloud formations awed me of God's greatness, splendor, and faithfulness. I saw with my own eyes (and not through a "screen," which is how many of us experience things) that: "The heavens declare the glory of God; the skies proclaim the work of his hands. Day after day they pour forth speech; night after night they display knowledge" (Ps. 19:1–2 NIV 1984).

How the sun never ceased to rise every day encouraged me too. These silent walks created an atmosphere free from devices and distractions in which I could worship God and focus on His greatness and the abundant resources that I have, instead of focusing on my limitations or what I do not have. Time in nature reminds our hearts to beat in rhythm with God's abundance, fostering contentment in a world of comparisons. Our God is a God of abundance not scarcity. Other times during a walk, He would nudge me to send a text or call someone after the walk or pray for someone while walking. Walking helped reset my focus from self to others. Silence resuscitated my decrepit and languishing prayer life and reactivated it.

Through my recovery journey, God showed me during these silent walks that quiet and silence needed to be developed in my life. Instead of struggling with what to write or do next or being driven by the need to feel productive, God said I needed to be quiet. He was saying that His way to build strength and clarity of mind is countercultural to the world's hustle. And His way is quietness. While walking, I started experiencing God giving me insights related to this book. After walking consistently at least four to five days a week for a few months, I noticed that my thoughts were clearer and more organized, and I did not feel as drained after periods of writing. A Bible verse that I memorized decades ago about quietness and trust being our strength (Isa. 30:15), I was now experiencing as the positive effects of quietness restoring and improving my ability to focus during my writing. Silent walks outside and daily time in silence have become priorities for strengthening myself spiritually, emotionally, mentally, and physically.

Beauty in Silence

Henri Nouwen, a twentieth-century writer, professor, communicator, and theologian known for his writings on faith, prayer, and spiritual formation, tells the story of his deeply transformative encounter with Rembrandt's *The Return of the Prodigal Son* in Nouwen's so-named book. He describes how God spoke to him through silent contemplation over the painting in a way that "brought [him] to a new understanding of [his] vocation and offered [him] new strength to live it."[71] His story paints a beautiful picture of communing with God in solitude and silence, despite being in a busy room full of people. It also serves as an invitation to us to set aside time for silent contemplation with God in our next visit to an art museum. Two years after first encountering a poster of Rembrandt's painting, the image continued to stay with him, and his mind would frequently drift back to that image. While on a 1986 trip to the Soviet Union with friends, Nouwen had the opportunity to see the painting with his own eyes in Saint Petersburg. With great anticipation of his longing fulfilled to sit in the presence of Rembrandt's *The Return of the Prodigal Son*, he penned,

> While many tourist groups with their guides came and left in rapid succession, I sat on one of the red velvet chairs in front of the painting and just looked. Now I was seeing the real thing! Not only the father embracing his child-come-home, but also the elder son and the three other figures. It is a huge work in oil on canvas, eight feet high by six feet wide. It took me a while to simply be there, simply absorbing that I was truly in the presence of what I had so long hoped to see, simply enjoying the fact that I was all by myself sitting in the Hermitage in Saint Petersburg looking at the Prodigal Son as long as I wanted.[72]

Indeed, he took great license with the permission to sit as long as he wanted. After sitting unaware of the passage of time, two hours lapsed in silence and contemplation before his friend Alexi approached him. After a short coffee break, Nouwen returned for another hour before being dismissed by the security guard who was closing the museum for the night. Four days later, Nouwen returned once more for a visit, spending another four hours that day, as he "became more and more part of the story that Jesus once told and Rembrandt once painted. [He] wondered whether and how these precious hours in the Hermitage would ever bear fruit."[73] The nearly eight hours of silent communion with God over that painting forever changed the trajectory of Nouwen's life and ministry and altered his theology in a profound way, which inspired his writing of his classic book *The Return of the Prodigal Son: A Story of Homecoming*.

Eugene Peterson seized on another aspect of silence in his book *Working the Angles*. Peterson differentiates a true, biblical Sabbath from a "day off" by calling the latter a "bastard sabbath."[74] Using a Sabbath for a day off is a secularized perversion of what God intended for the Sabbath because it is only for utilitarian means: to restore strength, increase productivity, reward effort, etc., which are good things in themselves. He notes that "it just so happens that the side effects of shored-up family harmony and improved mental health are also attractive."[75]

Sabbath instead means to quit, to stop and unplug, to cease from the busyness of the week. Peterson calls attention to the creation narrative and how the Hebrew understanding of a day is much different than ours—beginning in the evening and following through the morning. He adds,

> More than idiomatic speech is involved here; there is a sense of rhythm. Day is the basic unit of God's creative work; evening is the beginning of that day. It is the onset of God speaking light, stars, earth, vegetation, animals, man, woman into being. But it is also the time when we quit our activity and go to sleep. When it is evening "I lay me down

> to sleep and pray the Lord my soul to keep" and drift off into unconsciousness for the next six or eight or ten hours, a state in which I am absolutely nonproductive and have no cash value.
>
> Then I wake up, rested, jump out of bed full of energy, grab a cup of coffee, and rush out the door to get things started. The first thing I discover (a great blow to the ego) is that everything was started hours ago. All the important things got underway while I was fast asleep. While I dash into the workday, I enter into an operation that is half over already. I enter into work in which the basic plan is already established, the assignments given, the operations in motion.[76]

Peterson later adds that the "precedent to quit doing and simply *be* is divine."[77] When we Sabbath the way God intended, we enter into a silence of the heart; though the day may be filled with leisure, prayer, family time, or recreation, it is a stillness of soul where we recognize with weekly regularity that Jesus is King, and I am not, and the world will carry on better if I rest in His greatness and trust in His provision for me to simply *be*. The Sabbath invitation is to not *do*, but *be present*.

Another very simple yet helpful practice to mark the Sabbath as a contemplative retreat is to plan a clear-cut, twenty-four-hour period of time and mark the day as holy by the lighting of a candle or other such signifier. During that Sabbath period, removing as many external noises and voices as possible is crucial—limit social media, television and other media, non-essential apps on your phone (for example, you can use the iPhone's "Screen Time" or "Do Not Disturb" feature). Doing this one day a week can have a profound impact on your capacity to benefit from silence.

Giving yourself permission to stop, turn off the sound, and simply be in God's presence seems daunting at first. We're so accustomed to noise that silence can be intimidating, even frightening. Yet as you practice this discipline consistently and patiently, you will find it to be precisely what Nouwen and Peterson described: a pathway to the presence of God.

Practical Methods of Practicing Silence

The practice of silence does not come naturally to most people. If you find it difficult, even daunting, to pause and listen to God, you are not alone. Fortunately, a host of Christians over the centuries have developed simple ways to prompt us to silence. Here are a few you can use. Try them, but do not be discouraged if you don't immediately fall into a long period of communion with God. The pathway is long, and these are your first steps. Let them lead you closer and closer to God.

Lectio Divina

Lectio Divina is a Scripture-reading practice that predates Ignatius of Loyola and is not exclusively practiced by Ignatians. It is becoming increasingly popular among "eucharismatic" evangelicals. It is (along with the Prayer of Examen), however, a staple in Ignatian Contemplation Retreats hosted by Loyola.[78] It involves approaching a Scripture passage with four movements: *Lectio, meditatio, oratio,* and *contemplatio*.

- Lectio (Reading): Read the passage several times. Note phrases or words that stand out. Study the meaning and background.
- Meditatio (Meditation): Think about the reading and how it connects to your life. Place yourself in the setting of the narrative or in the place of the first recipients of the verse.

- Contemplatio (Contemplation): In silence, express love between you and God. Listen for what the Spirit is trying to teach through the passage and prayer.
- Oratio (Prayer): Dialogue with God about the Scripture. Thank Him for His Word and ask for a deeper understanding of it.

The following questions can be contemplated on in times of silent retreat:

- How did the Spirit move me? How did I feel? What is God saying to me?
- How am I being a channel of Christ's love, peace, and mercy in the world?

Examen[79]

The Prayer of Examen is intended to be a contemplative prayer to help people find God, God's presence, and His blessings in their daily life. It is a quiet looking back and a looking forward to the next day as we ask for insights for the next day so we can face challenges and opportunities with patience, wisdom, strength, trust, and peace. The purpose is to find the God moments and build God memories. These memories build God-based muscle memory, which affects every other moment, revealing God's thoughts about you and the forming of your self-perception.

Ignatius of Loyola created this to be a short, fifteen-minute prayer that can be prayed twice daily, and he required the Jesuits to practice Examen at midday and nighttime prayer. If practiced at lunch, then you would look back on your morning and look forward to your afternoon. In the evening, you would look back on your afternoon and look forward to challenges and opportunities for the next morning. There are five movements or steps in the prayer:

1. Give thanks (thanksgiving).
2. Ask God to fill you with His Spirit and for the Spirit to lead you through reviewing the day.
3. Recognize a "consolation"[80] and a "desolation"[81] from the day (review the good and the struggles of the day).
4. Ask for forgiveness and healing.
5. Pray for the next day.

Jesuit author and novice director for the Jesuits "in formation" Mark E. Thibodeaux, SJ, offers a helpful mnemonic for remembering the daily Examen:

- Relish the blessing and gifts of today.
- Request the Spirit to lead you though reviewing the day.
- Review the day.
- Repent of any mistakes or failures.
- Resolve to live tomorrow well and pray for that day.

The Jesus Prayer[82]

The Jesus Prayer is the most popular devotional prayer in the Orthodox tradition. It is increasingly popular among other traditions and is commonly referred to as the Jesus Prayer: "Lord Jesus Christ, Son of God, have mercy on me, a sinner."[83] This short, concise prayer that is composed of four elements:

1. the cry for mercy
2. the discipline of repetition
3. the practice of stillness (*hesychia*)
4. the reverence of the Holy Name

The theology of the Divine Name is rooted in the name of God as noted by Malachi: "From the rising of the sun to its setting my name will be great among the nations" (1:11 ESV). According to Judaism, even the speaking and writing of God's name represented its greatness, holiness, and splendor in the use of the four constants of God's name: YHWH (known as the "tetragram"). The exaltation or reverence for the name of God is included throughout the New Testament in the Lord's Prayer, and at the Last Supper Jesus instructed His disciples to prayer in His name (John 16:23–24). Later Peter testified before the Sanhedrin of the healing virtue of Jesus' name (Acts 4:10, 12).

While a regular recitation of the prayer is essential, for it to be truly a prayer of the heart, the Orthodox believe that it must be united with one's breath so that it becomes a way of life, a pattern of praying without ceasing just as one breathes without ceasing (consider 1 Thess. 5:16). In this way, the prayer is actually prayed in silence. "Lord Jesus Christ, Son of God" is prayed upon one's inhale. "Have mercy on me, a sinner" is prayed upon the exhale, and then repeated.

This prayer will help stop the thoughts scrolling through your mind. If your mind wanders, then do not give up; direct it back to focus on the words again. This prayer is not simply designed to aid in concentration but also to be an act of worship and an expression of one's faith in Jesus.

Silent Walks

Since the beginning of time, our biblical ancestors, such as Adam and Eve, Moses, and Paul, experienced God in nature. Knowing God through creation has been experienced throughout centuries as the Bible speaks of the heavens declaring the glory of God (see Ps. 19:1). Walking as an aerobic exercise improves the immune system, increases memory, promotes cardiovascular health, decreases back pain and fatigue, and decreases symptoms related to depression and stress levels.[84] Additionally, silent walks in nature along quiet, unpaved trails provide the most benefits as they stimulate relaxation and the quietening of the mind, increasing oxygen to the brain.[85] If you are unable to walk along a path due to a physical disability, illness, or injury, listening to nature sounds while closing your eyes and visualizing being in nature also stimulates the mind and provides the relaxation and peaceful margin to connect with God. Taking silent walks outside at least three times a week will improve your overall health and provide margin in your day to enjoy the beauty of creation; reflect on God's greatness, sovereignty, and loving care for His creation; and quiet your being to hear from God.

Here are a few suggestions for taking silent walks in nature:

1. Choose clothes that are loose and fabric that will not make noise.
2. Determine your walking path.
3. Do not listen to music or talk.
4. Focus on breathing from your diaphragm, and breath in as you lift your foot and exhale as you put your foot down.
5. Do not walk too fast where you can't keep your breathing slow and controlled.
6. Swing your arms and hips as you walk to release tension.
7. Pay attention and listen to your surroundings; take in sounds of nature and enjoy the beauty of the landscape. Attention is an avenue of devotion and love.
8. Reflect on the beauty of nature and enjoy it, and then praise God for its beauty.
9. Ask God to speak to you as you quiet yourself before Him in the beauty of His creation.

Structuring Periods of Silence[86]

Eswaran notes his visit to a Franciscan friary in Italy, where the brothers would spend the entire Lenten season in silence. His daily morning ritual of an hour of silence is broken into three sections: thirty minutes of goal setting, twenty minutes of learning and growth, and ten minutes of mindfulness. Christian mindfulness is learning to pay attention and listen to God. It is a practice to help us shut out the noise, focus on God, and listen to God. It is a way of realigning and reorientating our lives to our God, who is active and alive and longs for a relationship with us. We realign ourselves by listening for the knowledge of God and discerning His voice in the Bible and in our thoughts by the power of the Holy Spirit, and then by living like we are mindful of God in our thoughts, words, and actions. As we practice mindfulness, it creates the space for God's wisdom and hope in our lives and deepens the roots of our faith in the turbulent winds of our noisy culture.

This structure is very helpful and could be adapted or modified as seen below:

- 30 Minutes of Goal Setting
  - 10 minutes writing down short, medium, and long-term goals
  - 10 minutes assessing progress to goals
  - 10 minutes taking notes and assessing why unmet goals aren't reach.
- 20 Minutes of Learning and Growth
  - 10 minutes of reading
  - 10 minutes of writing a summary of what you read
- 10 Minutes of Mindfulness
  - For the Christian, this would be a time of silent contemplative prayer.

Nurturing Silence in Parenting[87]

Yelena Moroz Alpert's piece in *National Geographic* recommends several practices to nurture silence in the lives of one's children, which research suggests is crucial in a young person's psychological and physiological development.

- Model silent behaviors to your children. Children will be drawn to model what they see comforts their parents.
- Play the "quiet game." Alpert suggests that leveraging the practice routinely for short segments of quiet, whether for a set amount of time or until you reach a landmark, is helpful. She notes that with teenagers, one should resist the urge to do away with uncomfortable silence. Resist shallow questions or filling the house with noise unnecessarily.
- Tune in to nature. Research shows that experiencing silence in nature heightens feelings of relaxation more than silence indoors does.

PATHWAY 3

Confession

My soul was exceedingly melted, and I bitterly mourned over my exceeding sinfulness and vileness. I never before had felt so pungent and deep a sense of the odious nature of my sin as at this time. My soul was then unusually carried forth in love to God, and had a lively sense of God's love to me.

—David Brainerd[88]

One of the most dreaded Christian practices is confession. We avoid confession because it is hard and embarrassing to admit our failures and sins to God or another person. Shame and guilt are the padlocks on your heart's door, and the pathway or practice of confession unlocks the door. Exposing our failures and sins through confession, we fear, might cause God or others to withdraw their love. Our erroneous belief that if we were fully known, then we could not be fully loved keeps the chambers of our hearts darkened by sin rather than opening the chambers through admitting our sin and welcoming the light of grace into our inner being. A moment of temporary embarrassment and shame places us in a posture of vulnerability to confess our sin and receive forgiveness. Instead of feeling helpless or hopeless, forgiveness reaggregates us to a renewed position of strength and standing before God and others, knowing that we are still deeply loved in spite of our flaws and sins. Confession releases the freedom of grace to cover your sins and remove the padlocks of guilt and shame.

In this chapter, you will learn what confession is (so you can cast off the weights of sin) and then its benefits, which are freedom from guilt and shame. You will also learn that confession is the best turn along our path, even when it is hard, and regular confession of sin and your belief in the grace of God in your life will quell the fear of confession. Confession is also the right turn toward freedom.

Confession Is the Right Turn

Confession is generally understood as a personal admission of wrongdoing. In legal terms, a criminal confesses to a crime. In theological terms, a sinner confesses his or her sin. Confession is an admission of guilt. In a broader sense, a confession can be an admission of one's state of mind, belief, or being. For example, a "confession of faith" is an acknowledgement of what one believes, usually indicated by acceptance of a particular creed, or written statement of faith. We "confess" our faith in Christ. Confession, in Christian terms, is closely tied to repentance. Repentance is understood as a change in direction, a turning away from sin and toward God.

As a pathway to a deeper relationship with God, confession is all of those things—and something more. Confession is not a simple one-time admission of guilt nor a once-and-final change in the direction of one's life. The pathway of confession is a life oriented toward and in constant pursuit of God.

The late Christian anthropologist, Paul Hiebert, articulates the relationship between confession and repentance in a person's coming to faith in Jesus in his book *Transforming Worldviews*. He states that we, deriving our thought from modernity, think primarily in terms of "intrinsic, digital sets, and emphasize precise definitions with clear boundaries. In doing so, we define conversion in terms of what people are in and of themselves. In doing so, however, we risk thinking of conversion as something people believe or do."[89] In other words, we tend to think of our own repentant living in relation to some internal quality or right living. Is my "conscience" right before the Lord? An "internalized" conscience—the proverbial devil sitting on one side of our shoulder and an angel on the other, each depicting the internal struggle of right and wrong within a television character—was foreign to the biblical cultures. [90]

By contrast, these cultures had more of an "externalized" conscience. The honor or shame that would result from the action's exposure to the community established the standards of right and wrong rather than an internal barometer. Therefore, the biblical audience would have regarded repentance and conversion as a condition in relationship to other things and to history.

In other words, we think in terms of where our feet *are*, but they thought in terms of where our feet are *headed*. We are all on a path with God, and what repentance does is turn the direction of our life actions and thoughts toward Him.

The Hebrew term for repentance, *shv*, means to turn in the opposite direction, turning away from sin, or turning back to God.[91] Similarly, the New Testament uses words such as *metanoeo,* which also refers to turning and proceeding in a new direction, or to change one's mind.[92] Both convey the idea of physical movement. Hiebert argues that a biblical view of transformation is to regard conversion as both a point (confession) and a process (repentance).[93] Instead of viewing confession and repentance like simple verbal statements that are followed by doctrinal affirmations, they are more like a noble pledging fealty to a new king who has taken the throne (confession) and the outworking of that fealty in loyal service (repentance). In the same way, our confession—whether it be at the moment of our salvation or as we continue to live out our faith daily—is the spring from which the living waters of repentance flow. Similar to wedding vows, which precede a marriage yet don't summarize the totality of a marriage, so too confession precedes repentance, but repentance must be lived out.

Confession in the Old Testament is the throwing or casting off of sin and giving thanks in the form of declaring praise to God and agreement with YHWH's design for creation. The Hebrew word for confession, *yadah,*[94] means "to throw, cast" and is used with great frequency throughout the Old Testament (see Lev. 5:5; 16:21; 26:40; Num. 5:7; 1 Kings 8:33, 35; 2 Chron. 6:24, 26; 30:22; Ezra 10:1; Neh. 1:6; 9:2–3; Job 40:14; Ps. 32:5; Prov. 28:13; Dan. 9:4, 20. Additionally, it can be used to refer to the giving of praise or making thanksgiving. Another term for confession, *todah,*[95] means "thanksgiving, associated with the confession of praise in liturgical worship" as seen in Joshua 7:19 and Ezra 10:11.

In Leviticus 26:40–45, through His people's confession and repentance, God promises to restore the Israelites because of His covenantal faithfulness (v. 42). God calls them "to confess" sin, using the Hebrew word *yadah*, which, again, implies the "throwing or casting off" of sin.[96] To our modern individualistic sensibilities, the idea of needing to cast off the sin of our forefathers is a difficult concept, yet YHWH establishes this as a condition to His recalling the terms of His covenant and acting upon them. It is not as if God forgot, but it is the sense that He would put his covenant faithfulness into action in response to their casting off of sin. YHWH here is not only concerned with their individual unfaithfulness but with the pattern that they have inherited and continued to propagate from their ancestors.

It does not take long before a teenager notices family sin patterns. As a teen, I remember noticing the patterns of divorce within my family along with their pride in wanting to be right and their problems with forgiveness. The root sins of ancestors continue to be propagated in families, communities, and cultures in both systemic and internalized forms today in much the same way as spoken of here. So confession is a way of casting off the sin, or anything else, that weighs us down in our journey so that we can fully pursue God (see Heb. 12:1).

In the same way, the pathway of confession presents a moment of decision, a change in direction based on an acknowledgment of our sin and Christ's forgiveness, which leads to an ongoing relationship, similar to a marriage, in which both parties continually move closer to one another. Confession is a change of heart that leads to a lifelong pursuit of God. As with thanksgiving and silence, confession brings a host of benefits, both spiritual and psychological.

Benefits of Confession

Confessing your wrongdoings and sins reduces the feelings of shame and guilt. Confession releases the power and effects of forgiveness, which brings freedom from the weight of guilt and shame. Forgiveness sends the weighty baggage of shame and guilt packing. According to a research study conducted at Carnegie Mellon University, of the 4,167 people throughout the United States involved in five experiments, those who confessed partially to cheating expressed more negative emotions, such as guilt, shame, anxiety, and fear, compared to those who confessed everything or did not confess cheating.[97] Those who partially confessed felt more guilty that they did not take full responsibility and were still holding back a full confession. Though people might see partially confessing as more attractive, potentially guilt-relieving, and less of an emotional burden than not confessing at all, the result of the study concludes the opposite. Telling the whole truth relieves the feelings of guilt and shame, whereas a partial confession increases those feelings that people are wanting to mitigate.

Throughout history, confession has been a practice used in both legal and religious contexts. While in a legal context, confession has typically been an incentive for a guilty party to admit wrongdoing in exchange for a more lenient sentence, within the religious context confession offers several benefits:

1. **Relieves guilt and shame**

   Underneath the wrongdoings or sins lies shame and guilt. Shame is like a shadow that can follow us everywhere, lying to us about who we are. It can tell you that something is wrong with you, that if others knew who you really were, they would not love you. Shame erodes your sense of connection and security in your relationship with God. Our first ancestors in the Bible trusted the lies of the serpent, which said that God was holding out on them, and soon the shadow of shame became their unwelcomed friend. Instead of offering safety from the pain of vulnerability, it delivered the pain of alienation. Confessing our sins can stop us from falling into the spiral of shame. In 1 John 1:9, the Bible makes it clears that it is through confession that God forgives us and cleanses us from all unrighteousness. This cleansing means that He removes the penalty of sin and its nagging power of guilt and shame and draws us into a closer relationship with Him. We are washed in the water of forgiveness and, according to Romans 8:1, "There is now no condemnation for those who are in Christ Jesus" (NIV).

2. **Releases forgiveness and freedom**
   Confession and repentance clean the soul, kicking out the controlling power of sin that established residence prior to our becoming a Christian. Confession is housekeeping for the soul. As Romans 6 reminds us, we have been set free from the controlling power of sin in our thought life and actions through confessing and repenting of our sins. One of my favorite Bible verses about how confession is the picture of freedom is found in Micah 7:18–19 and describes the merciful nature of God as He delights to "have compassion on us" and to "cast our sins into the depths of the sea" (ESV). We are washed clean by God's forgiveness and freed from the blues of guilt and shame. Christ has set us free! (See Gal. 5:1.) In turn, those who understand the undeserved forgiveness they have received through Jesus' sacrificial death are more likely to show others the same grace and forgiveness they have received. Forgiveness calms the turbulent waters of an angry soul and diffuses the desire for revenge.

3. **Initiates the ongoing journey of reforming us and breaking old habits**
   The frequency of confession, whether it be confessing ancient creeds or our sin, possesses a powerful formative component of aligning our thoughts and actions with God's ways and breaking old habits. In the practice of confession, when it is in liturgy such as ancient creeds, prayer, or the Eucharist, we simultaneously bear witness to how we are to live as a Christ follower and how our life speaks in comparison or contrast to God's standards. It reminds us of who we are, though not despairingly, but also who we are always becoming through the power of the Holy Spirit. It is reforming us to reflect the light and goodness of God to a dark and lonely world. Over time, we experience the old ways removed from our lifestyle and the new self "made new in the attitude of your minds" (Eph. 4:23 NIV). The ongoing practice of confession will tear down strongholds in your life.

4. **Strengthens us in difficult circumstances**
   Specifically related to confessing one's beliefs, confessing who God is strengthens us when we are going through a difficult time. Reminding myself of God's truths and then confessing them out loud has built strength and endurance in me, showing me that God is with me. Some of the Scriptures I say out loud are Psalm 46:1, "God is [my] refuge and strength" (NIV); Psalm 41:3, "The LORD sustains [me] on [my] sickbed" (NIV); and 2 Corinthians 12:9, "My strength is made perfect in weakness" (KJV). Accepting my position of weakness rather than being angry or wishing things were different has realigned my heart to see my position of weakness as

the grounds by which old habits are uprooted and new habits formed, resulting in the strengthening of my faith.

5. **Forces us to slow down and think**
   Confession calls us to slow down the pace and invites us to examine our hearts. This margin gives the Holy Spirit the space to speak to us and to open our eyes to what is going on in our life. The slowed pace creates an inviting environment to reflect and examine your heart before God. Spending time in reflection positions you to feel less hopeless, so the investment in confession will empower you with hope.

Barriers to the Right Turn

Despite all we have to gain from confession, most of us staunchly resist it. Confession is probably the most avoided of all spiritual disciplines. We simply do not like to admit fault, to change our minds, or to place ourselves under the seeming control of anyone, including God. There are several reasons this is so. Understanding these reasons will help you recognize and avoid them in your own relationship with God.

Despair

Depicting an accurate but false narrative in our understanding of despair, the dialogue between Anne and Marilla in the 1985 Canadian Broadcast Corporation's production of *Anne of Green Gables* comes to mind. In it, Anne asks Marilla (Dewhurst), "Can't you even imagine you're in the depths of despair?" "No, I cannot," Marilla replies. "To despair is to turn your back on God."

Though we do not use the word *despair* in our culture as much, some people hold a similar viewpoint regarding worry or depression as not trusting God. How can we say that someone has turned their back on God because they have despaired, worried, or felt depressed? Despair, from the Hebrew *pûn*, refers to a state of distraction or perplexity or to "be darkened." Despair is a loss of perspective in which problems seem insurmountable and hope is lost, but it's not apostacy. It is the loss of hope that should be grounded in God and not in our feelings or circumstances.

In Psalm 32, David speaks of this kind of despair with groanings, describing it as his bones wasting away and his strength being sapped as in the summer's heat (vv. 3–4). Neither the sin nor form of suffering that David went through is identified, but we know that it was so severe and acute that it felt like his bones were wasting away through his groaning. Then David's confession of sin and assurance of God's presence and protection (that God alone was his hiding place) cast out David's feelings of despair (vv. 5–7). This confession reoriented his perspective so he could thank God for His presence in times of trouble and focus on God guiding and protecting him rather than on his sufferings or trials. Just as David cast out the darkness of despair, we too can cast out despair through reorienting our perspective on God.

Guilt and Shame

David, one of the most well-known figures in the Bible and esteemed as a "man after God's own heart," was just like us in that he was not immune to failures and bad decisions. For him, too, the weight of the shame and guilt erected a barrier to confession. David's sin of adultery with Bathsheba began well before the actual act of sleeping with another man's wife. David probably did not wake up one morning and think, "I am going to sleep with another man's wife today." Sin is more subtle and progressive. Second Samuel 11:1 tells us that David remained in Jerusalem while the other kings had gone to war. Why is this so significant? King David was supposed to be at war, not at home. Perhaps he was exhausted in every way and maybe even lonely, so it seemed natural for him to stay home instead of going out to war.

When we are tired, we are more vulnerable to temptation. David never would have dreamed that staying at home would have led to a series of terrible decisions. Being in the wrong place reveals more the condition of his heart. Had he been talking to God about his loneliness and exhaustion, would Bathsheba have been so enticing? We are most vulnerable when we are not open with God about our struggles and desires. The shadow of guilt and shame followed David around and whispered in his ear that he should hide from God. Shame is a liar; it told him not to come clean with God by confessing his sin and receiving the freedom of forgiveness. The thought of a public shaming for his actions seemed overwhelming and humiliating to David.

Many people would have been aware of David's actions toward Bathsheba and Uriah; multiple players are even mentioned in the narrative. According to Brandon O'Brien and Randolph Richards in their book *Misreading Scripture with Western Eyes*, it was not uncommon or outside of the culturally approved expectations for a king to do what David did. David's scheme to cover up his sin by sending Uriah home to sleep with his wife failed. David knew that his actions might be exposed publicly because of Uriah's resistance, and Uriah's words in 2 Samuel 11:11 were a sort of public challenge to David, shaming him for remaining at home when he should be fulfilling his duties as king and fighting with his soldiers. To end his fear over a public shaming, David ordered for Uriah to be killed. But the matter was not put to rest in the eyes of the Lord. The sin would be kept quiet, and everyone would move on—except YHWH.

God's displeasure concerning David's actions deserves more attention than our first response: "Well, of course it would displease God." Though a sin might be acceptable culturally, that does not mean that God will let your sin go. David had probably moved on and was truly caught off guard by Nathan's confrontation (2 Sam. 12). This convicts David and results in his confession and subsequent contrition. Though David deserved public shaming for what He did, God is so gracious that He does not treat us as our sins deserve. Confession releases forgiveness and freedom from the weight of guilt and shame. God loved David, and David loved God. Confession removes the barrier that sin creates in our relationship with God and also throws off the weight and entanglements of sin, which lead to sinful habits. God knows that if we think we can get away with something that we will probably do it again because the sin will not seem as real if it remains hidden. Confession is the pathway to removing guilt and shame.

Pride

Pride inflates the ego, resulting in the growth of a superiority complex. It can also cause you to think that you know better than others, and therefore, you do not have to follow the same rules as others in society, which can lead to all sorts of injustices, cheating, greed, corruption, or exploitation. Pride will justify one's action by saying competition is healthy. Statements such as "I take pride in my looks, home, or family" lead to vanity and overvaluing your physical appearance, money, status, physical things, and ultimately leading to self-absorption, self-centeredness, and narcissism. This sort of pride aids people in justifying their excessive spending on clothes, beauty products, and procedures or their frequent purchasing of accessories for their home. Pride is never satisfied and always wants more, spreading like a disease that disturbs our contentment and even our common sense. Pride also causes you to look down on others who may not have the same financial means or social opportunities. A practical sign of this attitude is reflected in the treatment of restaurant servers. Pride raises its ugly voice in demanding requests and snobbery toward servers or other workers in the service industry.

A prideful heart assumes that a person has a special license to do as they want, yet their speech does not reflect their actions. The Bible abhors the hypocrisy of saying one thing and doing another, or another way of expressing it: the inconsistency between your words and your actions. Chapter 4 of the book of James gives prominence to this problem of hypocrisy among the religious leaders and church body. In verses 9–10, James calls them to humble themselves by physically showing their repentance in their actions instead of parading around saying one thing while doing another. A prideful person is a vain person who is consumed with praise, approval, admiration, attention, and applause, while angling for position, often at the expense of others.

The Bible issues a warning of the dangers of pride in Proverbs 16:18: "Pride goes before destruction, a haughty spirit before a fall" (NIV). One cannot help recalling the many church scandals coming to light in a nearly incessant succession. The voice of pride says, "You are the exception." But in each of these scandals, whether from an abuse of power, money, or sex,[98] there exists an apparent pride wherein the church leader has believed that his (and occasionally her) capacity to live one way and preach another is not a spiritual or ethical problem.

Humility, the opposite of pride, is a chief virtue of a confessing heart and of the Christian life. In Wilmer Villacorta's book *Tug of War: The Downward Ascent of Power*, the author underscores the benefit of humility: "Although a sense of powerlessness and vulnerability can be extremely unsettling, accepting and embracing the end of our own strength helps us find our way to God's path of power."[99] In laying down our desire for power, wealth, esteem, and pride and then humbling ourselves by following Jesus' example, we find that God's strength and power enters and advances through this humility. Humility births wisdom, and pride leads to destruction and alienation in a dungeon darkened by selfishness.

Narcissism

In Greco-Roman culture, philosophers and teachers commonly employed "vice lists" and "virtue lists," as Paul additionally emulated in his writing. These lists were not meant to be exhaustive but were to be the starting point, provoking further thought, examination, and application for individuals and the community. The list of gifts or fruit of the Spirit from 1 Corinthians 12 and 14 and Galatians 5 are the starting points but not the total list. The emphasis on self-love as a precursor to loving another, even the ancient moralist teachers in Paul's day condemned that teaching. Plutarch even warned of avoiding the appearance of self-love.[100] Paul was calling attention to the ethical teachings of his Greek contemporaries, which would have been familiar to his audience, to prove the point that the vices of self-absorption and self-promotion were not virtues that aligned with the teachings of Jesus.

With regard to confession, this pride produces narcissism, which is rampant and celebrated in our culture. Who is held in high esteem but those with the most followers, likes, tweets, etc.? Someone always has more, so they are chasing the cultural worship of more. Take a look at "Christian influencers" on Instagram to see Bible verses or moralistic (though seemingly Christian) quotes plastered atop selfies. This sort of self-absorbed pride produces a slow-growing association between our own feelings of contentment and the faithfulness of God, while ignoring both a theology of suffering and the necessary role that confession plays in our spiritual development.

Casting Off the Weight

After my time of silence in my Seven Pathways experience, which God was working into my daily cadence with Him, I would spend time connecting with God through confession, which is the third pathway. Before writing the Seven Pathways for all of you, God guided me to create this Seven Pathways plan for connecting with Him while I was in a dark place physically as I struggled with many health issues. This Seven Pathways experience has become so life-giving to me, and it helped me chart my way back to better health and a deeper relationship with God.

No other story in the Bible reminds me more of the forgiveness and freedom of confession, which removes the weight of shame and guilt, than the story of the adulterous women in John 8. Jesus' response to the question posed by the religious leaders of what to do to the woman was something unexpected: He wrote a message in the sand. We do not know what He wrote, but we can read His verbal challenge to the Pharisees and scribes, saying whoever had no sin could throw the first stone at her. They dispersed one by one. With the street clear and only Jesus and the woman remaining, Jesus asked her if anyone condemned her. Just as there was no one who remained to condemn her, then He said, "Neither do I condemn you" (John 8:10 ESV).

The first step to confession is to stand before Jesus, just as this woman did. I imagine that she felt ashamed over her sin and expected that God was going to guilt trip her. Most of us think of confession like that too—that God is going to guilt trip us. It is the kind of trip that we do not want to take and comes at a price that we want to stop paying. Instead of guilt and shame taking us on a trip of lies and weighing us down with its baggage, confession casts off the weight of guilt and shame and brings forgiveness and freedom.

One day very early on in recovery, while I was moving from a time of silence to confession in my daily Seven Pathways time with God, God did not bring up my past mistakes, failures, or accusations in a harsh tone with me. Instead, He rather lovingly said, "Let's talk about them," and He put his finger on one particular sin. I remember thinking, He is going to be mad at me or say "I told you so." But instead, I felt like He was saying there's no judgment, that my sins were covered, and to remember that I was His. I felt surprisingly comforted, and I agreed with Him regarding those things I had said and done that were not right, and that I wanted to make some changes.

Confession is the act of bringing any darkness and sin from your life into God's light and agreeing with Him about your sin, and then repenting, which is changing a direction in your life and then adusting your daily thoughts and actions to reflect that change. In confessing my sins and receiving His forgiveness, I felt like the weights of varying degrees were being lifted. Some of the "skin" around the sins was sore from the pressure, so I knew that it would take some time for healing from old habits, for thoughts to change, and for new "skin" to grow. Other sins had broken the skin, so the wounds were deeper.

All of life is repentance because we continually sin based on having a sinful nature. But thankfully, we are no longer in bondage to sin because Jesus has set us free from its bondage through His sacrificial death. And His Spirit living inside of us can help us change our thoughts, actions, and affections so that we live and think more like a follower of Christ. The progressive nature of this spiritual renewal and transformation is a daily process and is indicated by the use of the present progressive verb tense, *renewing*, as found in Romans 12:2. Christians will still struggle with sin while "being renewed in knowledge in the image of" Christ (Col. 3:10 NIV), whose glory we reflect. This process is continuous throughout a lifetime and not fully experienced until Christ returns. (See Phil. 3:21; 1 John 3:2.)

We often think of sin as the bad things that we do, and yes, that is true, but the Bible speaks of sin as having dominion, or "reigning." More than being the bad things you do, sin can be a power in someone's life. Sin exercises authority: "For if, by the trespass of one man, death reigned through that one man, how much more will those who receive God's abundant provision of grace and of the gift of righteousness reign in life through the one man, Jesus Christ" (Rom. 5:17 NIV). The sin nature exercised dominion and had a power in your life before you became a Christian. And now, for those in Christ, you still sin, but you have the Spirit living in you, helping you to resist sin, and His power in you, changing your desires and affections as He makes you more into the image of His Son. Yes, you still sin, but the reigning of sin and the condemnation for your sins were paid for by Jesus Christ's shed blood. "You, however, are controlled not by the sinful nature but by the Spirit, if the Spirit of God lives in you" (Rom. 8:9 NIV 1984). And Romans 6:6–7 says, "For we know that our old self was crucified with him so that the body of sin might be done away with, that we should no longer be slaves to sin—because anyone who has died has been freed from sin."

Sometimes I have asked for forgiveness but then did not change my actions; this leads to the Lord and me continuing to revisit this sin. I had confessed my sins but did not turn back to the Lord. (Acts 3:19 speaks of true repentance as agreeing with God about the sin and then changing one's actions.) All of us have taken a wrong turn, perhaps leading us off course. Stubbornness and pride cause us to not admit that we are lost. What we need to do instead is to confess that we are lost. This is a picture of biblical confession, the admission of our need to change course.

The struggle with sinful habits can seem insurmountable, and knowing how to change direction can be obstructed by our cloudy vision from sin. I am so comforted by Paul's struggle with sin, which he speaks of in Romans 7:18–19, and by God's wonderful, merciful nature. The Bible does not say that God might *think* about forgiving your sins, but it says that He "delight[s] to show mercy," and He casts "all our iniquities into the depths of the sea" (Mic. 7:18–19). Casting my sins into the sea sounds amazing. It means we can forget and stop talking about them. I am in! I think that we could all use some more time at the ocean with God. I felt like, during my time of confession with the Lord, He dove into the waters of my heart and cleaned out some of the growing algae. I am not saying that the old habits were gone through that time of confession, but we did land on one particular habit, spent some time there, and then started the conversation on others. The release of the old sinful habit as I cast it out through confession felt so good, and asking God to help me develop strategies to implement the changes and set up some guardrails and accountability felt like a step in the right direction.

Old habits often die hard because, if we are honest with ourselves and God, we are not sure if we want to stop yet. If this is the case with you, pray and ask God to help you to want to stop this sin consistently. If you keep praying this regularly, you will either quit the sin or stop praying. Another option is to visualize the consequences of that sin, which can make the sin more real. The way I visualize this is to imagine what it would look like if I stopped this sin and then what it looked like if I did not.

Be totally honest with God. Let him know that you are really struggling and that a part of you deep down does not want to quit. Keep attacking your habit honestly before God. You will either break the sin over time or you will stop praying about it.

Taking these steps of confession is just the beginning of the journey to reform these habits, but it's also important for others who are further along in their healing journey. Remember that God's process of changing us, called sanctification, is ongoing; He is forming us as we are being renewed to reflect the image of Christ more than the world. According to 2 Corinthians 3:18, we are being transformed continuously throughout our lifetime to reflect Jesus Christ. So be patient with yourself even while you're attacking the sin; don't give up too quickly. Old habits are hard to break. Resist the temptation to try to smokescreen God by focusing more on the minor habits so He won't go meddling in your favorite habits.

Focus on one sin at a time. Then instead of focusing on breaking the habit and on what you can't do, focus on what you *can* do. Stop the replay that says, "I can't." Those are two words Satan will use to lure you back in because we are prone to want what we can't have. Start storing up God's word in your heart by memorizing verses about how God helps you in your weakness—or whatever topic He leads you to, which will speak life to you and attack your habit. Our habits are formed in our thoughts and then lived out in our actions, so fill that space with new actions.

Lastly, ask a friend to hold you accountable. Just as Jesus called out Peter's sin in Luke 22:31, we all need trusted friends who love Jesus and who will point us back in the right direction. We need to pray with them and enlist them to help us root out our bad habits.

Stop letting guilt and shame hold you back from getting close to God. Start welcoming Him into your real life through confession, and the load that you are carrying will lighten. When you confess your sins and ask for forgiveness and invite God into your life, you will experience freedom and a deeper loving and trusting relationship with God and others. You have spent enough on your guilt trips while God has been inviting you to freedom the size of the ocean. Ocean trip or guilt trip—which one will you choose? I choose the ocean. I hope that traveling the road of confession is no longer a guilt trip but a trip by the shore.

Picking up Grace

Confession is a casting off of sorts. We cast off sin, guilt, shame, bad habits, selfishness, etc. But we take up something, too, as children of God. We take on a new identity. We begin the daily pursuit of God. Confession is both an end and a beginning. In this sense, our ongoing "confession" is that of our new identity. We confess that we are the people of God.

May the people of God say so! The Hebrew term *yadah* appears numerous times in the Old Testament in the sense of "giving praise to your name" or "glorifying your name." The King James Version of the Bible renders the term as "confess your name" (*yadah sem*), while the New International Version renders it as "give praise to your name." The English Standard Version's rendering is much more neutral, "acknowledge your name," while the Common English Bible uses "give thanks to your name." The semantic range of this term is helpful to determining its meaning, which is less an "either/or" but more often a "both/and." The NIV's rendering invokes the worshipful element that *yadah* conveys, unlike the ESV. Yet there is also a superiority and reorientation that is implied in such praise, which the CEB falls short of conveying. Because the term *confession* itself is so frequently misconstrued in modern parlance as simply meaning to "fess up" or "admit wrongdoing," denying the biblically intended reorientation (repentance) that should follow, I'm less inclined to invoke the KJV. That said, it is perhaps the second-best rendering to that of the NIV, "to give praise to your name."

This emphasis on praising God correlates with the New Testament term *homologeó*,[101] which means to speak the same, to agree, and refers to confessing that God is God and worthy of praise. In the New Testament, the Bible uses confession primarily in the sense of declaring with one's mouth who God is and of processing one's sins (e.g., Matt. 10:32; Luke 12:8; John 9:22; 12:42; Acts 23:8; 24:14; Rom. 10:9–10; Heb. 11:13; 1 John 1:9; 4:2–3, 15; 2 John v. 7). And this confession of the heart transforms his or her life. In biblical terms the heart is the center of a person, encompassing the whole being—mind, will, emotions, and affections. Therefore, confessing that Jesus is Lord means embracing with the whole heart a loyal devotion to Him (Rom. 10:9–10).

At All Times

The voices that declared misdiagnoses over me and the uncertainty of the source of my physical pain weighed heavily on my heart at times. I felt the power of those words unlike any situation I had ever encountered. Not too far into my healing journey, it became clear to me that there was one person who could give me a correct diagnosis, establish a treatment program, and heal me. And that was God. I knew that God was the ultimate Physician and that He created my body—and everything! So He knew how to help me. Each night I started confessing in prayer God as my Physician, and I asked Him to be my primary care doctor, to give me a correct diagnosis and treatment program, and to heal me. Not long after I started praying this, I received a good diagnosis and started treatment and physical therapy for occipital neuralgia.

In recovery, even when you are moving in the right direction, there are ups and downs. Though my path was painful and unsteady, I would remind myself of these truths, speaking God's truth over my situation, through confessing personalized Bible verses during prayer:

- Trust the Lord and lean not on my own understanding. (Prov. 3:4–5)
- He will make my steps firm. (Ps. 37:23)
- The Lord will sustain me on my sickbed and restore me from illness. (Ps. 41:3)
- The Lord watches over me. (Ps. 121:5)
- Be content in all circumstances. (Phil. 4:11–13)
- When I am weak, I am strong. (2 Cor 12:9–11).

These verses reminded me that I did not need to fear or stress out about my weaknesses or the uncertainty in my recovery journey, but that I could trust in God, and through trusting, He would strengthen me, be with me, and help me as I work hard to recover. And He would help me to sleep, work, write, pray, and even laugh with friends and family, through nerve pain, ear infections, and gout. It was frustrating to feel so weak because I was accustomed to a much faster pace, but God was telling me, "You need to slow down."

As I adjusted my work pace into segments, I noticed that I was getting stronger and was processing my thoughts into writing more quickly. I was also building more strength in my muscles as I targeted and focused on them.

So I encourage you to attack what you are going through with the Bible, as there is strength and power in His words. Speak life, trust God, and do your part with every fiber of your being. Never give up! The Bible speaks of its power as a weapon, a sword, so pick it up and learn to fight for your life, the life of your family, and generations to come.

No other person in the Bible, aside from Jesus, suffered more than Job. Job's first children were all killed tragically by the mighty winds of a storm, which caused the house to collapse on them. Then Job developed some type of sickness that was very painful and caused sores all over his body, along with a fever. The severity of his sores left him unrecognizable to his own friends. Just like us, when God allows bad things to happen, Job believed that he must have done something wrong for God to have aimed poisonous arrows at Him.

Suffering from chronic pain pulled Job down into the quicksand of misery and depression, where he lost his sense of purpose. He relentlessly voiced His dreadful situation and called out God's injustice to have allowed this. Yet still Job did not deny God (Job 6:10), nor did he curse God (10:2). Amid his suffering, Job recalled his faith in God in this confession that has been sung throughout the ages: "I know that my Redeemer lives, and that in the end he will stand upon the earth" (19:25 NIV 1984).

Job's faith continued despite all his suffering and the taste of bitterness in his soul (Job 27:2). His continued discourse in chapter 27 and his poem in chapter 28 are windows into his struggle and inner dialogue with God about his situation. Then, to end his case before God, Job denied having engaged in a list of sins. Like we do, Job did not see his own sin. In all the thousands of years since then, human nature has not changed from diverting one's guilt by pointing out good things. If your responsibility was to take out the trash, then instead of admitting that you failed to do it, you might instead mention how you put your dishes in the sink this morning or moved a neighbor's trash can from the street and back to their driveway.

After listening to Job's relentless appeal, God spoke very clearly to Job, asserting His ability to administer justice and His supreme power to care for His creation (see chs. 38–41). In response, Job repented of his arrogance and even prayed for his friends, who had misguided and hurt him. Lastly, the Lord blessed the latter years of Job's life even more than the first (Job 42:12). Just as Job never knew the reason for his suffering, we have to trust that God does not allow us to suffer for no reason, even when the reason is never revealed (Isa. 55:8–9). We must trust that God only does what is right and that He never does evil.

Keep clinging to Jesus, and do not give up on Him. Instead of getting bogged down in your case, listen to God when He speaks (as Job eventually did). All Job's former talk about God became real because he wrestled with how God could allow injustice in the life of one who loved Him. We learn from Job that God is not unjust and that we can thank Him for being patient with us when we are slow to understand. Just as Job never knew the reason for his suffering, we can thank God that He is just, infinitely good, and powerful even while we are suffering, and He only does what is right. God stayed with Job through all the trials, accusations, and complaining, so God is not going to give up on you either. God is all about restoration, and He promises that He is always working for your good. I am sure that it was hard for God to watch someone He loved like Job endure such afflictions.

Confession is a declarative act of worship that is done in communion with God alone and with God and other believers or as a church. It affirms who God is and God's restorative work in Jesus and aligns us to his sense of order, wholeness, and righteousness. Walking in darkness is persisting in unbelief. First, sin is devasting, but God is gracious, making a way through the costly sacrifice of Jesus' death. While walking in the light, our life speaks, says that Jesus is God, and that Jesus changes lives (1 John 1:5–8). Jesus' blood makes our forgiveness possible (Heb. 9). Jesus made full atonement for our sins, so, "If we confess our sins, he is faithful and just to forgive us our sins and to cleanse us from all unrighteousness" (v. 9 ESV). Forgiveness is grounded in Christ's redemptive work. To paraphrase Martin Luther: The entire life is repentance.

In All Circumstances

Early in my struggle with head and neck pain from the injury to my head, I decided that I was not going to let this take me down or out. What has helped me climb through the pain and continue on my recovery journey has been celebrating the small steps and small wins rather than focusing on how far I still have to go for a full recovery. I altered my vision to focus on the small steps. I knew that small steps with God right beside me, behind me, and before me would take me far and eventually to a full recovery, whether in this lifetime or the next. I have had my share of setbacks and really painful and sleepless nights, but I have learned to set up guardrails to protect myself from evil that would try to set me back, hurt me, or make me focus on what I was missing—or how my hair was falling out—which could fuel anger and bitterness. At the time of this writing, this suffering has been a marathon of about four and half years, and I have never been more certain that God is still with me and that I will not be disappointed as I wait and hope in God's faithfulness. But until my full recovery, I will keep watch and not give up the fight in the darkness of the night.

Sadly, our churches are languishing and atrophying due to little emphasis put on the role of confession of sin; the thoughtful, historical and theological teaching on sin, confession, and repentance; and the role of suffering in the Christian life. When I think on the most concise and extensive teaching on repentance, the pain of suffering, and the state of the human soul in relationship to God, I think of Psalm 130. The psalm opens with the phrase "out of the depths," the place from where the psalmist cries out to the Lord for mercy. With the rise of depression and sadness among adults and now among teens, more research funds are being allocated to identify and treat this burgeoning crisis. While focusing on symptoms and seeking treatment through our medical system is a good thing and a good step in healing, it must be coupled with treatment for the primary problem—and the root of all problems: our existence as guilty sinners before God.

To help avoid depression in my own life, I employ strategies to remove triggers for depression, and I have learned new ways of speaking to myself and viewing myself that are necessary in a holistic treatment program. These all help my emotional and mental states, but I know that we can't leave out the "soul" problem.

You are not just a mind living in a body. You can stop engaging in activities that stimulate sadness, or you can use strategies that will help combat a spiral of negative emotions, but activities and strategies cannot change your inner soul identity or dialogue. You can make all the positive changes yet still see yourself as guilty. This is where the real problem resides: that the soul of man screams guilt. Guilt will eat you up and rob you of the freedom of Christian repentance. The good news for Christians is that our primary human problem from which all other problems propagate is that sin does not have to rule our lives; Jesus took all our guilt and shame through the cross, which silences the guilty voices that speak against us. We need to be just as concerned with employing strategies and creating habits that address our spiritual being as we do for our mind and body.

In Psalm 130, David doesn't ignore or try to cover up his feelings of despair. He admits them forthrightly. He openly and passionately calls out his suffering to God. Because he does not identify the sin that put him in this situation, this psalm can easily be applied as our own prayer when needing forgiveness. David cries from "out of the depths," essentially saying, "I'm drowning in guilt," and it is a metaphor for total misery and sin. David believed that God heard his prayer and that his prayer would change things. As Christians, we can approach God with the same assurance and security of our relationship. Do you believe that God hears your prayers and that they make a difference?

In verse 2 of Psalm 130, David cries out for God to hear him and to be attentive. Psalm 5:2 also speaks of God "hearing" David's cries. This urgent request or petition of God is based on God Himself and His mercy.

Going back to Psalm 130, the phrasing found in verse 3 represents a traditional Hebrew conditional clause known as an "if, then" clause. This conditional means that *if* God kept a record of sin, *then* no one could withstand the punishment. The term in Hebrew for "sin" refers not only to the act of sin but also to its guilt. The purpose is to show how endless God's mercy is that He doesn't focus on David's fault or guilt. This Hebrew idiomatic statement best represents that the source of David's request and confidence is in God.

Psalm 130:4 goes on to talk about fearing or revering God. This does not mean dread or trepidation, but the word "feared" in the KJV and "reverence" in the NIV mean "to inspire reverence, godly fear."[102] God's forgiveness inspires far more gratitude than the fear of punishment. What the psalmist is saying is without a real awareness of forgiveness, a person cannot worship God. The psalmist emphasizes the rising degree of his hope by the repetition of the act of waiting and watching (vv. 5–6). The psalmist does not ground his hope in wishful thinking but in God's faithfulness to His word (v.5). This refers to God's covenant with Israel and His promise to fulfill His covenantal promises (Ps. 10:5, 11; 51:4, 6; 56:4; 105:8, 42; 106:12, 14).

This type of waiting and hoping in God means holding onto hopeful expectation in God during much pain or suffering. This is holding on to hope when you hit rock bottom and endure physical suffering or when you see no light at the end of the tunnel for you or your family. David's comparison to a night watchman (v. 6) may not be easily understood in our culture. A night watchman's duties were to be alert, to maintain a watchful eye, and to defend the city from any enemies or threats to the safety of its inhabitants. It was a physically exhausting job to keep your eyes scanning for threats all night, and it was quite dangerous. The comparison of David waiting *more than* a watchman waits for morning depicts the extreme urgency and longing that David had for God's mercy to relieve his pain and suffering. When you feel like you have hit the bottom, and you do not see how you can get a new outcome or situation, be a watchman; look for the danger in the night, and call for God's faithfulness and love. Ask Him to turn things around. As a watchman, keep up your work and your responsibilities. God wants you to keep living; do not let this suffering or pain stop you from living with the hope that light is coming each morning. His redemption is just as sure as the sun rises.

Through Jesus' sacrificial death, which paid our debt and removed the penalty of death, we can have hope that whatever pain or suffering we experience in this lifetime, it will not be our end. Those who believe in Christ will never die. Jesus suffered unto death so that we do not have to. In all eight mentions of God in Psalm 130, the context is that God is not absent or ambivalent toward His people, but that He is working in their lives, for good. Remember, David does not share one word in this psalm about the source of his suffering. No one can escape suffering. The difference is not *what* you suffer but *how* you suffer. Suffering is not the ultimate; redemption is. We need God's lens by which to see our suffering as a watchman's eye in the darkness of the night.

The Cost of Confession

Confession brings great freedom. There is also a cost. We know that intuitively, which is a primary reason we avoid confession. We understand that it will mean turning away from the past, letting go of old thoughts and behaviors, and turning ourselves fully toward God. That's hard to do, but it is the pathway to freedom—the pathway to God.

Upon arriving in Ephesus, in Acts 19, Paul found a disturbing, growing economy that involved the monetization of the sexually promiscuous cult practices and the writing, selling, and *using* of spell books to cast spells on people. As a cultural center, Ephesus was known for the cult worship of Artemis, and the Ephesians believed that these magical spells gave them power personally and over people. First, we meet with some of the followers who had a very limited understanding of the gospel. They had received John's baptism but did not know about the coming of the Holy Spirit. Seeing the great spiritual need and its great influence in culture in Ephesus and beyond, Paul spent two years lecturing in the hall of Tyrannus.

Through the proclamation of the gospel, God performed miracles, as some were healed from sickness, and others freed from evil spirits. Others who were not followers of Jesus were taking advantage of people for money, claiming to have the power to cast out evil spirits in the name of Jesus. Then one day, "seven sons of Sceva" (Acts 19:14 NIV) tried to cast out an evil spirit, and the evil spirit responded to them: "Jesus I know, and Paul I know about, but who are you?" (v. 15). Then the evil spirit jumped on them and beat them so that they ran out naked and bleeding. As this terrifying story spread throughout Ephesus, the Bible says, "They were all seized with fear, and the name of the Lord Jesus was held in high honor" (v. 17). As a result, many "believed now and openly confessed" their evil practices (v. 18).

The confession of their sin led them to also throw out their evil sources and practices. They went so far as to burn them publicly, validating their inward act of repentance. Their act of confession and then repenting—no more writing, selling, or teaching from spell books or making idols—was costly. It had been a lucrative business. The value of these spell books totaled "fifty thousand drachmas" (v.19 NIV), which was a lot of money. Many had profited from this business and were living in nice villas, so repentance cost them their lifestyle. But they believed that saying yes to Jesus was worth the great cost to them and their families. Through the proclamation of the gospel and the power of Christ, strongholds were torn down. After this Paul spent much time teaching the Ephesians about spiritual warfare (read in Ephesians 6) to prepare them for the challenges and temptations that would come to their cultural capital. In order for them to follow Jesus' ways and be a light in a dark world, Paul taught them that they must continually repent when the Holy Spirit points out sin (see Eph. 4).

When has your confession and the act of repenting cost you something? Are there some things that you physically need to put in the garbage? You might not have books to throw in the garbage, but what apps do you need to delete on your phone or websites that you need to block or media services that you to unsubscribe from? What are some sins that you need to uproot in your life? How can you more regularly confess your sins?

Don't fear this process. Confession is the pathway to healing, redemption, and freedom. It is your pathway to knowing God.

The Practice of Confession

Christians have practiced confession in a variety of ways over the centuries, so the word itself may evoke a number of images. To many people, confession means sitting in a confessional and recounting your sins to a priest. To others, the word evokes the image of kneeling at an altar at the front of a church, tearfully confessing to God. In fact, there are a number of ways you can practice this discipline. Here are a few that will get you started.

Private Confession

Confession can be awkward, as it feels like we are exposing our "dirt"—the things that we are ashamed of—even when we know God is compassionate and loving. Think about a time when you confessed something to your spouse, parent, or friend. Their unconditional love made it easier, but it was still hard. Since our salvation is both an event and a process (Phil. 2:12), the practice and the discipline of confession will help us in that process of growing in our faith and experiencing transformation more in this life (Eph. 4:13). I found it helpful to start a prayer of confession with some verses from Psalms, before I confess specific sins to God. Two of my favorites are,

- Out of the depths I cry to you, O LORD; O Lord, hear my voice. Let your ears be attentive to my cry for mercy. (Ps. 130:1–2 NIV 1984)
- Then I acknowledged my sin to you and did not cover up my iniquity. I said, "I will confess my transgressions to the LORD"—and you forgave the guilt of my sin. (Ps. 32:5)

As you read the verses, imagine breathing the words into your soul, and then pause quietly for a few seconds, letting the belief soak in. Next, as you confess it in prayer out loud, breathe it out.

Corporate Confession

Before communion each week, Glenn Packiam, while serving as associate pastor of New Life Church, would pray a few verses from Psalm 51. Here, he describes what his congregation began to experience, the beautiful intimacy of confession as a church community and the power of receiving and announcing the good news to one another:

We began to notice an intimacy, vulnerability, and honesty we hadn't experienced before. We had found and committed to the tension. Husbands and wives stood next to one another, saying that they had sinned. Parents and children, friends and neighbors, were all on level ground before the cross. It was hard, and it hurt, and sometimes we even cried with one another.

But then something beautiful happened.

Because the tension had become real, the experience of resolution became visceral and powerful. On the heels of confession, we turned corporately to a moment of recognizing God's forgiveness. We asked people to turn to one another and to announce the good news by saying, "Your sins are forgiven in Jesus' name."

Can you imagine the raw beauty and spiritual intimacy of husbands and wives, friends and roommates, brothers and sisters, coworkers and strangers, saying that to one another? It was powerful. . . . And we need a community to remind us of God's grace.[103]

Since the first Anglican prayer book of 1662, Anglicans have opened the celebration of the Eucharist with a "Collect for Purity," followed by a "Humble Access Prayer." Each prayer follows a pattern of orienting our unworthiness in light of God's holiness and thanking Him for His cleansing work. Some examples of the Collect for Purity are as follows:

- *Book of Common Prayer*, 1662: Almighty God, unto whom all hearts be open, all desires known, and from whom no secrets are hid: Cleanse the thoughts of our hearts by the inspiration of the Holy Spirit, that we may perfectly love thee, and worthily magnify thy name. Amen.

- *Melanesian English Prayer Book*, 1973: Almighty God, all hearts are open, and all desires known to you, and no secrets are hidden from you; cleanse our thoughts by the breath of your Holy Spirit, so that we may truly love you and worthily praise your holy name; through Jesus Christ, our Lord. Amen.
- *Kenyan Our Modern Services*, 2002: Almighty God, you bring to light things hidden in darkness, and know the shadows of our hearts; cleanse and renew us by your Spirit, that we may walk in the light and glorify your name, through Jesus Christ, the light of the world. Amen.[104]

Creeds

In the field of ritual studies, confession as a corporate act can function both as a rite of communion and as a rite of affliction.

For a rite of exchange, a person or an object is temporarily set apart to aid in corporate unity. Related to the ancient Creeds, the corporate recitation of these confessions of faith functions as a rite of communion. The creed acts as a "bonding agent" that provides cohesiveness to the community of faith.

When we recite the creeds together, we're reminded that we are joining the voices of Christians throughout centuries, declaring our great heritage of faith and our one and true God. The creeds solidify our identity within the community of faith, and our religious identity as a Christ follower, affirming our belonging to God and as a social group. Additionally, it is spiritually and psychologically empowering to affirm our standing, loyalty, and love before God together.

The Apostles' Creed was created around AD 150 in response to circulating heresies of the time and as a symbol and confession of faith "whereby Christians could distinguish true believers from those who followed the various heresies circulating at the time, particularly Gnosticism and Marcionism."[105]

Eventually the Apostles' Creed was integrated into the baptismal rites (each of which, ritually speaking, is called a "rite of transition" or "rite of passage"). In baptism, candidates are asked to respond to a section of the Creed in question form: "Do you believe in God the Father almighty?" Their response to the question affirms the confession of faith. In addition to the rite of baptism, the season of Lent focuses on spiritual reflection and confession of sin. Corporate confession, especially in ritual and liturgical contexts, is a catalyst for transformation and spiritual formation.

Morning and Evening Prayers

The practicing of praying regularly at set times of the day, morning and evening, derived from Christianity's Jewish roots and has continued its primacy in Christian prayer practices. Here are a few examples from various Christian traditions of corporate confessions for morning or evening prayer.

- The Anglican Church in North America (ACNA), *Book of Common Prayer*, 2019[106]: Almighty and most merciful Father, we have erred and strayed from your ways like lost sheep. We have followed too much the devices and desires of our own hearts. We have offended against your holy laws. We have left undone those things which we ought to have done, and we have done those things which we are not to have done; and apart from your grace, there is no health in us. O Lord, have mercy upon us. Spare all those who confess their faults. Restore all those who are penitent, according to your promises declared to all people in Christ Jesus our Lord. And Grant, O most merciful father, for his sake, that we may now live a godly, righteous, and sober life, to the glory of your holy name. Amen.[107]

- (Roman Catholic) *Saint Augustine's Prayer Book*, 2014: Lord Jesus Christ, you bought our condemnation on the cross; give me a heart that is broken for the wrong that I have done, the harm that I have caused others, the good I have not done, and, most of all, that I have turned away from you. For these, and for any sins I cannot now remember, and for any failure to recognize and acknowledge my sins, I truly and humbly repent and ask mercy. Give me a sorrow for all my sins and trust in your forgiveness.[108]
- (Eastern Orthodox) *Ancient Faith Prayer Book*, 2014: Oh Lord, my Savior and Master, I, your unprofitable servant, with fear and trembling give thanks to you for your loving-kindness and for all the benefits you have poured so abundantly upon me. I fall down in adoration before you, oh God, and I offer you my praise. Enlighten my mind and guard all my senses, that henceforth I may walk in righteousness and keep your commandments, that I may finally attain eternal life with you, the source of life, and be admitted to the glory of your unapproachable light; for you are my God and to you I give glory, to the Father and the Son and the Holy Spirit, now and forever, and to the ages of ages. Amen.[109]
- United Presbyterian Church in the United States of America (UPCUSA),[110] *The Book of Common Worship*, 1946: Most holy and merciful Father; we acknowledge and confess before thee; our sinful nature prone to evil and slothful in good; and all our shortcomings and offenses. Thou alone knowest how often we have sinned; in wandering from thy ways; and wasting thy gifts; and forgetting thy love. But thou, Lord, have mercy upon

us; who are ashamed and sorry for all where in we have displeased thee. Teach us to hate our errors; cleanse us from our secret faults; and forgive our sins; for the sake of your dear Son. And our holy and loving Father; help us, we beseech thee; to live in thy light and walk in thy ways; according to the commandments of Jesus Christ our Lord. Amen.[111]

Declarations of Faith

The following declarations of faith during my recovery journey strengthened me and reminded me of God's goodness and to not dwell on my situation but, instead, to speak faith over it and pray through it. I would encourage you to write down your own list of scriptures (which could include some from the list below), pray them, work on memorizing them, and then believe them.

1. **I can trust in the Lord in all circumstances.** "Trust in the LORD with all your heart and lean not on your own understanding; in all your ways acknowledge him, and he will make your paths straight." (Prov. 3:5–6 NIV 1984)
2. **My emotions are safe with God.** "Cast all your anxiety on him because he cares for you." (1 Pet. 5:7)
3. **God is not mad at me.** "The LORD is compassionate and gracious, slow to anger, abounding in love. . . . As far as the east is from the west, so far has he removed our transgressions from us." (Ps. 103:8, 12)
4. **I am not alone. God is with me.** "Fear not, for I have redeemed you. I have summoned you by name; you are mine. When you pass through the waters, I will be with you." (Isa. 43:1)
5. **My guilt is removed and no longer weighs me down.** "Your guilt is taken away and your sin atoned for." (Isa. 6:7)

6. **My heart is safe with God.** "The LORD is close to the brokenhearted and saves those who are crushed in spirit." (Ps. 34:18)

PATHWAY 4

Song

Beautiful music is the art of the prophets that can calm the agitations of the soul; it is one of the most magnificent and delightful presents God has given us.
—Martin Luther

I will sing to the Lord*, for He has been good to me.*
—Psalm 13:6 NIV 1984

Sing and make music in your heart to the Lord.
—Ephesians 5:19 NIV 1984

Turn on the radio. Feel the music's beat in your bones, and feel it uplift your spirit and infuse you with hope and energy. I can't imagine my days without music. Music is the first thing I hear when I open my eyes. Prioritizing music in my morning routine was not intentional at first. One cold December morning a few years ago, I heard music coming from my alarm clock instead of the alarm sound. I am not sure how the setting was changed from the buzzer to the radio on that particular morning, since I never changed it. But ever since then, I have been using a clock radio. It had been so long since I had woken up to anything other than a buzzer, not since the third grade. Because I love to sleep in order to feel ready for my day, I was under the assumption that I needed the annoying sound of a buzzer to wake up. Well, I discovered that I was mistaken. (Although I do set a buzzer to go off about fifteen to twenty minutes after the radio on days when I have an early work meeting or urgent responsibilities.) It so happened that morning, that the station playing was a Christian music station. I just lay there, soaking in all the uplifting and hopeful tunes, and I thought, *Why haven't I done this before? I have been missing out.* I think of it like a spiritual shower to refresh, realign, and restart my day before the stressors in the day beckon for my attention. So I have never stopped. Each morning, I awaken to uplifting songs of worship, both instrumental and classical.

The power of music is undeniable, proving by how we can forget a lot of things over the years, but we can still remember a favorite song from college. And who does not remember their first concert in an arena or performance venue? Music has profound power to affect our lives. It can transport us back in time or propel us forward, giving us a vision and confidence of where we want to go. It also speaks to our hearts when it is hard to find the words to express our fears, failures, disappointments, hopes, dreams, and loves won and lost. Embedded within its language are values and beliefs about faith, God, family, life, death, violence, trials, happiness, loss, joy, etc. In some of our favorite songs, we find our story within their story, and other times the longing for that story to be true in our lives. Additionally, the rhythm and tempo might hook us, even when we don't connect with the message of a song.

Yet somewhere between the childhood days of playing Capture the Flag in the neighborhood, riding bikes to the drugstore to buy gum, searching for bluebird eggs, and stopping to pick up a beautiful leaf or shell, we have lost our ability to hear, see, and be curious about the power of melody. Even fewer of us are involved with making music. Very few people sing, even in church, where most music is now performative. At some point, we traded in our band instruments, guitars, and living room pianos for MP3 players. Before the technological age, for entertainment, families would sing together in the evenings or listen to the radio. Even with the widespread popularity of cable TV during my earlier teens, most holidays would find my family gathered in my grandparents' living room singing together while my grandmother played the piano. While we are surrounded by music everywhere we go, such as in public spaces like offices, restaurants, gyms, etc., and streaming through our earbuds, many people have little involvement with it beyond pressing play. Along with that, we have lost more than the ability to produce sound from an instrument. We have also endangered our ability to think, learn, explore, and create. For me, that loss happened somewhere in the course of my education.

I had never seen a long, narrow sheet of paper with boxes (called a scantron) until college. I thought that filling in a box was a very strange way to determine my comprehension. My tests, for the most part, in high school were all essay, short answer, or fill-in-the-blank, so this was one of my first experiences of the changing values of a culture elevating efficiency, and productivity. The scantrons would be fed into a machine, and then out came our grades. I am not saying that all standardized testing is bad, as certainly there is an appropriate place for it. But it is equally important in our personal formation that we learn to think, hear, and see through all types of educational disciplines, and then to thoughtfully evaluate and draw conclusions and to grow personally. We are learning how to be uncreative while our society demands more creativity in order to solve our complex and mental health problems. We still hear the music, but I am afraid the voices of the world that demand productivity, influence, and success, say, "Look at me, follow me, and be like me." We have access to see and hear anything we want. Our days are filled with a glut of information; it's no wonder many are sick. The loss of participation in music has left a void in both our intellectual and spiritual formations.

God is creative. Our internal soundscape needs a way to connect with God's creativity, His greatness, and His great love and actions in this world. We need songs to express our longings, sufferings, pains, fears, hopes, love, and victories. These songs build a connection between our entire world, from the inside out to God. We need to see God in the songs of our life, which is what songs do: they invite you into the story.

Art awakens us to the world and guides us to see what we could not see without its voice. It reawakens us to hear and to desire to tune into some music that is restorative and honest yet hopeful. We can first be awakened to this kind of music through creation. In Thomas Hardy's novel *Under the Greenwood Tree*, Hardy speaks of the voices of creation singing of God's glorious wonders as the fir trees sob, or the holly whistles, and the singing of creation inspires and models the call of all creation, including humans, to sing.[112] William Blake's poem "Auguries of Innocence" opens with, "To see a World in a Grain of Sand / And a Heaven in a Wild Flower / Hold Infinity in the palm of your hand / And Eternity in an hour." The poem speaks of the breadth and depth of the universe and increases our awareness of brokenness and of God's beauty across all of creation. The language of his poem is resonant of Psalm 65:12–13: "The hills are clothed with gladness. The meadows are covered with flocks and the valleys are mantled with grain; they shout for joy and sing" (NIV); and Isaiah 55:12: "You will go out in joy and be led forth in peace; the mountains and hills will burst into song before you, and all the trees of the field will clap their hands."

This second verse, Isaiah 55:12, is describing the joyous departure of the Jews after many years in Babylonian captivity. Their experience of joy in their long-awaited deliverance is compared to mountains bursting into song and trees clapping their hands. No doubt this was one of the best days of their lives. Just as all of creation sings worship to God, humans are created to voice songs of worship with a variety of voices and in different musical compositions and contexts and for different reasons.

So our fourth pathway to a deeper relationship with God is song. By learning to offer our songs to God, we enter into another level of communion with him. Just as a stirring symphony or a haunting melody can inspire your heart or quiet your soul, so our spiritual songs can lead us to new places in relation to God. We need the pathway of song to know God fully.

In this chapter, you'll discover the various types of songs that God's people have found meaningful through the centuries, and how they have used them. You'll also learn ways to incorporate song into your spiritual practice, even if you're not a skilled singer or musician. In the end, you'll be well equipped to use song as a pathway to a deeper relationship with God.

The Benefits of Music

Do you want to keep your brain young? Turn on the radio or wherever you listen to, stream, or store your music and sing along. According to research studies concerning brain function during an fMRI (functional magnetic resonance imaging), Johns Hopkins researchers concluded that playing and listening to music is a total brain workout.[113] Music engages your brain in interconnected and complex computing across various disciplines such as math, architecture, English, and engineering, to name a few. Music improves physical, mental, emotional, and spiritual health, increasing a sense of belonging and confidence.

Music can make you healthier and happier with fewer calories. A research article from the University of Oxford supports the many benefits to all human beings of singing, such as improving overall health including better breathing, posture, and muscular tension.[114] Additionally, music can help sustain a healthy immune system as it reduces the production of the stress hormone cortisol and boosts the immunoglobin A antibody. Singing also improves our sense of happiness and well-being in maintaining and developing our social networks and mood, which is connected to the release of endorphins, dopamine, and serotonin. A study conducted by researchers from McGill University in Montreal discovered that dopamine, the chemical that sets a good mood or the feeling of love, happiness, or enjoyment, is released from listening to music, particularly at the moment when the music evokes the highest emotional response, called the "chill" or "musical frisson." [115] We have all had those moments when a song gave us the "chills." This chemical of enjoyment is released by other tangible stimulants such as sweets or other favorite foods. Music can also increase your energy and physical health, including lung capacity, reduced heart disease, improved immunity, and a longer lifespan.[116] Singing is also a good prescription for chronic pain, as it lowers the levels of cortisol and enhances a sense of belonging and connection, which calms the body and mind and elevates overall well-being and happiness.

Since hearing is sometimes the last sense to go, music positively meets social, emotional, and spiritual needs of terminally ill or palliative care patients. Music is increasingly used in the care of such patients. Although it has a vast history of use, it is relatively young as a clinical discipline. Music in combination with medicine has been utilized from the Middle Ages to current times. During the Middle Ages, hospitals invited musicians to play for the patients, and in the Renaissance, physicians used music for preventative care. In the aftermath of World War II, music therapy in the United States became a more established profession as it met the great demand of veterans in hospitals who benefited from music to soothe pain and anxiety and restore hope, health, and wellness.[117] A research study published in *Scientific Reports* found that for most individuals, even if they do not respond physically to music, their brain continues to process auditory information. This was found after measuring the EEG brain responses to five different auditory patterns. The three groups of participants were young and healthy patients, hospice patients who were conscious, and hospice patients who were unresponsive.[118] Go ahead and keep talking and play music for your loved ones in palliative care, as this offers them support, love, and comfort.

Sing the anxiety or tension out of your body. Who would have known all those concerts in your youth were good medicine for your mental health development as a teen and are still good medicine no matter what your age? Group singing reduces stress and anxiety[119] and even mitigates the effects of dementia.[120] Researchers have discovered that music is the perfect tranquilizer, as it is both calming, reducing your nerves, and energizing, uplifting your spirit.[121] In addition to the endorphins and dopamine released by singing, lifting your voice releases another hormone, oxytocin, which is proven to alleviate anxiety and reduce stress. Oxytocin elevates the feeling of togetherness and lessens the feelings of depression and loneliness. Just like physical exercise, the more consistently singing is incorporated into your lifestyle, the more benefits you will experience in your mental, emotional, and spiritual health. If you want to lower your stress, turn on the radio, join a choir, go to a concert, or listen to music through your favorite streaming service.

Group singing forges social bonds, unifies a group, and forms a corporate identity. Just as noise can pervade the soundscape and decrease your physical and emotional health, group singing can alter the soundscape with its positive effects, slowing down the heart rate and decreasing stress or anxiety.[122] The value of music needs proper attention in the church for the role it plays in supporting discipleship in a person's spiritual growth, building community, and forming a corporate identity. It is not hard to discover the value of music in the development of a young child. However, somewhere along the way, music education in the church became a thing for children and older adults. According to Chorus of America, 32.5 million adults sing in choirs, and there are more than 270,000 choruses around the country.[123] When the article in *Time Magazine* citing the study was written in 2013, the number of adults in choirs had risen by almost ten million over six years. Sadly, according to a study, 85% of people think that they can't sing. The benefits of singing are not based on the professional level of your voice.[124] If you have a voice, you can sing. A most enjoyable and cost-effective way to improve your health is to join a choir. We need to get back to singing together!

Singing is important for people of all age groups and social groups to engage in regularly for their spiritual, physical, social, and emotional health and to restore the health and integration of communities due to this growing monolithic technological culture. Interwoven throughout the Bible is the role of music at worship services, celebrations, festivals in the tabernacle and temple and in the New Testament church, and more. Music was played for all kinds of celebrations and gatherings in the Bible, such as coronations (2 Sam. 15:10; 1 Kings 1:39), processions (2 Sam. 6:5), worship gatherings (Ps. 4:1–8; 33:2–3; 43:4; 92:1–15), and social gatherings (Job 21:12; Isa. 24:9; Lam. 5:14; Amos 6:4). It was sometimes accompanied by dancing (Ex. 15:20; 1 Sam. 18:6–7). Music played a central role in the celebration of a victory, baptism, holiday, or family gathering and in a wide range of solemn events for a community, preparing them for battle or to mourn a death. Ubiquitous in religious, social, and political life, music resounded in homes, hallways, streets, schools, and battlefields.

Singing school songs that recall common beliefs forms unity, even in a diverse group. Battle songs educate or give voice to a message, strengthen support of a common goal, and rally the community together, giving a voice to all. In my old church, each Sunday morning the choir would proceed down the aisle singing "A Mighty Fortress is our God" to open the worship service. Hearing the tempo, timbre, and rhythm combined with the lyrics made me feel and believe the strength of God in those moments, and it reminded me that God is strong and real, and I can trust in Him. For various celebrations, such as baptisms, births, weddings, or social gatherings, songs create a celebratory mood, making us feel happy and hopeful. In more solemn events, such as a death, or in worship services that remind us of Jesus' sacrificial death and our sinfulness, songs give comfort. They can speak to what we are going through, which makes us feel heard, and they can carry us through a difficult time.

Singing is both an enactment and a public display of the church's unity to the world and aids personal and corporate spiritual formation. When believers sing together in worship, they release corporate praise to God, strengthen the faith of individuals, unify the body of believers, and testify to the unity of believers to an unbelieving world. While the people sing, the Holy Spirit gets to work revitalizing and realigning our hearts with love and thankfulness to the grace, love, provision, and faithfulness of God. Through recalling and celebrating what we believe, in song, our hearts and minds are being renewed and reformed to look more like Jesus and to help us live more as followers of Jesus. In general, it is assumed that music has to do with feelings and emotions, which it does, but it is rarely associated with growth in wisdom or as a means of spiritual formation or discipleship. I would assert that music forms us—our thoughts and values. We are becoming what we sing. In Paul's letter to the Ephesians, he exhorts believers to sing "psalms and hymns and spiritual songs" (5:18–21 ESV). The best portrait of this unity of believers is displayed in the singing band of pilgrims ascending up to Jerusalem, praising God, during the annual religious festivals three times a year. These songs are called the Psalms of Ascent (Pss. 120–134). In John 17:20–24, Jesus, in His prayer for believers, taught that unity is the mark of believers to the world. Through believers' unity, the world will know that God sent Jesus and that they are loved as much as Jesus is loved by God. This unity testifies to the glory of Jesus and the unity of the Father and Son, and this unified community of believers is a living image of Jesus Christ. Jesus is the "image of the invisible God" (Col. 1:15 NIV), and Christians are the image of God to the world through our unity as we sing together.

The Music of God's People

The Bible's explicit references to music are fragmented, yet we know that music was vital to the life of God's people. The references to singing and playing instruments arise often in the context of worship. Perhaps because of music's broad scope in the social fabric of the culture and the fact that it was not decisive among the people, the Bible does not address its role comprehensively; perhaps there was not a need to educate on this matter. Music was a harmonious social action.

Since the Bible does not address a theology of music involving the role of instruments, musical composition, music makers, music hearers, and contexts in relation to God, we will look here at the broader theological perspective of God's creative and redemptive purpose in everyday life and worship. What we do know is that listening to music for pleasure alone would have been foreign to ancient Jews. Music was connected to actions and events of the day in social, political, personal, or religious life. The Israelites sang victory songs, covenant songs, songs of mourning or lamenting, love songs, songs of entertainment, songs with dancing, songs of instruction, songs of prophecy, and more.

Let's look at two Psalms of Ascent to see the rich history of the Psalms used as the hymnbook of early believers. The journey would have involved ascending due to Jerusalem's topography and ranking as the highest city in Palestine. But Eugene Peterson notes that the ascent was not only literal, but it was also metaphorical: "The trip to Jerusalem acted out a life lived upward toward God, an existence that advanced from one level to another in developing maturity."[125] The pilgrims knew the psalms well and sang them together as their caravans ascended the road to the holy city. The diverse themes, from praise and thanksgiving to repentance, sorrow, help, and hope, found in the psalms has resonated with audiences throughout the ages.

The idea of a pilgrimage is foreign to most of us in our technocratic culture, which has trained us for immediate gratification and the quick and casual. We want the Cliffs Notes version of Christianity and shortcuts to growing our relationship with God, and we are impatient to see the results in our lives. Soon after you become a Christian, growing in your faith, allowing the Holy Spirit to apply God's Word to your life, and really trying to start living differently, you realize that transformation is not instant. The language, form, and rhythm of the psalms used as songs throughout history teach us that transformation is a process, and they remind us that we pilgrims worship and grow progressively on our journey to be home with the Lord and His people forever. John Calvin refers to the power of the Psalms to express an array of human emotions, describing them as "an anatomy of all the parts of the soul, for there is not an emotion of which any one can be conscious that is not here represented as in a mirror."[126]

Three reasons to elevate your devotional use of Psalms are that it restores the deep musical and poetic roots of the Psalms in worship and in worshiping communities, it has a role in our spiritual formation, and it has the holistic purpose of helping to express the inner state of man to God, which causes us to grow our spiritual life and enrich our worship.

While there are many psalms to choose from, I will highlight two below and draw out the truths and applications found throughout history. The poetic form and structure of each song have given voice to our ancestors and continue to give voice to all believers as we express our need to God for help in life's circumstances. They also act as model prayers for all kinds of occasions such as thanksgiving, praise, and hope. I hope that you use them as models in your own prayer life. Many of the pathways in Psalms are interconnected, as the songs can be prayers, or the prayers can be songs. Some musicians have composed songs based on the

Psalms, which is helpful since the ancient instrumental compositions of the songs have been lost. You may want to create a playlist of current artists playing or singing the Psalms, some of which are the Gettys, Sandra McCracken, Ellie Holcomb, and Phil Wickham. Also, check out The Psalms Project, which is composed of over 70 musicians who have put all 150 psalms to music.[127]

To help you understand how to use Psalms in your life, I have expounded on some psalms below, where I focus on a psalm and/or a contemporary song of similar theme that has been impactful on my life. Listen to and sing these songs for yourself, meditate on and study the meaning of them, and then ask the Holy Spirit what the song should mean to your life. Do not miss the joy and comfort of singing your story and prayers to God. Sing your way to a closer relationship with Jesus, and sing your way to better overall health on your way home. A closer relationship with Jesus is only a song away!

Songs of Providence and Hope

Psalm 121. Read Psalm 121, then read the reflection below.

Not far into the Christian journey of faith, we fall down, sprain an elbow, or break a foot. One of the greatest misconceptions is that a Christian will not have troubles. We break bones, get sick or receive a bad diagnosis, get in a fight with a loved one, have feelings of sadness and loss, and experience health, emotional, work, and family problems in this life. The question the psalmist raises is: Where do I go for my help?

Psalm 121 is an example of a Song of Providence. The start of this psalm reflects humans' first reaction to difficulties—Help! We want the quickest solution to our problem with the least amount of pain. The psalmist does the same thing, looking to the hills for help. This reference to the hills does not appear clear unless you know that pagan worship permeated the hilltops throughout

Palestine. Shrines were constructed on the hilltops where people could engage in sexual rituals to appease the gods and invoke other spells and enchantments to help solve their problems. Sometimes we do the same thing by engaging in pleasure to get our minds off the pain or a problem, or we follow the culture's wisdom. To the complex and most difficult problems of life, we want instant or easy promises to solve our problems; we'll use anything such as ignoring the problem, doing things that are destructive to numb the pain, making rash decisions, or engaging in distractions through pleasure-seeking or retail therapy. This is not trustworthy, and true help, as our experience attests, does not provide true or lasting solutions to our problems.

In 1 Kings 18, Elijah exposed the fraudulent religion and practices of Baal worship when he challenged the priests: "Maybe [Baal] is sleeping and must be awakened" (v. 27 NIV). The priests of Baal frantically called out to Baal, but silence persisted. Then Elijah called out to God, who answered. The people fell to the ground and said, "The LORD—he is God!" (v. 39). Our God answers our calls for help. His phone is never on silent or do not disturb. The psalmist is saying that the help we need for wisdom, healing, and strength in difficult situations is not in trusting ourselves, nor is it in worldly wisdom, but it is in the One who is the Creator of the heavens and the earth. Beware of seeking immediate relief in the world, or religions that worship false gods. Seeking help in the world leads to more trouble, just as was for the Israelites in Psalm 121 when they sought relief in hilltop pagan temples.

No illness, disease, crime, financial problem, or loss of a loved one, marriage, or child can separate us from God because God is always guarding your life from evil trying to destroy you or take hold of you (Ps. 121:5). He will not allow more than we can bear. The comfort and hope we can bank on is that, though the pain may be great and the loss seems unbearable, God says it will not break or kill us. When we are God's children, we are forever His children in this life and in heaven. We have great hope because the difficulties, pain, and trials will end one day. We are not helpless or hopeless because we have a God who always picks up our call, so make Him your first call.

"It is Well with My Soul" is a hymn penned by Horatio Spafford in 1876, after he tragically lost all four of his daughters when the ship they were on sank after colliding with another sea vessel. His wife, Anna, survived and sent him the now famous telegram: "Saved alone." Shortly after receiving that telegram, Spafford traveled to meet his grieving wife, and with a heart wrecked with sorrow, he wrote this song as a comfort to his heart:

> When peace, like a river, attendeth my way,
> When sorrows like sea billows roll;
> Whatever my lot, Thou has taught me to say,
> It is well, it is well, with my soul.

I cannot even imagine writing a song such as this after losing all of one's children. If Spafford could say that He still trusted God after this tragedy, then we can all sing these words, knowing that God will anchor our soul when the storms of life roll. This song can anchor and lift us by strengthening us with hope and comfort during dark days.

Songs of Humility

Psalm 131. Read Psalm 131 and then read the reflection below.

What was your first job? My first job was as babysitter, starting in my neighborhood and then for a family at my swim club. Continuing this through college and then moving on to other roles as a camp counselor and then assistant and director of a camp, my days were filled with tennis, swimming, singing, painting, making bracelets, and playing shuffleboard, along with the laughter and smiles of kids, and some battles of the will. One day a camper persisted to not participate in their group activities and would disrupt the group. His counselor asked if I could talk to the child and enforce some consequences. As the assistant director, one of my roles was dealing with discipline problems. After speaking to him about following his counselor's rules and the benefits of doing so, he looked at me and said, "No one can control me, not even my parents, and you are not the boss of me." I responded, "At camp, I am your boss." After speaking to his mom when she picked him up from camp, she assured me that he would have better behavior when he returned. The next two days, he was absent, and when he returned, he was on good behavior. Our pride can get the best of us when we think that we know better or the rules do not apply to us. Or we think that we have worked hard for the life we have and are doing a good job of it. That all may be true, but ambition, status, and wealth do not define us.

Our greatest temptation and the oldest sin in the Bible is pride. Satan tempted Adam and Eve to doubt God's goodness, and he told them that God was holding out on them, that they *could* be like God. Adam and Eve's actions said to God, "You are not the boss of me." How has status or power lured you to say the same to God? It's not long until we lose a job, money, our health, or a relationship before we realize God is the Boss, and we need Him to be all powerful and mighty. We need God.

Psalm 131 identifies the problem underneath the Israelites' desire to look to the hilltops for help: pride. The warning is to not take matters into your own hands. Pride can be difficult to identify and root out of our lives due to our culture's virtues of achievement, power, status, and maintaining youthfulness. The Bible encourages hard work by speaking about eating the fruit of one's labor (Ps. 128:2), and Psalm 90:17. One of my favorite verses, says, "May the favor of the Lord our God rest on us; establish the work of our hands for us" (NIV). And Proverbs 14:23 warns against talking without action. Give your thoughts and dreams legs by creating an action plan. Jesus and His disciples kept a rigorous schedule helping people and sharing the good news from city to city. So work hard, and do not freeze God out of your work.

In addition, pride can underscore our unwillingness to ask God for help or the tendency to build our identity or self-worth on our achievements. Often, we think that we know better, or we feel comfortable with the ways that we deal with matters, even if we know that they are not good. Watch for pride when you start taking matters into your own hands, compromise yourself or your integrity to get ahead, and are generous with your time or money—but only spending them on yourself. Pride is the me-first attitude. Pride will say you deserve this; it inflates your ego by bragging, embellishing the truth, and flaunting one's power and authority as superior to others. Christians are not to be proud, arrogant, or self-centered people.

When pride is aroused, the biblical defense is to have a still and quieted soul (Ps. 131:2). The Bible portrays the model of Christian faith with the image of a weaned child with his or her mother. A Christian is not supposed to be like a child in the sense of needing constant feeding, attention, and care, but, like a weaned child who loves mom for who she is and not for what she can give. We can be the same way; we can view God as our genie or a vending machine. We bring our needs, wants, and plans to God, and we want Him to give His stamp of approval. Do you love God for His gifts or because He is the Giver of all gifts? Do you love God for what He does for you, or do you love Him for who He is?

Though Psalm 131 is brief in length, its lesson is continuous as we waiver between being a runaway and being a baby. We are either taking matters into our own hands or running to God in a panic to help us with our problems. A false sense of confidence beguiles us into thinking we can solve a problem or handle a situation, telling God, "I have got this, and I do not need you." One of the cultural mottos that I get so tired of hearing is, "You got this." I want to turn around and say, "I do not have it, but God does." Then when we have exhausted our failed solutions, we run to God like an unweaned baby. This psalm is telling us to grow up. When challenges, complex problems, or hard times arise, quiet your soul and rest knowing that God is with you; confess your trust in God. This is a lesson that we never stop learning. Who's the Boss? God is God, and I am not.

Rich Mullins's "Hold Me Jesus" is still one of my favorite songs; it's composed with raw and poetic language portraying the temptations of life, confession of sin, the need for grace, and the longing for peaceful rest all in the arms of Jesus. Rich Mullins was one of the most prolific songwriters and was writing worship songs before the rise of modern worship music in the church. I love the opening lyrics of this song: "Well, sometimes my life just don't make sense at all / When the mountains look so big / And my faith just seems so small."

When you are tired, you feel like God is far away, you keep hitting walls, you feel like you are stuck in your sin, or you're struggling with pain and suffering, listen to this song and pray, "Hold me, Jesus." In a culture where *sin* is a taboo word, we need to be reminded, through Rich's authentic and raw voice, that we are all sinners in need of God's mercy.

Songs of Victory

2 Samuel 22. Read 2 Samuel 22:2–7 and then read the reflection below.

A common practice of the ancient Semitic society was to compose and sing songs in response to God's help in achieving a victory. In 2 Samuel 22, David composed this song to celebrate God's help in delivering him from his enemies. From the first half of the third millennium an array of songs was composed. David speaks of God in figurative language in his song, referring to God as a rock: "The LORD is my rock, my fortress and my deliverer; my God is my rock, in whom I take refuge" (2 Sam. 22:2–3 NIV). To symbolize God as being a rock—something that gives security and safety to His people—would have been appropriate in their cultural and geographical context. David sought refuge among the rocks; they became his hiding place, resting place, and shade from the heat of the day as they did for many Israelites in the desert. The rock in the Old Testament often symbolized security and the defense of an impenetrable refuge. In the late second millennium BC, Anatolian and Palestinian deities such as El, the divine creator, were described as deified mountains.[128] David is not saying that God is just like any other rock, as other deities claimed, but David is saying God YHWH is the deliverer, the only rock of security.

A few victory songs that stand out to me are "Chain Breaker," by Zach Williams, and the hymn "O God, Our Help in Ages Past," by Isaac Watts. When we feel stuck in our life circumstances or feel hopeless that we cannot break repeated sins, we can cling to the hope that God alone has the power to deliver us and that the grace of God is our strength. We can do this through singing these songs. Watts' hymn reminds us of the power of celebrating past victories. It strengthens our faith by reminding us that just as God was faithful in the past, He will be faithful today. Singing of past victories will give you hope that you can experience victory today.

Songs of Praise

Throughout the Psalms, the people of God praise and thank God by singing of His provision and faithfulness, even during trials. Praising God can change the course of your day and reframe your perspective. Praising and thanking God will remove roots of ingratitude and spread seeds of contentment. Here is a list of some of my favorites when you need God's light to break through a gloomy day or need to be reminded that you have much to be thankful for. I would recommend listening to one of the most widely sung worship songs of modern times, "How Great is Our God," by Chris Tomlin.

To praise God, using His word and to sing "Sonshine" into your heart and day, read, sing, and reflect on these Psalms:

- Psalm 34:1–9
- Psalm 47
- Psalm 84
- Psalm 89:5–8
- Psalm 92:1–8
- Psalm 95:1–7
- Psalm 100
- Psalm 103:1–6
- Psalm 111:1–5
- Psalm 139:13–17
- Psalm 145:1–9

Songs of Prophecy

While there are numerous songs in the book of Revelation, two are explicitly called "songs" and were possibly sung in their early years. The first is the "New Song" of Revelation 5:9–10:

> You are worthy to take the scroll and to open its seals,
> because you were slain, and with your blood you purchased men for God
> from every tribe and language and people and nation.
> You made them to be a kingdom and priests to serve our God,
> and they will reign on the earth. (NIV 1984)

The second is called "the song of Moses the servant of God and the song of the Lamb"; it is found in 15:3–4:

> Great and marvelous are your deeds, Lord God Almighty.
> Just and true are your ways, King of the ages.
> Who will not fear you, O Lord, and bring glory to your name?
> For you alone are holy.
> All the nations will come and worship before you,
> for your righteous acts have been revealed.

Other musical sections include the hymn of the living creatures (Rev. 4:8), a song of the elders (4:11), praises of the angelic hosts and living creatures (5:11–13), a song of the elders (11:17–18), the throwing down of the accuser (12:10–12), the justness of God (16:5–7), and the final Hallelujah (19:1–8). While not always, these hymns often function as transition devices between various aspects of John's vision.

Scholars differ in their views concerning the progression of time of the events in Revelation. Some view Revelation as unfolding in a linear progression, others view it as cyclical. The difference in interpretation is that, while the former would hold that the events of chapter 19 naturally follow chapter 18 and so on (like watching a movie), the cyclical interpretation is more akin to John examining a diamond from a variety of angles.

In Revelation, similar themes exist in the relationship between God's people and music as the relationship between music and slave spirituals from the American South. The content of slave spirituals is often rooted in the images of the Exodus narrative, demonstrating a close identification that enslaved Black Americans felt with the Hebrew children and the hope of eventual liberation.

Slave spirituals were eschatological in their focus on the future reign of Christ upon the earth, turning one's attention toward God's liberating act. CeCe Winans's song "The Goodness of God" also speaks about seeing the faithfulness of God in hard times. Esau McCaulley explains,

> These are the stories of a God who fights for us and against the enemies of his people. These are stories of a God who turns his compassionate eye toward those whom society forgets. Rome knew this and so did Herod.[129]

What does this have to do with Revelation? Much of Revelation is set against the backdrop of a Roman empire that was increasingly growing weary and worried of a political and religious uprising posed by the Jesus sect pejoratively called "little Christs" (the term which eventually evolved into "Christians"). Throughout his shorter commentary on Revelation, G. K. Beale makes frequent and regular references to the increasing political and social pressure being placed upon Christians in this time period to participate in pagan festivals and pagan worship. Their use of terms like "son of God" and "prince of peace" that were originally designated for Caesar but were being applied to their messiah, was a friction point. As new followers of Jesus surged throughout the Roman world, their protections as a sect of Judaism were threatened. In some of the Roman empire, financial and social isolation were forms of retribution, while in others places, outright persecution and threats of violence were increasingly common. Rome held the keys of life and death over it all. However, Rome was nothing more than the empire of the day who embodied the spirit of antichrist. Centuries earlier, another empire stood in oppressive force over God's people along the banks of the Nile River. Egypt was the "Rome" of its own day. In every age since, there has existed a "Rome" motif, some granting favor to Christians and luring them with extravagance and power, others oppressing and persecuting Christians. Same spirit, different empire.

Beale rightly points out that the dominant theme of Revelation is often missed in today's discussions of the end times but can be encapsulated in John's encouragement to stare death directly in the face and sing away. He encourages them throughout his vision to remain steadfast against persecution, against the allure of false teachings, and against immoral living. He calls for a strengthened faith to persevere with the certain knowledge that King Jesus was returning. And just as God in Moses delivered the Hebrews from the oppression of Egypt, so too God in Christ would deliver the church from the oppression of a new Egypt.

Amid whatever trials or persecution endure, we have the assurance, through the hymns of Revelation, that they will end. A future-oriented exaltation of who the Lamb of God is shows how He alone holds the keys of creation in His grip. It is the reminder, as Pope John Paul II famously stated, "Do not abandon yourselves to despair. We are the Easter people and hallelujah is our song." Revelation and its hymnody is a helpful reminder of the power of focusing *through* the muck and mire of present circumstances into the certain hope of the return of Christ in glory.

Mary's Song

Luke 1. Read Luke 1:46–55 and then the reflection below.

Mary's song, known as the Magnificat, in Luke 1:46–55 expresses humility and devotion to God after Mary receives, reflects on, and welcomes this life-changing and world-changing news that she would give birth to the Son of God. Without a doubt, only someone of deep faith and knowledge of the Old Testament and of the traditional structure of biblical hymns could have written such a masterpiece that is both a hymn and a prayer. Following the traditional Old Testament "Thanksgiving Hymn," the first strophe of the Magnificat (vv. 46–49) is the call to praise, and the second strophe (vv. 50–55) reflects on the cause for praise, referring to God's covenant faithfulness in the past, present, and future. I would encourage you to sometime study this hymn verse by verse, looking back to the Old Testament themes and images, to experience the depth and beauty of this hymn of thanksgiving to God for His loving-kindness and mercy (*hesed*) toward His people. Amy Grant's song "Breath of Heaven (Mary's Song)" beautifully captures Mary's humble words of love and devotion to God. The meaning and applications of Mary's song will be discussed more in-depth in the prayer chapter.

Song in Worship

Despite the fact that most people don't consider themselves good singers, everyone can engage in song as an act of worship. This pathway is for everyone, not just graduates of The Julliard School! Here are some of the ways we practice the pathway of song.

The Bible's collectivist culture contrasts to our individualist culture. These two cultural types hold different approaches, perspectives, and values. Without diving too deeply into the anthropological differences, at their foundation, collectivist cultures think of themselves in light of their community, while individualists think of ourselves in distinction from our community. So, when we read Peter's words that we are "living stones" (1 Pet. 2:5 NIV), we think of *our* stone first—my personal placement in the broader whole. By contrast, Peter's first hearers would have thought about the broader whole and how they each are personally an important, but relatively indistinguishable, part of a much larger whole. We think of our own, personal quiet time with the Lord as the foundational practice of our spiritual walk, which it is, but our participation in gathering corporately as the church is just as important. Their personal time of worship or prayer was an overflow of what they had received in community, rather than the other way around.

Additionally, the attitude concerning doing something alone or with others is much different in collectivist cultures. We instinctively prefer to do something ourselves and solicit help only if necessary. Collectivist cultures, by contrast, think, *Why do something alone when you can do something with others?* So, collectivist cultures, including those which gave us the Bible under the inspiration and guidance of the Holy Spirit, placed tremendous value on corporate prayer, corporate worship, and corporate singing and less on those personal expressions. It is not that they were not important, only less important than we consider them to be. We see remnants of this in the ancient traditions of the church. The Roman Catholics, Anglicans, Orthodox, and many mainline Protestant denominations place a high value on corporate worship. Their prayer books, especially those of the Anglican Communion, are intentionally crafted for corporate rather than private use (though certainly they can apply to private use!).

The practice of worshiping corporately, including in song, is a fundamental process of spiritual formation, which in their view should be done in community. The famous motto, *lex orandi, lex credenda, lex vivendi* ("the law of what is prayed, is what is believed, is what is lived"), used by these traditions, is a fundamental belief in ancient Christian worship. Mary's Magnificat is an example of personal singing or private worship, and David's psalms were codified for public use. Biblically speaking, there is an inextricable link between private song, worship, and prayer and its impact or benefit to the shared life of the Christian community.

Theologian Jeremy Begbie (a Thomas A. Langford Distinguished Research Professor of Theology at Duke Divinity School and writer on the theology of music) elucidates several critical points that function as a well-rounded theology of worship. I will summarize these briefly in short points, so for more in-depth discussion listen to his interview:[130]

1. Corporate worship should be diverse.
2. Corporate worship should be well-theologized.
3. Corporate worship should form us holistically.
4. Corporate worship should be emotional, but not emotionally manipulative.

Through music we can reflect, be inspired, gain hope and wisdom, and connect to another's story. A song can express what a heart feels but has a hard time expressing our deepest pains and longings and our greatest joys.

After struggling with pain in my heel one night, making it hard to sleep, Lauren Daigle's song "You Say" woke me up the next morning. The words that aroused me were, "You say I am strong when I think I am weak." God knew that I needed to hear those words because I felt weak and exhausted physically from a sleepless night, but also from the arduous recovery journey. It brought a smile to my face, reminding me that God is with me and that I am stronger than I think because He is my source of strength. I did not physically speak in words that morning, but my heart sang along with her, lifting up this song as a prayer to God.

I would implore you to reevaluate your morning wake-up routine and prioritize adding music and singing into your lifestyle. Stop your first thoughts of a to-do list scrolling across your mind, or what you haven't accomplished from yesterday, or worries and anxieties. Start waking up to music that will ground and center your thoughts and inspire you, give you hope, and remind you that you are loved. It's the best way to wake up. I recommend everybody pull out that old clock radio in the closet or go order one online, so that you can start your day feeling loved, strengthened, and encouraged. Music has changed my mornings, days, and nights, and I think that it can change yours too.

Practical Ways to Practice the Pathway of Song

Practical considerations for observing personal song and musical worship as a spiritual discipline can include the following.

- Listen to music to wake you up instead of an alarm or timer.
- Have a list of morning songs to listen to when you're getting ready for work.
- Be intentional to turn on Christian radio, listen to Christian music on Spotify or other steaming services, such as Apple Play, IHeartRadio, SirusXM, Pandora, etc., and sing along. Singing songs of hope and truth is like depositing money in your spiritual bank account. Try it for thirty to forty-five days.
- Sing the songs out loud, and then the ones that you want to stay in your memory sing a few times a week for a few weeks until you feel like you have almost memorized the words.
- Download a worship playlist and sing along.

- Listen to music and sing on your commute, and listen to music at work.
- Dig out your grandmother's old hymnal and start singing; get a family member to play the piano and have family sing-alongs.
- Listen to music while you work out.
- Create themed Christian music playlists.
- Sing to your kids at bedtime.
- Go to a concert and have fun—sing and dance.
- Go to a symphony, opera, or play.
- Join a choral group at your local church or join ChoirPlace or ChoralNet.
- Check out the New York Choral Consortium that has links to choral networks.
- Sing the Psalms (see resources mentioned earlier in the chapter).
- Engage in a Seven Pathways study plan and benefit from the recommended songs related to the theme for the day.
- If you play a musical instrument, use it in your worship and corporate worship.
- Volunteer at church to help with a children's or youth choir.
- Volunteer at music events and at a senior adult home to play music.

PATHWAY 5

Prayer

The one concern of the devil is to keep Christians from praying.
He fears nothing from the prayerless studies, prayerless work, and prayerless religion.
He laughs at our toil, mocks at our wisdom, but he trembles when we pray.

—Samuel Chadwick

Human beings were not created to do life alone. We all crave relationships. Perhaps the most prominent description of this need comes from American psychologist Abraham Maslow, who published his view of human needs, called "Maslow's Hierarchy of Needs." Maslow's writing, dating back to 1943, explains human motivation through a series of basic human needs in ascending order, which has become the bedrock of Psychology 101. Maslow's hierarchy provides a basic and clear indication that humans are called to live life in community with one another, but all too often overlook the principle of human need. The need for belonging and relationship is foundational to human existence, only to be outdone in priority by the need for physical safety and physiological provision. The line between growth needs and deficiency needs is between self-esteem and self-actualization.

Sadly, all too often we try to meet this basic need for relationship in ways that seem promising but are ultimately unsatisfying. Currently, the best example of this may be our profound addictions to social media. It affords our brain a near endless supply of mental satisfaction for both esteem and belonging. Likes, shares, follows, retweets—they all tell our brain that we are loved, we belong, and we are esteemed and valued. If my need for belonging and esteem is met through social media, then it decreases my motivation to seek out in-person relationships or gatherings, especially if I have experienced a lot of conflict, trauma, or pain from past face-to-face, personal relationships.

So social media provides a low-risk, high-reward perception in our brains. Only it's an illusion, as our brains are being fed quick stimulating signals of belonging. It's like eating candy for a quick boost, but you would not get your nutritional needs met for the day by eating candy. Do "follows" really mean deep, meaningful, long-lasting belonging? Or have our brains been tricked by Silicon Valley and driven us toward engagement on various social platforms, ultimately, to drive revenue? Are they making money through our online socializing? Innately, we know that socializing online is far from the same as meeting in person, and an online hug is not the same as feeling someone's arms around you. This is precisely how the most interconnected generation in human history is simultaneously the loneliest. Because, while our brains may be temporarily led to believe we've had our need for belonging met, our souls are empty and dehydrated for the lack of contact. It's like turning to salt water to quench one's thirst or drinking sodas all day. They will only make you thirstier. Humans were designed for face-to-face relationships, so no number of likes, shares, follows, retweets, or smiling or hugging emojis can satisfy that need.

Beyond that, social media and even genuine human contact cannot fill our most basic need for connection because our deepest desire is connection with God, our Creator. That hunger to know God and be known by Him is the starting point for each of the Seven Pathways. Yet our fourth pathway, prayer, is the one that most clearly and consistently brings us into contact with our Maker. To enter fully into a relationship with God, you must become familiar with the Pathway of prayer.

In this chapter, you'll learn where this deep hunger to know God originates, and how prayer fulfills that need. Many people have questions about the effectiveness of prayer, so we'll walk through some of the basic intellectual problems people have with this practice. You'll also learn practical ways to enter into prayer, a discipline that most people are eager to practice but simply don't know how.

The Instinct to Pray

Most people pray. As we'll see, it's one of the most basic and prevalent religious practices in the world. Yet most people report finding little satisfaction in prayer. Research on expectancies of prayer, referring to if people feel like their prayers were answered, reveal that without belief and trust in God, prayer expectancies can easily discourage their faith.[131] Faith and trust in God are grounds for a higher level of satisfaction in prayer. If belief in God is essential in feeling satisfaction in prayer, then the decline from 87% (2013–2017) to 81% (2022) in the United States affects people's belief that their prayers matter.[132]Also, according to Gallup, of those who believe in God about half (42%) say God hears and can intervene. Then among all Americans, 28% believe that God hears prayers but cannot intervene. Four out of ten Americans feel like their prayers are heard and God can intervene, which leaves many Americans dissatisfied with their prayer life. In comparison to a poll by *Newsweek* in 1997, 87% of Americans said that God answered prayers, [133] so the number of Americans who believe that God answers prayers now has dropped almost 50% in twenty-five years.

For many, the reason for lower satisfaction in prayer is that they don't understand the relational nature of prayer. We are made for a relationship with God. Contrary to our usual urge to see prayer as a way of petitioning God, it's really a way to know Him better.

The Prevalence of Prayer

According to a poll by ComRes for the Christian charity Tearfund, one in five adults in the UK pray despite identifying as nonreligious.[134] Instinctively, nonreligious people cited the most common reason for prayer was personal tragedy, and the primary reason to pray is for family. After praying for family, 41% pray out of thankfulness, followed closely by 40% who pray for healing and friends, and lastly 24% pray for global issues and natural disasters.[135] Of Catholics, 42% pray more regularly, compared to 23% of Anglicans who pray regularly. In America, prayer is the most common faith practice among adults. According to Pew Research, in America, 79% of evangelical Protestants pray at least daily, followed by 69% of Muslims, then 59% of Catholics, and 54% of mainline Protestants, while 20% of nonreligious pray. The importance of religion determined the frequency of prayer. Pew Research[136] results found that for those who said religion was very important, 79% prayed at least daily, while daily prayer declined dramatically to 16% for those who said religion was somewhat important, and 3% for those who said religion was not too important. Weekly prayer was equally important to both groups, who said religion was very important and somewhat important, the former (43%) and the latter (45%). The group who said religion was not too important may not pray as frequently, but evidently, they believed in the value of prayer, as 19% prayed monthly. The results suggest that those who consider religion important pray more frequently than those for whom religion is not too important.

Also, belief in God was a determining factor in the frequency of prayer. Of those who said they believed in God with absolute certainty, 85% prayed at least daily, while daily prayer declined dramatically, to 12%, among those who were fairly certain and 2% for those who were not certain at all. Monthly prayer was equally important to both those who said belief in God was absolutely and fairly certain, the former (43%) and the latter (45%).

The results regarding religious attendance and frequency of prayer revealed that of those who attend church at least once a week, 54% pray at least daily, and 30% pray a few times a month or a few times a year. So, for 70% of once- or twice-a-month (or a few times a year) church attendees, prayer is not a daily priority, but they still see the value of weekly prayer, as 47% pray weekly. Of those who seldom or never go to church, 25% pray weekly. The research shows that even for the group who seldom or never go to church, people are praying monthly at a rate of 35%, which is about a 75% increase from those who said religion was not too important, as they prayed monthly at a frequency of 19%. So, gathering with a community at a church for worship does increase the frequency of prayer, but there are still just under 50% who attend church weekly but do not see the value of praying daily. Yet, of those, one in four pray weekly.

In conclusion, the research suggests that a lot of people are praying weekly: 47% who attend church a few times a month or year and 25% who seldom or never attend church. One in five nonreligious people pray weekly and one in four people who seldom or never attend church pray weekly. Among all groups discussed above, the greatest number of people are praying weekly. Those praying weekly experience a lower level of satisfaction in prayer because a weekly prayer request time to an unknown God (if they do not believe in God) is not fulfilling. Prayer is designed to build a relationship with God, as it is communication and an experience with God rather than just lifting requests to the "universe" or searching for "whatever" through prayer, which will leave one dissatisfied and empty. We are not just seeking some "thing" but rather seeking God in prayer. If you are not seeking God in prayer, then you can't experience God in prayer.

Made for Relationship with God

God shaped man from the clay of the earth to reflect the beauty of His image as an artist. You were created to bear a distinct image and likeness of Him. God has always been concerned about your image. God is interested in you bearing His image to the world.

When God creates male and female in Genesis 1:27, He uses a Hebrew verb (*bārā'*) that most commonly means "to create" but also means "to shape or fashion, exclusively of divine activity."[137] Other passages in the Old Testament use *bārā'* when the object of God's work is the heavens and Earth (Deut. 4:32; Isa. 40:26; 45:18; Amos 4:13), while Isaiah 43:1, 7 and Malachi 2:10 use *bārā'* to refer to creating man. The root *bārā'* also means "to form" in the sense of "carving or cutting out"[138] man in God's image (Gen.1:26–27). In the three lyrical lines of Genesis 1:27, God's excitement resounds with the repetition of the word, *bārā'* ("to create").[139] The root *bārā'* in Genesis 1:26–27 differs from the word *yāsar* ("to fashion or to form") found in Genesis 2:7.[140] Though the word *yāsar* is synonymously parallel with *bārā'* ("create") and *'āśâ* ("make"), the shaping and forming of an object of God's attention, whether it be man or mankind, is its primary meaning.[141]

The Hebrew word for "image" is *selem* (Gen. 1:26) and refers more to a teleological function than a material one. It means "likeness" or "of resemblance[142] and is derived from a Hebrew root that means "to carve" or "to cut."[143] The two terms *image* and *likeness* are complementary ideas indicated in the Hebrew parallelism in verses 26 and 27 and Genesis 5:3. There is no "and" between "image" and "likeness" in the Hebrew Scriptures, debunking the error that people make of drawing distinctions in the meaning between the two terms.[144] In Genesis 5:1, "likeness" is used without "image." The words *image* and *likeness* independently used without the other in the verses above affirm the complementary nature of the terms.

The closest semantically related word to *selem* ("image") is *tabnît* ("image" or "model").[145] The metaphor of "image" used of the creation of man means man is a "reflection" or "small-scale copy" and was cut or made like God, who is invisible. How are we a "reflection" or "small-scale copy" of God? A synonym for "copy" is "imitation," and in the Bible, the term carries forth the meaning in a positive sense of humans bearing a likeness to God and a negative sense of referring to idols. In the ancient Near East, kings would establish images (idols) of themselves to act as boundary markers on the borders of their kingdom.[146] So, whenever someone approached the dominion of the king, they would see the idol and call to mind into whose kingdom they were entering. In speaking of humans imaging God, the images are not wood, clay, or stone; we are living and active bearers of His image, with a mind and emotions. And unlike the stationary idols of the ancient Near East, we cultivate the expansion of His dominion throughout the earth, wherever we go in His name.

Making man in God's "image" and "likeness" means that man is carved and crafted as an image bearer, His representative, or God-likeness, to the world. How many times has someone said, "Your child looks like you/your spouse"? Or you could tell that child belonged to a certain parent? Just as many children look like their earthly parents, do we look like our heavenly Father? Since our childhood, we have been imitators of values, principles, and truths as that is how we grow as humans. We are by nature imitators but not simple copies that are lifeless. But we are meant to imitate God by mirroring and reflecting His character in our thoughts and actions. The Pharisees followed the religious laws but failed to live them out, so they never generated real-life transformation and real spirituality.

To bear God's image can be more properly understood as a calling than a designation. Imaging God is something we are called to do as our created purpose along with being in relationship with God. Unlike idols, we have a voice, and God gave us a voice to speak words of life and to be the hands and feet of Jesus. First, we image God by imaging or "reflecting his likeness" to the rest of creation—His goodness, holiness, wisdom, and stewardship—in how we are caring for culture and contributing toward its renewal. Second, we are to call creation's attention to God, worship Him, and be in relationship with Him.

In her book on faith-rooted organizing, Alexis Salvatierra tells the story of the power of prayer in promoting action:

> The San Diego Interfaith Committee for Worker Justice (ICWJ) was part of a broad coalition working to pass living wage legislation. The coalition attended city council meetings every week and used the public commentary period to raise its concerns. As it's common practice, the coalition carefully crafted talking points to ensure that the comments all communicated a common and clear message. But the San Diego ICWJ decided that they needed to participate in an alternative, faith-rooted way. So every one of their leaders that approached the podium used their time (one to three minutes) to pray. They prayed for the poor, for the community and for the city council. They prayed in whatever way they felt called to pray. When the legislation passed, a journalist asked a conservative council member why he had voted for the living wage. He responded that he could not take being prayed for one more week. He had armed himself against the talking points, but he had no armor against the prayer. The prayer reached his heart.[147]

We become active in changing society and caring for culture as God called humans to do, after we are changed by the Scriptures. We are to be fair in wage, expectations, and treatment. Remember God gave you all that you have and holds you accountable for how you care for your employees.

Experiencing God Through Prayer

Prayer is instinctively a human response, but there are differences in what is the essence of prayer, its priority, and the growing in its practice and experience. To reflect God's image means that we are designed to image his likeness to the world in our thoughts, words, and actions and to relate to God and worship Him. Therefore, since all humans are made in God's image, humans innately have an awareness of their Creator. The sixteenth-century reformer John Calvin called this *divinitatis sensum*, the sense of God that all humans have. "There is within the human mind, and indeed by natural instinct, an awareness of divinity."[148] Experiencing the power, beauty, and brokenness of creation triggers the awareness of God (Rom. 1:19–20) and His presence. So prayer is communication with God in response to the knowledge of Him or an awareness of Him. There can be prayers of adoration, confession, contrition, entreaty, intercession, petition, and more. But with a general and limited knowledge of God, one will also miss what prayer is: a conversation with God. You can't easily have a conversation with someone you don't know. However, God does sometimes, in His mercy, answer the prayers of unbelievers as He did for the Ninevites in Jonah 3 and King Ahab, one of the cruelest kings in the Old Testament (1 Kings 21:27–28). Engaging in a conversation with God through prayer activates the Holy Spirit to clear the fog of unbelief. "For it is by grace you have been saved, through faith—and this is not from yourselves, it is the gift of God" (Eph. 2:8 NIV).

What fundamentally happens when a person comes to faith is that they have responded to what God has already done by paying for the sin of humanity in full (because He loved us) so that our relationship with Him might be restored. So, in that sense, hearing from God precedes asking in prayer. Now, all who believe are sons and daughters of God:

> You are all sons of God through faith in Christ Jesus. . . . If you belong to Christ, then you are Abraham's seed, and heirs according to the promise. (Gal. 3:26, 29 NIV 1984)

> It is not natural children who are God's children, but it is the children of the promise who are regarded as Abraham's offspring. (Rom. 9:8)

According to Galatians, we do not have to prove anything to earn God's love as one might do to gain social status, rank, or approval, because through Christ we receive adoption as sons, and "since you are a son, God has made you also an heir" (Gal. 4:7 NIV 1984). Through Christ, you are heirs of God. And 2 Corinthians 6:18 says, "I will be a Father to you, and you will be my sons and daughters."

Cultivating this new relationship as sons and daughters of God takes time just as building any relationship requires time and investment. During my teens, God became very real to me, and I spent quality time with Him almost daily, but then as time marched into my thirties, I stopped investing as much time in our relationship and was drawing from spiritual savings and yesterday's bread, until the savings got low and the bread stale.

Prayer is communication with God, communion with God, and an encounter with God. The essence of prayer is experiencing the presence of God and requesting God to work powerfully according to His plans and purposes to fix brokenness in your life, your loved ones, and the world.

To further build on, from the last chapter, the different types of songs or prayers in the Psalms, the prayer book of the Bible, it is important to understand a majority of the songs or prayers are cries for help about personal problems and circumstances or issues in the world, and people are calling on God to exercise His power and authority to make things right. These prayers are birthed from raw and genuine need and not sugarcoated. First, prayer functions in our lives to draw us near to God and experience God's presence, and this encounter transforms us to love

God, enjoy God more, and live like a follower of Jesus. Second, prayer functions as a call; think of it as your own direct line to God to bring His plans and purposes into your real world and restore the brokenness in the world.

In his book *Righteous Brood*, missional practitioner Hugh Halter gives several personal examples of impactful moments in prayer. In 2021, one unexpected encounter with a stranger who was hosting the church leaders' event he was attending in Queens, New York, was a turning point for him and an appointed meeting to encourage Hugh. His son's declining health with frequent seizures had left Hugh feeling angry at God and without the energy to continue his normal work and to be a husband or dad. After unloading his frustrations to a wise and loving man, George, Hugh saw a tender smile and tears stream down George's cheeks as he knelt to the ground, placed his hands on Hugh's shoes, and began to pray:

> "Father, Hugh is having a hard time trusting you because he's tired. He sees Ryan's disability as a limitation. Would you show him the beauty, the power, and the ministry that must now flow from his home, from his weakness, from his brokenness. May he see your power and freedom through these very real constraints."[149]

George reminded Hugh that God's mission is not about him doing great things for God or even about feeling good; God's mission is to work through our normal life and the ordinary when we are feeling weak and exhausted. In other words, "when you sign up your family to live for God's purposes in the world, brokenness isn't something that hinders mission; brokenness is the bedrock of mission."[150] Brokenness does not hinder prayer but entreats God's power and freedom to be displayed through them.

Small Steps

Several years before my injury, I left a city that I loved, a career opportunity with a company that I had dreamed of working for, and another job splitting my time between NYC and Florida. I left my small, cozy apartment in NYC, wonderful friends, and my church community because I could see some opportunities that were leading me to compromise my integrity and take my life in a direction that was not God's plan. Not long before God gave me clear direction to expand my master's comprehensive paper into a book. God and I were rekindling our close relationship through my writing, so when I experienced that freak injury that has required several years of recovery and led to other health issues, immediately I knew that God allowed this for a reason. God and I have had a long history, so He would not have allowed this injury, which would cause me not to complete my book that was about 75% complete, and pause my normal life, if it was not for a very good reason.

God knew that we needed a lot of me-and-Him time to get my heart in a better place and remind me of our old relationship. When I was a teen, I had an encounter with God that changed my life. I will share more about that in the next chapter on Bible study. I had several needs, and I believed that God could help. My mom modeled prayer. After Mom and I would discuss a situation, instead of going over it again and again as teens like to do, Mom would say, "Let's pray and ask God." She would say, "I do not know the answer, and God can help us." God helped us in big and small ways as a family and then for me personally.

One of our neighbors borrowed our ladder and kept it for months. When he returned it, he gave my mom $100 for all the time he had kept it. She said that was not necessary, but he insisted that she keep it. Mom said that money came at just the right time because she needed money for our electric bill. She was single at the time, and even though she had a good job as an accountant, it was still hard to care for the needs of our family. Mom shared many stories with my brother and me about how God would answer her prayers and provide for our family.

So I started making prayer a priority in my life, spending about thirty to forty minutes almost every morning before school in eigth grade, reading and learning verses from the Bible, which could help me, and then praying for others. I prayed that God would help me love some difficult people and bring me some new friendships. As I continued to pray, I discovered it was easier to love some of those people, and He brought several new friends into my life. Some of these friends were so fun and loving and also genuine in their prayers for people. A large portion of my prayer time was devoted to praying for family and friends. In addition to close friends, I prayed for my larger network of friends, and since I did not know their specific needs, I prayed Ephesians 3:16–18:

> I pray that out of his glorious riches he may strengthen you with power through his Spirit in your inner being, so that Christ may dwell in your hearts through faith. And I pray that you, being rooted and established in love, may have power, together with all the saints, to grasp how wide and long and high and deep is the love of Christ. (NIV 1984)

Additionally, I prayed Philippians 4:6–7 over my own life:

> Do not be anxious about anything, but in everything, by prayer and petition, with thanksgiving, present your requests to God. And the peace of God, which transcends all understanding, will guard your hearts and your minds in Christ Jesus. (NIV 1984)

Then looking back into my years in college in my twenties, I can still see just like it was yesterday: my college roommate and me sitting on one of our twin beds, either her bed with the cool plaid bedspread or mine with the floral bedspread, praying for our needs, dreams, desires, family, and friends.

I did not intentionally stop praying as much, but I let the busyness of life and work distract me from continuing to invest more in my relationship with God. God quieted my life through this recovery journey, so we could strengthen our relationship. Let me tell you, it came through hard times and good times. There were a lot of quiet moments, and then God filled them. He brought back our communication, and really, that is what prayer is: communication with God, listening, speaking, and hearing through the silent moments that then move into thanksgiving. Feeling as a shell of myself, it would have been easy to let bitterness take root or for me to focus on my limitations and pain. But instead, God said, "You still have much to be thankful for, and there are still many things that you can do. Focus on your steps forward and not how far you have to go."

A lot of small steps with God in the right direction will take you far. Just like when I was in my teens and twenties, I started praying for family, friends, extended family, and the needs in the community and globally. Then, because I needed exercise, since it hurt to bend my knees from all the steroids and part of my back and my shoulder were frozen, I started taking walks. And then thought that I would walk-pray. So, on many days, for months and months, I could easily spend about two hours in prayer. Then God gave me a clear structure to my prayer time, and this is the Seven Pathways plan for deepening your relationship with God. This plan helped me chart my way back to a deeper relationship with God and better health, and I pray that it will do the same for you.

The Practice of Prayer

Prayer is an interconnected relationship and involves a cadence of hearing, listening, and responding to God. The practice is found among thanksgiving and praise, silence, confession, song, petitions and intercession (along with many others forms of prayer), Bible study (reading, studying, and thoughtful life application), and Scripture focus (meditating, pondering, memorizing, etc.). Prayer is interwoven into all of the Seven Pathways, so this discipline is foundational for practicing the rest.

The following are the concepts related to prayer that will guide your practice. I lay them out in the order in which God revealed them to me, which I believe will apply to the experience of most people. This structured plan is what God gave me for prayers of petition and intercession.

Prayers of Petition and Intercession

As we've seen, most people approach God through prayer in order to ask for something, either for themselves (petition) or on behalf of someone else (intercession). These prayers are a starting point because they do come naturally to us. Let's begin here and allow these types of prayers to become a gateway to your larger practice of prayer.

This simple structure is a way for weaving prayers of petition and intercession into your prayer practice.

- Monday: Pray for yourself, immediate family, and one to three nonbelievers.
- Tuesday: Pray for yourself, immediate family, and extended family.
- Wednesday: Pray for yourself, your friends, and one to three nonbelievers.
- Thursday: Pray for yourself, your church, community, and world leaders, and needs around the world.

- Friday: Pray for yourself, immediate family, and one to three nonbelievers.
- Saturday: Pray for yourself, immediate family, and extended family.
- Sunday: Ask the Lord how He would lead you to pray, and also pray for Christians around the world who are persecuted for their faith.

Praying through Scripture

As I began writing this Seven Pathways guided journey, I was continuing to connect with God through these practices, starting with thanksgiving and so forth. I was still very weak and tired after about one and a half hours, so I would have to take a break. I used to be able to sit at a computer for hours on end without taking breaks. When I said yes to God, that I would write this study, I thought that I had all my study notes from John 1–15, which I used for teaching a small group Bible study. Unfortunately, they were located in a box at the back of a storage unit, making them impossible to recover. I revisited that conversation with God and said, "I don't think that I can do this now." Then He assured me that He would show me the way and give me small steps.

This was the strategy He impressed upon me. First, listen to one chapter of the Gospel of John a day, and then voice-text three application questions. After that, listen to a chapter of John a day and voice-text a short prayer. That took about two months, and then God said, "I want you to start listening to John again, and then ask your nephew if he could help you type a summary of each chapter of John." I did, but then my stepfather transitioned to being my scribe when my nephew went back to school. I needed this help since I still struggled with a lot of pain around my ears from the occipital neuralgia that made wearing glasses painful.

Listening to small segments of direction from the Lord and then taking those steps, I found that taking lots of steps even if they're small will take you a long way.

I would encourage you to stop thinking that now is not the right time because you might be struggling with an illness, some type of hardship, or a difficult season in your life. I would encourage you to start praying and start taking the steps that God shows you. Start praying for others. Through prayer, you will experience the joy of fellowship with God, stronger relationships, and the strength and confidence to take steps, even when you don't feel like it or you feel inadequate. Be consistent and keep showing up. God will meet you.

The Language of Prayer

The language of prayer is forged in the crucible of pain, trouble, and where there is a need. Our language is direct, personal, and honest. Henri Nouwen, in his book *With Open Hands*, paints the picture of prayer in the opening of our hands:

> To pray means to open your hands before God. It means slowly relaxing the tension which squeezes your hands together and accepting your existence with an increased readiness, not as a possession to defend, but as a gift to receive. Above all, therefore prayer is a way of life which allows you to find a stillness in the midst of a world where you open your hands to God's promises and find hope for yourself, others and the whole community in which you live.[151]

The Psalms humanizes and normalizes problems that forge the forty-two laments in the book. Problems or troubles are not unusual or something to hide from others; they are a normal part of the faith journey. Experiencing suffering, pain, or difficult circumstances is not a sign of a lack of faith but is intrinsic to the nature and growth of faith. Half of the laments in Psalms turn to praise in the end. The laments, difficult trials, pain, or suffering that we want to avoid or ignore rather than pray through bring us back to joy.

Our culture promotes the masking, hiding, or ignoring of problems through presenting a false self to the world through social media, where only the good trips, awards, or fun experiences are shared. Prayer starts with being real and genuine with God and often starts with a trouble or need. That was true for me as well. I prayed out of my need for God to help me love some difficult people and for me to gain some new friendships.

Enlightenment's thinking that gave rise to the autonomous self has forged a culture of individualism and relativism. If an individual views his or herself as autonomous, then there is no need to confess or acknowledge sin nor the accountability to and relationship with God. The rising concern for social justice, which is valid, has forged our culture's reinterpretation of "sins" between individuals or groups (normally the word *sin* is replaced with *injustice*) instead of personal "sins toward God." The social sciences have usurped the meaning of *sins* from biblical theology. Recognizing sin as self-centeredness and self-isolation and our need for self-preservation is a social action, which separates us from God and others. It is a social action in the sense that lamenting or confessing sin will open you to God, progressively changing you to become more concerned about the needs of others, which in turn will heal and improve your relationships and contribute to solutions and cultural renewal. These all reflect the character, actions, and purposes of God.

May the language of the psalms, and other prayers in the Bible that record biblical lament, confession, and repentance, help us to become more open with God and ourselves and reassure us that

God is safe for us to pour our hearts out to Him and to heal us from the false narratives we sometimes believe—that a Christian does not have pain, trouble, or suffering in life. Remember, there is no resurrection without death. We need to embrace grief and lament, making space for us to feel more deeply, so that we might be healed from the inside out and reject our culture's discomfort with grief as a subject.

Prayers in the Bible

The Bible contains good examples of various prayer practices. And by studying and imitating them, you can improve your own practice of prayer. Here are some of the types of prayer found in Scripture, and some of the most well-known prayers. Some have taken a cherished place in the worship of the church and the saints for centuries. Let them enrich your prayer life as well.

Spoken Prayers

Prayers of praise and thanksgiving are focused on worship and professing great love, humble devotion, and adoration of His majesty and power, grace, redemption, and His goodness and blessings in your life. Though not exhaustive, here are several examples of praising and thanking God: (1) Jesus models first praising God in His prayer known as the Lord's Prayer, where He teaches us to pray (Matt. 6:9–13). (2) Another example is praising God for sending a mighty Savior (Luke 1:46–47) and (3) for casting our sins into the depths of the sea (Mic. 7:18-19). (4) Then, Psalm 29:1–11 and 77:14–20 praise God for His glory and majesty as the King of Creation. (5) Psalm 63:3–5 speaks of praising God that His love is better than the richest food or anything of this world, for only God satisfies our deepest need. (6) Lastly, Psalm 30:2–3 teaches us to praise the Lord for the times when He has shown up when we really needed him, helping us, and pulling us out of a pit. No "pit" is too deep that the Lord's mighty arm can't reach.

Note that the difficulties and trials of life can eclipse our ability to see the goodness, greatness, and majesty of God when we are fixed on the problems of our world. First, look for the rays of light in your world and the goodness of God, even in hard times, and pray that the Lord help you to see them and then celebrate them and praise God for His grace and goodness. Second, start your prayers with, "I praise You for . . ." Third, to give words of praise to your prayers, look up "praise" in your concordance and then focus on the verses with "praise" in them, particularly in the Psalms. Perhaps, make a list of five to seven of these verses, and start your prayers each morning with one of these verses; then rotate them daily. After a period of perhaps six to eight weeks, add some more verses to your list, and start your prayers with those new additions. You are creating a library of praise verses to give words to your praise, and these will frame your thoughts and draw out other reminders of God's goodness in your life.

Prayers of confession are an acknowledgment of sin or proclamation of who God is. Here are some examples of prayers of confession and the need for God's forgiveness:

- Psalm 19:12–14: "But who can discern their own errors? Forgive my hidden faults. Keep your servant also from willful sins; may they not rule over me. Then I will be blameless, innocent of great transgression. May these words of my mouth and this meditation of my heart be pleasing in your sight, LORD, my Rock, and my Redeemer." (NIV)
- Psalm 38:4 (speaks of the oppression and weightiness of guilt): "My guilt has overwhelmed me like a burden too heavy to bear."

- Psalm 25:7: "Do not remember the sins of my youth and my rebellious ways; according to your love remember me, for you, LORD, are good."
- 1 John 1:9: "If we confess our sins, he is faithful and just and will forgive us our sins and purify us from all unrighteousness."

Note that confession is a gift of God to cleanse us, so that we will stop the frequent guilt trips that our minds take. First, relax; telling your sins to God is safe because He is your safe harbor where you can unload them forever, and He remembers them no more. Second, perhaps follow the sequence of the Lord's Prayer by starting with praise and thanksgiving and then confessing your sins before God. Lastly, the more that you confess your sins regularly, the more grace you will experience in your life and the more thankful you will become. A more grateful person is a more gracious person.

Prayers of supplication (focused prayers) are prayers turning to God with a request. Below are several topic-based examples of these types of prayers:

- Guidance: "Direct my footsteps according to your word." (Ps. 119:133 NIV)
- Wisdom:
    - "If any of you lacks wisdom, you should ask God, who gives generously to all without finding fault, and it will be given to you." (James 1:5)
    - "Gracious words are a honeycomb, sweet to the soul and healing to the bones." (Prov. 16:24)

- Trust: "Some trust in chariots and some in horses, but we trust in the name of the LORD our God." (Ps. 20:7)

- Doubt/Comfort: "When doubts filled my mind, your comfort gave me renewed hope and cheer." (Ps. 94:19 NLT)
- Endurance: "Therefore, since we are surrounded by such a great cloud of witnesses, let us throw off everything that hinders and the sin that so easily entangles. And let us run with perseverance the race marked out for us." (Heb. 12:1 NIV)
- Temptation: "No temptation has overtaken you except what is common to mankind. And God is faithful; he will not let you be tempted beyond what you can bear." (1 Cor. 10:13)
- Healing:
    - "'But I will restore you to health and heal your wounds,' declares the LORD." (Jer. 30:17)
    - "Is anyone among you sick? Let them call the elders of the church to pray over them and anoint them with oil in the name of the Lord. And the prayer offered in faith will make the sick person well; the Lord will raise them up. If they have sinned, they will be forgiven." (James 5:14–15)

Note, be specific in your prayer requests. Remind God of His promises in the Bible by praying back those prayers to Him. Do not give up too easily; be persistent in your prayers. Write specific verses beside prayer requests in your prayer journal.

Prayers of intercession appeal to or petition God for help on behalf of others. Two prayers from the New Testament that I have prayed for people since my teens are found in Philippians and Ephesians:

- "And this is my prayer: that your love may abound more and more in knowledge and depth of insight, so that you may be able to discern what is best and may be pure and blameless for the day of Christ, filled with the fruit of righteousness that comes through Jesus Christ—to the glory and praise of God." (Phil. 1:9–11 NIV)

- "For this reason, ever since I heard about your faith in the Lord Jesus and your love for all God's people, I have not stopped giving thanks for you, remembering you in my prayers. I keep asking that the God of our Lord Jesus Christ, the glorious Father, may give you the Spirit of wisdom and revelation, so that you may know him better. I pray that the eyes of your heart may be enlightened in order that you may know the hope to which he has called you, the riches of his glorious inheritance in his holy people, and his incomparably great power for us who believe." (Eph. 1:15–19)

Note that in praying for your friends and family, perhaps develop an organized weekly prayer plan like the Seven Pathways plan. Developing a plan helps organize all the needs and people you're praying for so that you will not become as easily discouraged in your prayer life and give up praying. Do not be rigid, because everyone has interruptions, and the devil will try to use that to discourage you. Be consistent, and do not be discouraged if you do not see results quickly. Remember that transformation is progressive. Lastly, write your prayer requests for all you are praying for in a journal, as this will keep you organized and accountable, and will build confidence. Include answers and updates to prayers, which will also encourage your faith.

In addition to praying for the needs of people you know, pray for other believers who are suffering around the world for their faith. (See Heb. 13:3) As you pray, keep the following things in mind: (1) Pray that God strengthens them to endure persecution and that He supplies His strength in their weakness. (2) Pray for them to find grace and favor before their persecutors. (3) Pray for their protection. (4) Pray that the Lord will help them forgive their persecutors. (5) Pray that their faith and that the gospel will be shared in this dark place. (6) Pray that they hold onto the hope and love of God.

Pray also for those you know and love who are not Christians. Pray that you will be sensitive to the leading of the Spirit to pray for them regularly. Keep these in mind: (1) Pray that they see their need for salvation and feel gratitude for the free gift of salvation, which cost Jesus His life (see John 3:16; Rom. 6:23). (2) Pray that God will reveal Himself to them in a way that makes sense and will help them understand the truth about God. (3) Pray that God will remove spiritual blindness from their eyes. (4) Pray that God helps you and other Christians in their life to represent Jesus to them in words and actions, and to love them well. (5) Lastly, choose one to three nonbelievers to pray for this year, and commit to praying for them several times a week.

To highlight the different types of prayers above, I would like to draw your attention to one of the best-known prayers of supplication for our country, which was delivered by President Franklin Delano Roosevelt on the night of June 6, 1944. He addressed the nation on national radio for the first time after the invasion of Normandy, and his address was mostly a prayer:

> Almighty God: Our sons, pride of our Nation, this day have set upon a mighty endeavor, a struggle to preserve our Republic, our religion, and our civilization, and to set free a suffering humanity.
>
> Lead them straight and true; give strength to their arms, stoutness to their hearts, steadfastness in their faith.
>
> They will need Thy blessings. Their road will be long and hard. For the enemy is strong. He may hurl back our forces. Success may not come with rushing speed, but we

shall return again and again; and we know that by Thy grace, and by the righteousness of our cause, our sons will triumph.

They will be sore tried, by night and by day, without rest—until the victory is won. The darkness will be rent by noise and flame. Men's souls will be shaken with the violences of war.

For these men are lately drawn from the ways of peace. They fight not for the lust of conquest. They fight to end conquest. They fight to liberate. They fight to let justice arise, and tolerance and good will among all Thy people. They yearn but for the end of battle, for their return to the haven of home.

Some will never return. Embrace these, Father, and receive them, Thy heroic servants, into Thy kingdom.

And for us at home—fathers, mothers, children, wives, sisters, and brothers of brave men overseas—whose thoughts and prayers are ever with them—help us, Almighty God, to rededicate ourselves in renewed faith in Thee in this hour of great sacrifice.

Many people have urged that I call the Nation into a single day of special prayer. But because the road is long and the desire is great, I ask that our people devote themselves in a continuance of prayer. As we rise to each new day, and again when each day is spent, let words of prayer be on our lips, invoking Thy help to our efforts.

Give us strength, too—strength in our daily tasks, to redouble the contributions we make in the physical and the material support of our armed forces.

And let our hearts be stout, to wait out the long travail, to bear sorrows that may come, to impart our courage unto our sons wheresoever they may be.

> And, O Lord, give us Faith. Give us Faith in Thee; Faith in our sons; Faith in each other; Faith in our united crusade. Let not the keenness of our spirit ever be dulled. Let not the impacts of temporary events, of temporal matters of but fleeting moment let not these deter us in our unconquerable purpose.
>
> With Thy blessing, we shall prevail over the unholy forces of our enemy. Help us to conquer the apostles of greed and racial arrogancies. Lead us to the saving of our country, and with our sister Nations into a world unity that will spell a sure peace a peace invulnerable to the schemings of unworthy men. And a peace that will let all of men live in freedom, reaping the just rewards of their honest toil.
>
> Thy will be done, Almighty God.[152]

Though not specifically a biblical lament in its structure, President Roosevelt's prayer does have some structure. This prayer first addresses God and then expresses the problems. Then he calls on God in His mercy and grace to help our warriors and our country, and he calls the nation to rise up in fervent prayer. In the closing of his prayer, the president expresses confidence that God will help save our country and our sister nations against the forces of our enemy, and then he prays for a world unity that reflects the heart of God.

Mary's Prayer and Song

Mary, the mother of Jesus was a teenage girl from a poor community of Nazareth; she was an ordinary girl chosen for an extraordinary task and gift of birthing the Son of God. She was a virgin and pledged to be married to a man named Joseph. To be pledged in marriage to a man meant that the couple had a public ceremony in which they were legally married, but they would not live or sleep together for about a year. The only way to break the engagement was through a divorce.

Mary was about to receive news that would change her life and the world.

An angel appeared to Mary and delivered the news that she was highly favored by God and that she would birth the Son of God through a miraculous conception. She had thoughts racing through her mind concerning what the angel could possibly mean. This phrase, "highly favored," as found in Luke 1:28 (NIV), means that Mary received a special grace from God, His unmerited grace, and was given the privilege of serving as the mother of the Messiah. This phrase in no way singles Mary out as one who has any prerequisite grace. While the angel was telling Mary about the Son of the Most High, who will reign on the throne of David forever, she was becoming more and more aware that the Messiah, the one Promised in the Old Testament and a descendant of David (2 Sam. 7:13, 16; Ps. 89:26–27; Isa. 9:6–7), would be entrusted to her to raise as well to birth.

A better definition for Mary's response of feeling "greatly troubled" (Luke 1:29 NIV) is "thoroughly stirred up, confused, and perplexed."[153] What you and I would say is, "She is freaking out." She knew accepting what God said came at a cost—her life. How would she be able to care for her son? Would she lose her fiancé? What would her family think? What would the people in the community say? A single, pregnant, poor woman had very little hope of taking care of herself, let alone a child. She would face both alienation and rejection. The word for "wondered" (v. 29) in the Greek carries a different connotation than a common English meaning of "to be curious about something," but it means to use logic and reasoning to understand a difficult matter. The maturity of her faith is evident as she used her mind to weigh against the Scriptures what the angel had spoken and in her openness to honestly ask questions to gain God's wisdom and understanding. She asked the angel how she could have a baby since she had never "known" a man. Her questions expressed her belief that what the angel said was true, but she was confused about how she might conceive a baby. She was not asking questions to find a reason to reject what God was saying.

I love this about Mary—that the first time we are introduced to her, the mother of Jesus, she is trying to understand what God has said to her. I could identify with her because I like to ask questions. I have found that asking questions is the best way to get to know someone. Asking questions says, "I want to get to know you, and you matter." The people whom I feel most comfortable asking questions of are my closest friends and family members. Asking questions develops intimacy. Often, we are uncomfortable expressing our questions because we think it shows unbelief. It can sometimes, but often, we can't believe without asking questions first. Questions lead us to an understanding, which leads us to deeper faith.

Mary, after thinking through all of this and remembering that God was and has always been faithful, responds, "I am the Lord's servant . . . . May it be to me as you have said" (Luke 1:38 NIV 1984). What she was saying was, "I am yours, God—I submit all of who I am to you." This is a statement of identity, much like we might say, "I am a daughter or a mother." She is assuming the implications and challenges with her identity and trusting that if she is God's servant, then He will protect and guide her to carry out the tasks and plans that He has for her. These two statements in Luke 1:38 affirm her intelligence and deep-rooted knowledge, faith, and trust in God.

Moving on through Luke 1, Mary leaves her home to visit her cousin. Without studying the geography, we might forget that Mary's trip from Nazareth to Elizabeth would take several days, so during that time, she had to think, reflect, and compose her response of prayer or song of praise to the annunciation.

Mary's song (Luke 1:46–55), which is also a prayer, is preserved for God's people when they might receive shocking news or experience life-changing situations. Her prayer reminds us to reflect rather than to react to situations and to allow faith to triumph over fear. When you receive bad news about your health, a loved one, your work, take the time to reflect, then respond . Ask God to help your faith triumph over the fear of the worst-case scenario, fear that you do not know how you can make it, fear that this situation is going to be a disaster, or fear that there is no recovery from this situation. Mary's high-caliber character shines through her thoughtful responses and faithful heart to embrace God's design for her life with joy, knowing that it would not be an easy road. May we cling to our faith during those hard times, that God's grace and faithfulness will get us through and give us the faith to trust that God will work all situations for our good.

Laments

More than one-third of the Psalms are laments. Laments are a way of praying, which can be grieving, but most of them are birthed out of raw, genuine faith, as a passionate call for God's help when things are going badly. They are more than simply expressions of sorrow and grief or a release of emotions. They are prayers aimed at God when grief or pain makes you want to blame, reject, or run from Him. It is a prayer birthed in deep despair, loss, or heartache. Those who lament discover that their pain is not hopeless, but in going through the pain and lamenting, they find strength and renewed confidence in God. Jesus lamented, calling out to God in despair and pain before enduring the agony of the crucifixion.

Laments might seem disrespectful or demanding, but they are one of the forms of prayer practiced prominently in the

Old Testament, as the Israelites, God's covenant people, were surrounded by pagan nations with their hostility. Laments reflect upon the difficulties of life, sufferings, fears, and aspirations, as well as act as confession and repentance by the worshiper before God. Lament and confession are interrelated as a prayer of petition to God to intercede on the behalf of His people, and confession is trust in God, whom they are calling upon.

In our 24/7 global media culture, tragedy and destruction have usurped the role of lament in the lives of individuals, the community, and the world in which God's sovereignty is being questioned. In the Psalms, most of the laments (except for a few) circle back to deep trust in God, even during the darkest of days. The role of lamenting in the life of a believer needs to be restored and taught in our churches. If you don't lament over sin or brokenness in your life or in the world, then you miss resurrection. Through bringing our brokenness to God, He works good through the pain or difficulties and can restore and resurrect what seemed hopeless or impossible. God is working for good in our lives and in this world, and one day, all will be made right, and all the evil will be undone when Jesus returns.

Psalm 88, a song of lament, is one of the two psalms in the collection of laments (the other being Psalm 39) that end without hope. It will give you a model of bringing your raw emotions and brokenness to God and will encourage you that you can trust God to help you endure and navigate through darkness and pain in this world. About half of the laments in Psalms end with hope and a sense of God's faithfulness or power, yet these two do not. Psalm 88 is for all of us who have felt so hopeless or that our life is falling apart.

Perhaps you can't see any way out of a bad situation; you can't seem to get a break from the same struggle with health, family, or finances; or your child is out of control, distant, and you think struggling with addiction. Maybe you feel trampled by addiction yourself, or you are in a bad relationship, and you honestly do not like your life. Perhaps you try to pray, but God does not seem to be answering your prayers; you are angry at God for allowing sickness, injury, or some type of health issue to happen; or you are struggling in life, while it looks like others who do not follow God's ways are succeeding and doing well. Some of you might be thinking, *well, a Christian should not think that way.* That is precisely why Psalm 88 is in the Bible. God is saying, "Bring your raw emotions and honest thoughts to me." The psalmist speaks bluntly to God, to paraphrase verses 14–16: Why are you ignoring me? What are you doing, God? Why have you allowed me to suffer for all these years? Why are you afflicting me this way? The psalmist is weak, angry, overwhelmed, and desperate, even though he may be trying to fake it, by acting like things are not that bad. He is at the end of himself and with no hope, yet he is still talking to God. He knows that God is the only One who can help.

After a series of misdiagnoses and seeing more than ten doctors without a clear diagnosis, I had exhausted all my known resources. I was feeling hopeless. My mom suggested that we start praying that God would be my primary care physician and give the doctors wisdom to give me a clear, accurate diagnosis. Since He is the great Physician, God knew what I had, and that I needed Him to help the doctors. So, don't give up so easy, as you have a big God who is powerful, majestic, and all-knowing. Keep crying out to Him when you feel broken or like your life is falling apart.

Be like the persistent widow from Luke 18:1-8 who prayed with tenacity and would not let her request go unanswered. Almost every night, I reminded God that I am still praying like that persistent widow prayed. I am praying for my full recovery from head and neck pain that has persisted for several years now.

Peter knew this well, too (despite denying Jesus later), that God was the only Person he could run to for peace and security (John 6:68). Peter was saying that when life seems hopeless, or your road seems more than you can handle and is intolerable, God is your only safe harbor and can save you and turn things around.

Jesus' prayer on the cross, while He was suffering excruciating pain and feeling the cosmic abandonment of God, reminds us that He understands our pain and can relate to us during those times (Matt. 27:46). Jesus faced the ultimate darkness of abandonment from God so that we would never experience the agony of this abandonment and that all people might be justified and restored through faith in Jesus (Rom. 3:25–26).

The psalmist's very insightful question from Psalm 88—"Do those who are dead rise up and praise you?" (v. 10 NIV 1984)—points to Jesus' death and resurrection, and is a reminder of the resurrection of all believers. All the pain and suffering will be undone, for there will be no more death, mourning, crying, or pain in heaven. The answer to his question is Yes! Because of the resurrection, we can count on God to restore all things broken in this world when He returns. In this life, we can experience God restoring brokenness.

This prayer is included to give us hope that we can come to God with our raw emotions and be honest, and we do not have to get our life together first. Also, it reminds us to bring our real self to God, the unscripted and unedited self. Brennan Manning offers this as consolation:

> His love, which called us into existence, calls us to come out of self-hatred and step into his truth. "Come to me now," Jesus says. "Acknowledge and accept who I want to be for you: a Savior of boundless compassion, infinite patience, unbearable forgiveness, and love that keeps no

score of wrongs. Quit projecting onto Me your own feelings about yourself. At this moment your life is a bruised reed, and I will not crush it; a smoldering wick, and I will not quench it. You are in a safe place".[154]

Even when God seems absent or unjust, He is not. Because sin has affected the whole of creation, humans experience the effects of sin, such as suffering, pain, tragedy, disease, trials, disasters, etc. God does not explain why He allows suffering, pain, or injustice in the lives of His children, but He does say that you can count on this: He is a restorer and will restore all things to health and wholeness fully when He returns.

General Lament Structure

This basic structure of laments in the Psalms can serve as a model to pray your own laments. Most of them follow a general structure; however, a few do not include a statement of confidence or praise to God to conclude the prayer. Psalm 88 is one such psalm. Using it as an example, note the following structure of a lament.

Address: Turn to God. (vv. 1–2)
Complaint: Tell your complaint or problem to God. (vv. 3–5)
Confession: Confess your internal struggle with the complaint or problem. (vv. 6–9a)
Affirmation of Trust: Recount that you can trust God and why. (vv. 10, 12)
Petition: Boldly ask God for help as you pour out your heart to Him. (vv. 9b–13)
Statement of Confidence: Express that you know God hears and your confidence that He will intervene.

Praise: Praise and thank God related to what you know about Him. (This might be a truth that has grounded your request above.)

The Lord's Prayer

Among the many questions that we would like to ask God, Jesus answers one of our primary questions: How should we pray? His specificity and detail is for the purpose of helping us to communicate and build a relationship with Him, worship Him, experience His power of transformation, and know how to effectively engage and experience prayer. Think of prayer like language. Prayer is God's language of communication with us and us with Him. Jesus is teaching us the language of prayer in His model prayer; it continues to be the best-known of all Christian prayers and is prayed frequently throughout the world. Some of the great theologians and writers of prayers, such as Augustine, Luther, and Calvin, devoted extensive study on the Lord's Prayer and developed their teachings on prayer based on Jesus' model prayer. We will understand and explore the language of this prayer in sections, so that this prayer will help give you the direction that you have been wanting to strengthen your prayer life. This is the prayer recorded in the NIV in Matthew 6:9-13:

> Our Father in heaven,
> hallowed be your name,
> your kingdom come,
> your will be done on earth as it is in heaven.
> Give us today our daily bread.
> Forgive us our debts, as we also have forgiven our debtors.
> Lead us not into temptation,
> but deliver us from the evil one.

The *Address/Invocation* to "our Father in heaven" is to remind us who God is—our Father—and who we are—children of God. This address helps us to resist the urge to start asking God for things and to remember to whom we are directing our prayers: God, our Father. The address invites us to pause to allow grace and gratitude to arise through our speaking to our Father.

The *First Petition*, "Hallowed be your name," signifies His transcendence. He is not like other gods, and this phrase underscores His immanence, His nearness and ability to hear all who call out to Him in prayer and holiness. The word *hallow,* infrequently employed in our modern culture, refers to the holiness of God. In praying this petition, we are asking God to help us (and all Christians) to honor Him through living as a follower of Christ in our words, thoughts, and actions and for help that by our witness more people would experience the grace of God transforming their lives to also live as followers of Jesus. And we are asking for a heart of gratitude for this undeserving grace.

The *Second Petition* and *Third Petition*, "Your kingdom come" and "Your will be done on earth as it is in heaven," represent a calling on God for His "kingdom" to come in us through reshaping by the Holy Spirit of our thoughts, affections, and actions and to come into the world and end our death, suffering, pain, and injustice. We are asking God to rule in our hearts and help us to surrender all of who we are to God. Also, they are petitions of yearning for the consummation of the kingdom of what we only partially experience now to be completely established on the Earth.

After the first three petitions as our framework that redirect our hearts from self-dependence to God-dependence, we now bring our "prayer list" to God. We come to God in prayer with this *Fourth Petition*, "Give us today our daily bread." Here we are now remembering that we are speaking to God who loves us like a Father who provides for His children and to Him as the God over all the resources in the world. The grace and love of God melts the arrogance of our hearts and quells the scarcity mentality that we project onto God. This petition is grounded in thanksgiving, reframing our prayers with a thankful heart to our faithful God, who is the Provider of all our needs. Praying this also reduces our desire to accumulate more things, reduces the lure of consumerism, and cultivates contentment.

The *Fifth Petition*, "Forgive us our debts as we also have forgiven our debtors," concerns our relationship with God in which we regularly confess and repent, which increases our faith, trust, and joy, and does not undo us with guilt and shame. This petition is also linked to our relationship with others. Confess feelings of anger, resentment, or hurt that are blocking the waters of forgiveness. Next, lay down any desire for retaliation toward another and cling to God's role as Judge of the person (Rom. 12:19). When you realize that you have been forgiven much, then you are more willing to forgive others. Forgiveness frees you from bitterness.

The *Sixth Petition*, "And lead us not into temptation," is a request for Him to help us not to "enter into temptation," meaning to start entertaining thoughts or desires that might lead to sin. It is also a petition to help us with our disordered desires so that a good thing becomes an "ultimate" thing, which can lead to greed, pride, resentment, fear, and more. We are asking God to reveal hidden sins to us, so that we will not be forced to the test by trials or circumstances, which expose our heart.

When we pray the *Seventh Petition*, "And deliver us from evil," we are asking for God to deliver us from the evil in the world, such as death, anger, greed, injustice, poverty, and more. When we become a Christian, we are released from the power of sin and death, but because we still live in a fallen world, we still experience the effects of evil—all the brokenness and injustice—in the world. And so, with confidence and hope, we pray that we might experience more freedom from these forces during our lifetime and look forward to the end of the reign of evil in the world.

I would encourage you to look back to Jesus' model prayer to guide your prayer time. First, I would read the prayer. Then I would meditate on each petition and ask the Lord to reveal to you how that petition applies to your life and how you can personalize this prayer. Next, I would pray what He reveals for that petition, and then move to the next petition. For example, when meditating and praying "your kingdom come," ask the Lord to reveal to you what you might be holding back from Him or how you are still trying to control your life instead of surrendering and asking for God's purposes and plans to prevail in your life.

Prayer Dilemmas

Of the Seven Pathways, prayer is probably the pathway that draws the most doubts and questions. I find that many people come to this discipline with a great deal of disappointment over seemingly unanswered prayers, and others bring intellectual doubts about some aspect of prayer. Let me say first that prayer, like everything related to knowing God, depends on faith. Without faith, even a small amount, it is impossible to make progress in the practice of prayer. So I offer answers to these prayer dilemmas, not to provide irrefutable proof of prayer's efficacy, but to offer biblical, theological, and personal perspectives on these questions.

Working through the follwoing questions has greatly aided my faith and my practice of prayer. I believe it can do the same for you.

Does it work?

1. Scriptural Context

   James 5:16: "For this reason, confess your sins to each other and pray for each other so that you may be healed.

The prayer of the righteous person is powerful in what it can achieve." (CEB)

2. Scriptural Example(s)
   - Elijah's prayer for rain: 1 Kings 18:41–45
   - The healing at the Beautiful Gate: Acts 3
   - "Ask and it will be given to you; seek and you will find; knock and the door will be opened to you." (Matt. 7:7 NIV)
3. Theological Response

   Since many of us bring a host of unmet expectations to prayer, we are skeptical concerning its effectiveness in our lives and the world. What we are really wondering is if prayer is going to move God to action and if it is going to bring about change. Those who have written extensively on the subject (Keller, Foster, Rohr, Nouwen, etc.) largely agree that the effectiveness in prayer is what it does to us more than what it does to God. As noted in the scriptural examples, our prayers matter—they call God to activate His power and His will. Yet at the same time, we know that God's plans are sovereign. This is a divine mystery of how God works His sovereign and infallible plans and invites us to be a part the execution of His plans through prayer. If we believed that God is sovereign, and our prayers do not matter, then why pray? God allows us to be a part of the power by asking Him to act on our behalf and then watching Him work. This encourages our faith to believe that our prayers have power and do matter.

   I think that we miss the effectiveness of prayer because we do not focus on *how* we should ask. What I mean by that is this. Look back to the Lord's Prayer model; are you asking God to fulfill your desires from a self-focused state, or are you asking God to do something or fulfill your desires from a place of surrender to God and wanting His will and wisdom in your life? God instructs us to ask the desires of our heart and those things that fulfill His will. So, how do we know if our desires are right? J. I. Packer gives us some practical insight when we petition God. He says to lay out before God the reasons why this is a good thing that we are asking for and how this lines up with what we know is right, what delights and honors Him from Scripture, and what He wants and how He works in the world.[155] The habit of doing this will either deepen or lessen your prayers, and it will give you great strength in your prayers because you have lined them up with Scripture and what you know about God.

On the effectiveness of prayer, Tim Keller notes, "Prayer is the only entryway into genuine self-knowledge. It is also the main way we experience deep change—the reordering of our loves. Prayer is how God gives us so many of the unimaginable things he has for us. Indeed, prayer makes it safe for God to give us many of the things we most desire. It is the way we know God, the way we finally treat God as God. Prayer is simply the key to everything we need to do and be in life."[156]

The act of praying consistently and rhythmically attunes us to the voice of God and His ways and conforms our will to His. As we are conformed into the image of Christ, we find that our prayers are met with ever-increasing cadence and effectiveness because we are praying attuned to God's will and in step with His heart, and He fundamentally knows what is best for our lives. We can be confident that God hears our prayers and will answer. His answer might be what we ask if it is in accordance with His will, or He might answer it in a way that we did not expect and give us what He desires for us.

What should I pray for others?

1. Scriptural Response
   - "I urge, then, first of all, that requests, prayers, intercession and thanksgiving be made for everyone." (1 Tim. 2:1 NIV 1984)
   - "Therefore, confess your sins to each other and pray for each other so that you may be healed." (James. 5:16)
   - "After Job had prayed for his friends, the LORD made him prosperous again and gave him twice as much as he had before." (Job 42:10)
   - "And pray in the Spirit on all occasions with all kinds of prayers and requests. With this in mind, be alert and always keep praying for all the saints." (Eph. 6:18)
   - "In the same way, the Spirit helps us in our weakness. We do not know what we ought to pray for, but the Spirit himself intercedes for us with groans that words cannot express." (Rom. 8:26)
2. Theological Response
   - We can pray a lot of things for others, but here are some main categories from Scripture. First, Paul lists several things we should pray over others: 1) requests; 2) prayers (general); 3) intercessions (specific); and thanksgiving (blessings). Second, in James, we see a relationship between authentic openness and confession coupled with prayer. Amid our transparency with one another, we find healing through praying over one another. Third, Job's response to pray for his friends is in the broader context of the conclusion of YHWH's

dialogue with Job. YHWH tells Eliphaz that he is angry with him and his two friends because they have falsely spoken about YHWH to Job. He commands the three to take an offering to Job (a demonstration of repentance and seeking the restoration of *shalom* between them). He then tells Job to pray for them, functioning as a mediator. It is through Job that YHWH chooses to restore the honor of the three foolish friends. Verse 11 and forward describe Job likely eating, with his family, the very sacrifice that had been brought by the three, demonstrating God restoring to Job through the very means that made his trials go from bad to worse.

- This Scripture demonstrates something much deeper in its original cultural context than simply letting go of hard feelings through prayer. It demonstrates that God's people possess the power to mediate the restoration of honor to those who have become shamed—even when that shameful activity hurts or maligns us in some way. God restored the standing of the friends through Job's functioning as a Christ-type figure, mediating restoration between the wayward and YHWH (see 2 Cor. 5).
- The Ephesians and Romans passages highlight the role of the Spirit to pray through us on all occasions, even when we do not know what to pray. This emphasizes the functional responsibility of the Spirit to do the praying and our responsibility to simply yield. We do not receive an answer to our prayers because we prayed the right formula. We receive answers to our prayers when our yielded hearts pray in accordance with the mind of the Spirit, even when such prayers are nothing but groans.
- This is not an exhaustive list; see also the section "Spoken Prayers" for more examples of the various types

of prayers for others, those of intercession and supplication. Praying for others is a privilege and to be a part of God's work in their lives, and it strengthens your faith and deepens your relationship with God. It also gives you a broader perspective of how God works and gets your focus off yourself.

Can we really ask God for anything in Jesus' name?

1. Scriptural Response
   - "You may ask me for anything in my name, and I will do it." (John 14:14 NIV)
   - "'Lord,' Martha said to Jesus, 'if you had been here, my brother would not have died. But I know that even now God will give you whatever you ask.'" (John 11:21–22)
   - "If you believe, you will receive whatever you ask for in prayer." (Matt. 21:22)
2. Theological Response
   - So what does asking God in Jesus' name mean. First, it does not mean that God will answer whatever you ask if you end your request with, "In Jesus' name." Using Jesus' name is not like speaking a magical incantation as in pagan worship in the first century for the purpose of manipulating the spiritual forces. Using the Lord's name to further selfish desires or purposes is using the Lord's name in vain.
   - John 14:14 speaks to our responsibility to ask in accordance with God's character and as his authorized representative. Consider the cultural backdrop of John 11; we are to ask in a respectful and direct way as Martha did, challenging Jesus to be true to His authority and the name of His Father who He claimed as His own. This was (and still is) a common practice

in honor-shame cultures to entice powerful and influential people to exercise their power for the benefit of the one requesting. Jesus' response in verse 25 ("I am the resurrection and the life. The one who believes in me will live, even though they die" NIV) demonstrates that He doesn't simply appeal to what she wants him to do. He recognizes she is appealing to who He is. He is the resurrection and the life. And because of who He is, He responds to her request in kind. Martha asks in accordance with the name of Jesus, which He affirms, and then responds accordingly. Jesus states the same promise in Matthew 21:22 in the context of those who trust in His authority over nature and all things.

- For those who ask of Jesus, respectfully trusting in His authority and appealing to who He is, He will do what is in accordance with His will. Pray with a heart that desires to please God. First, we must remember that prayer is not just about asking God for things but is about communication and fellowship with God. In response to our asking, He does what is in accordance with His will.

Ways to Practice Prayer: A Collection of Prayers

A Prayer for Healing

Oh Heavenly Father, Physician of our souls and bodies, who has sent Your only begotten Son and our Lord Jesus Christ to heal every sickness and infirmity, visit and heal also Your servant (*name*) from all sicknesses of soul and body to the grace of Your Christ. Grant him/her patience in sickness, strength of body and spirit, and recovery of health. For you, Oh Lord, have taught us through Your word to pray for each other that we may be healed.

Therefore, I pray, heal Your servant (*name*) and grant him/her the gift of complete health. For You are the source of healing and to You I give glory, Father, Son, and Holy Spirit. Amen.[157]

A Prayer for Those Afflicted with Mental Suffering

Almighty God, whose Son took upon Himself the afflictions of Your people, regard with Your tender compassion those suffering from anxiety, depression, or mental illness, especially (*name*); bear their sorrows and their cares, supply all their needs, help them to put their whole trust and confidence in You, and restore them to the strength of mind and cheerfulness of spirit, through Jesus Christ our Lord. Amen.[158]

A Lament for the Death of Someone Killed in the Neighborhood

Lamb of God, You take away the sins of the world. Have mercy on us. Grant us peace. For the unbearable toil of our sinful world, we pray for remission. For the terror of absence from our beloved, we pray for your comfort. For the scandalous presence of death in your creation, we pray for the resurrection. Lamb of God, You take away the sins of the world. Have mercy on us. Grant us peace. Come, Holy Spirit, and heal all that is broken in our lives and on our streets, and in our world. In the name of the Father, and of the Son, and of the Holy Spirit. Amen.[159]

A Prayer for Our Enemies

Oh Lord, You who command us to bless our enemies, protect us, we pray, from turning our neighbors into enemies, worthy only of hatred and deserving of nothing but insults and curses, and grant us instead the heart of Jesus so that we might love our neighbor as You love them. We pray this in the name of the One who causes the sun to rise on the evil and on the good. Amen.[160]

Practical Steps to the Practice of Prayer

1. Set a time and pick a quiet place where you can be alone daily for a longer time to pray.
2. Start your prayer time reading the Lord's Prayer.
3. Follow the Lord's Prayer model to structure your prayer time: Adoration (praise God); Confession (confess your sins to God); Thanksgiving (thank God for His salvation and the many blessings in your life); Supplication (petition God with requests for yourself, family, friends, community, and global community).
4. Be specific in your prayers.
5. Keep a prayer journal or prayer cards to record your requests; date those requests, and then update the cards with the answers to your requests. This will encourage you to know that praying is effective.
6. In addition to praying alone, pray regularly with a group (recommended with a small group of friend once a week).
7. Pray the Psalms.
8. Pray Scripture.
9. Pray a written prayer from a collection, such as some of the examples above, or pray a creed.
10. Pray at mealtime.
11. Start your day with a short prayer, and end your day with a short prayer.
12. Pray consistently, and pray frequently.
13. Write a card to someone, or send them a text to let them know that you are praying for them.

PATHWAY 6

Bible Study

If you are ignorant of God's Word,
you will be always ignorant of God's will.
—Billy Graham

While the Bible has sold over five billion copies worldwide, and more than three-fourths of American households own a Bible, biblical literacy continues to decline. The good news is that two-thirds of Americans express curiosity about the Bible. However, according to Barna's State of the Bible, 2018, only 48% of Americans use the Bible at least three to four times a year. Churches and Christian organizations need to capitalize on the curiosity of people about the Bible and the 75% of Americans who have a Bible in their homes but need an invitation and help to engage with it.

Despite the overwhelming access to content, people are more biblically illiterate and feel less confident about studying the Bible and having meaningful time with the Lord. Many people, both raised in the church and new to the faith, have difficulty understanding the Bible and developing a relationship with God. According to a Pew Research study in 2019, only one in five Americans know that Christianity teaches that salvation comes through faith alone through Jesus.[161] Among evangelical protestants just over one-third—about 37 percent—answered the question correctly in the Pew Research study above about salvation that comes through faith in Jesus. Another study revealed that just over half, 53% of Americans, believe that they have an average knowledge of the Bible.[162] Perhaps people are overly confident in what they think that they know in contrast to what they actually know; this was affirmed in the results of the Pew study. The Seven Pathways approach to Bible study gives people a plan of engagement that turns curiosity into discovery and uncertainty about how to relate to God into steps to building a relationship with Him.

Bible study is observing, interpreting, and applying the text of the Bible to your life. It involves studying the meaning of words, grammatical and literary relationships, and themes throughout the Bible. It is also studying the key characters and places, along with their significance, and then interpreting the meaning of a passage within its cultural context. And lastly, it is applying the text to your life.

Bible study is also different from just reading the Bible because study makes you slow down to ask questions, take notes, and investigate the meaning and applications. You can read a passage one time quickly and then come back to it years later and see connections to other Scriptures and how it relates to the overall message of the Bible better. Also, God has given us His Spirit to live within us and to help us understand the Bible. Prayer helps you understand what you read, its purpose for the intended audience, its purpose for us today, and how you can apply it to your life. Bible study is most effective when you study an entire book of the Bible to see how each part fits into the overall structure, purpose, and meaning of the book. Studying the Bible will show you God's heart, character, and action. And through studying the Bible, you will encounter Jesus, grow to love Him more, and be transformed by the beauty of His grace.

In this chapter, you'll discover what the Bible is and the tremendous benefits of studying it for yourself. You'll also gain confidence in the Bible as a source of truth about God, by learning where this amazing book came from and how it is intended to be used. Finally, you'll gain practical information, practices, and resources for digging into the Scriptures on your own or with your community.

What Is the Bible?

The most common definition of the Bible is that it is God's Word. Yet often, when New Testament writers speak of the "word of God," they do so in a manner that is slightly different than we speak of it today. When we hear phrases like the "authority of the Word," we think of preachers pounding the pulpit with one hand while holding up their leather-bound copy of the Bible in the other. While it is certainly true to call canonical Scripture the "word of God," its ability to be so-called is derived from its inspired nature. Scripture is the Word of God because it is first and foremost the *words* of God. Reading the New Testament references to the "word of God" as a list of Scriptures that would one day become "the Bible" misses the point and is anachronistic, as its origin is derived from the inspiration and testimony of His love for His people and mission of renewal and reconciliation of all creation.

For example, when Paul says, "Take the helmet of salvation and the sword of the Spirit, which is the word of God" (Eph. 6:17 NIV), he is referring not specifically to a future determined canon but to the *message* of the gospel itself, which is illuminated and transmitted through the testimony of Holy Scripture.[163] Does that mean that the Bible is not the "word of God"? Absolutely not. When Paul refers to the "word," he is drawing a connection to the widespread agreement among Jews of the inspiration of the Hebrew Tanakh (what Christians refer to as the Old Testament). He is speaking of the Tanakh as the Word of God and connecting it to the testimony of the gospel message in Jesus attesting to the connection in the New Testament authors' minds between the Old Testament as God's Word, while reading the Old Testament in light of Christ. Jesus became the lens through which they reread the Word of God, and the testimony of His resurrection power became the unfolding sequel of the gospel of the kingdom first recorded in the Hebrew scrolls, which were taught to them as children.

The Bible, as the Word of God, is a collection of writings that bear witness to the gospel, that is, the good news of God's gift of salvation through Jesus' death and resurrection. Tim Keller succinctly summarizes our misguided approach to reading the Bible and clarifies how to do so:

> We usually read the Bible as a series of disconnected stories, each with a "moral" for how we should live our lives. It is not. Rather, it comprises a single story, telling us how the human race got into its present condition, and how God through Jesus Christ has come and will come to put things right. In other words, the Bible doesn't give us a god at the top of a moral ladder saying, "If you try hard to summon up your strength and live right, you can make it up!" Instead, the Bible repeatedly shows us weak people who don't deserve God's grace, don't seek it, and don't appreciate it even after they have received it.[164]

In God's love and kindness a way was made for sinners to be forgiven and restored in relationship to God through Jesus' bearing the penalty of our sin on the cross. He satisfied our debt, and through faith in Him, we receive forgiveness of sin and a restored relationship with God that was originally broken by sin. Given that claim, it's quite natural to ask where the Bible came from. In other words, how did the Bible come into being, and how do we know that this is the Word of God? This leads us to three important factors about the origin and reliability of the Bible: inspiration, historical reliability, and canonization.

Inspiration

The doctrine of inspiration, simply put, is the belief that the content of the Bible originated with God Himself. The Bible is God's revelation of Himself and His purposes, and God inspired the content.

When God called out Abraham and established His covenantal promises, He initiated into salvation's history a language to communicate, relate, and reveal Himself and divine truth. Paul's reference to Timothy's knowledge "from infancy" of the Old Testament Scriptures points to the unfolding inspiration of testimony of Jesus (see 2 Tim. 3:14–17 NIV). In a sense Paul was tying the thread of God's revelation in Old Testament history to the thread of revelation in the New Testament and the unfolding of God's salvation story in his statement that "all Scripture is God-breathed" (2 Tim. 3:16). The term that Paul used, "God-breathed," in reference to the inspiration of the Bible is *theopneustos*. "God-breathed" refers directly to the concept of inspiration. This inspired quality was commonly attributed to prophetic writings, both in Judaism and in the faith systems of other Mediterranean cultures. It was also applied to poetry and music (though in a somewhat different sense).[165] One can see the reason for the English rendering of *theopneustos* in the breakup of the Greek: *theo*, meaning God; *pneuma*, meaning breath and spirit. The term conveys an understanding that Holy Scripture is Holy Scripture because it has been discerned by the church that God has breathed His Spirit upon it, within it, and through it.

Unlike the ancient Judaic and Greek thinkers' view of inspiration as divine possession or frenzy, the Old Testament prophets used their minds and language (see 1 Cor. 7:40; 14:1–2, 14–19; 1 Pet. 1:10–12) under the inspiration of the Holy Spirit as a mouthpiece for God.[166] Dr. Scott Horrell, my seminary professor, offers a succinct explanation of inspiration:

> The Bible can be said to be theanthropic—authentically human yet infallibly superintended by God himself. With all the peculiarities of what constitutes language—grammatical quirks, cultural influences, and continual

flux—God assumed the Hebrew and Greek languages to communicate the weighty truths of his own reality."[167]

As noted earlier, this prophetic unction is confirmed, vetted for its reliability, and discerned as trustworthy, through the discernment of the community, which is also guided by the Spirit. This also recognizes that the Spirit was inspiring the writers throughout the construction of Scripture.

There are two factors about the emerging recognition of the inspiration of the New Testament that we see within its own pages. First, we see in the writings of Peter an early agreement of the inspired quality of Paul's writings:

> Consider the patience of our Lord to be salvation, just as our dear friend and brother Paul wrote to you according to the wisdom given to him, speaking of these things in all his letters. Some of his remarks are hard to understand, and people who are ignorant and whose faith is weak twist them to their own destruction, just as they do the other Scriptures. (2 Pet. 3:15–17 CEB)

Peter here remarked about Paul's writing as Scripture in an assumed manner that suggests his audience would have already presumed them to be inspired and scripturally equivalent in authority to the Old Testament.

Second, André Muzinger notes in speaking of prophetic unction that only the Christian community, not any one individual, could rightly determine whether any particular writing was indeed inspired by God:

> Discernment, then, establishes a spectrum of authority in which all prophecies find their correct place. The

> burden lies on the shoulders of the whole congregation to decide how authoritative prophecies are. Community discernment, then, is the means by which authority is granted or rejected.[168]

This collectivistic approach to discernment is foreign to our individualistic worldview but was the practice du jour (and still is, in many Christian communities to this day). Munzinger notes that in early Christian communities, a word, a prophecy, a letter, an unction, etc., would not have been deemed "of God" or "not of God" per se, but would have been scrutinized by the community, which would determine the degree of reliability or inspiration it possessed from the Spirit.

We'll see more about this later in the discussion on the canonization of Scripture. For now, the important point is that we know the Bible is inspired by God for two reasons. First, the Bible itself shows that God has made a practice of speaking to individuals throughout history. So their writings can be said to have been inspired by, or originated from, God. Second, the judgment of the Christian community affirms this inspiration. In other words, the great majority of Christians have discerned in these writings the voice of God.

Historical Reliability

Is the Bible historically reliable? This is a critical question because it gets at the overall reliability of the Bible as an authoritative source for knowing God. If Moses did not cross the Red Sea, then should we believe that God gave him the Ten Commandments? If the Bible cites the wrong ruler when Jesus was born, why should we believe in the virgin birth? Biblical history and biblical theology are intertwined. The fall of man in Eden, the exodus, the giving of the law, and the birth, crucifixion, and resurrection of Jesus are all historical events as well as doctrinal events. If the Bible is not accurate in the mundane details it reports about the past, how could we trust it in speaking of God, human nature, or salvation?

The Bible is accepted based on its historical reliability in bibliographic tests both internally and externally, and further archaeology findings attest to its truthfulness. Our belief in the reliability of the Bible is based on facts, not fiction.

When evaluating for reliability, the bibliographic external test examines the quantity, quality, and time span. Old Testament manuscripts are not numerous, as many Jewish scribes buried imperfect manuscripts, and many were lost or destroyed when different foreign powers occupied Israel. But in the sixth century AD, Masoretic Jews standardized the Old Testament text, and "all manuscripts that deviated from the Masoretic Text were evidently eliminated. But the existing Hebrew manuscripts are supplemented by the Dead Sea Scrolls, the Septuagint (a third-century BC Greek translation of the Old Testament), the Samaritan Pentateuch, and the Targums (ancient paraphrases of the Old Testament), as well as the Talmud (teachings and commentaries related to the Hebrew Scriptures)."[169] Some archaeological findings confirm the truthfulness of many Old Testament accounts.

For example, when Nineveh was excavated, thousands of clay tablets were found from the library of King Ashurbanipal of Assyria, who ruled from 688–626 BC, and among those was a creation Epic that corresponds to the biblical account. For another example, many critics concluded the story of Abraham's rescue of Lot in Genesis as historically inaccurate, saying that the names of the kings were not confirmed by other sources and that it was ridiculous that a king of Babylon served a king of Elam. Archaeology has identified the four kings, and there is evidence that a king of Babylon served a king of Elam.

Regarding the quality and time span of the manuscripts, the Jewish scribes meticulously transcribed the Hebrew text, and a manuscript was destroyed if a mistake was made. The discovery of the Dead Sea Scrolls in 1947 has confirmed no substantial changes to the Old Testament text throughout the centuries. Experts in paleography evaluated the manuscripts, and this indeed was one of the greatest findings in history. Prior to discovery of the Dead Sea Scrolls, the earliest manuscripts known (the Masoretic text) dated back to AD 800–1000. The Dead Sea Scrolls date from 200 BC to AD 68. Dr. Gleason L. Archer concluded that the two copies of Isaiah in the Dead Sea Scrolls discovery are word-for-word identical in 95% of the text.[170] According to the Bible Archaeology Report, more than 980 manuscripts dating from the third century BC to the first century AD were found in eleven caves at Qumran near the Dead Sea between 1947–1956 during the excavations.[171] The explosion of archeological discoveries in the twentieth century has provided strong external confirmation of the Bible's reliability. Some of the most notable sources substantiating the biblical claims are the Nuzi, Mari, and Ebla tablets. Other archaeological findings related to the New Testament support the geographic and historical details of Jesus' life and ministry. For further reading, check out the Top Ten Archaeological Finds in 2021.[172]

The quality of the Hebrew Bible exceeds all other ancient manuscripts, as the oldest manuscripts of Plato and Aristotle date back to AD 1600. There are only forty-nine manuscripts by Aristotle and seven by Plato compared to the more than 6,000 in Greek (24,000, including translations in other languages). Also, the small number of variants due to visual or auditory errors do not affect the meaning. Scholars use the textual variants to determine the original meaning of text. Earliest copies of documents of antiquity are five hundred to one thousand years newer than the originals, such the copy of Caesar's Gallic Wars. The earliest manuscript of Caesar's Gallic War that ended in 50 BC was not written until 900 years later. Surprisingly, with all the thousands of copies of the Bible, and its proven historical reliability with few errors over centuries, people are still questioning its truthfulness.

As for the New Testament, it's important to note that the Gospels were written thirty to sixty years after the life of Jesus, or AD 65–95. Jewish oral tradition stringently followed the guidelines of memorizing accurately large amounts of text. So, when the Gospels were recorded, they could draw on eyewitness accounts and large amounts of Jesus' words and deeds preserved in the churches. Richard Bauckham, in his book *Jesus and the Eyewitnesses,* attests that the whole of the Gospels is rooted in the testimony of eyewitness accounts. He suggests recovering the Gospels as testimony, meaning the "kind of historiography they are is testimony. . . . Understanding the Gospels as testimony, we can recognize this theological meaning of the history not as an arbitrary imposition on the objective facts, but as the way the witnesses perceived the history, in an inextricable coinherence of observable event and perceptible meaning."[173]

One of most noted passages in appealing to the role of eyewitnesses is the testimony of those who witnessed the resurrection as well as the witness of the women and apostles who saw the empty tomb (see 1 Cor. 15). The eyewitness accounts in the Gospels are the retelling of the events as the author recollected and described to their intended audience. Furthermore, we would do well to pair the existence of these eyewitnesses with the internal appeal to their authority within the writings of Scripture, but also to note the extent of the insistence as to the truthfulness of their testimony. By this, I mean that one of the chief types of evidence of the Scriptures' truthfulness is the lengths to which these witnesses were willing to go to stand by their testimonies—lengths that included torture, exile, and martyrdom. Their commitment to their testimony—even unto death (Rev. 12:11) is a testimony to the truthfulness of their claims.

Current events afford us with modern examples of individuals and groups who propagated large-scale deceptions, but who ultimately wavered, pivoted, or even reversed their testimony when pressured with imprisonment or other punishments. Examples like these demonstrate how little many people are willing to stand by falsehoods when the falsehood no longer benefits them. In the case of early Christian testimony, there was seemingly zero benefit to propagating a large-scale deception. Even early on, Christians experienced social pressure and persecution, and yet remained unmoved in their testimony.

One final point should be made regarding eyewitness testimony: it is how the whole missional enterprise—God's reconciling work through the death and resurrection of Jesus–is moved forward based upon testimony. Christianity has endured and spread all over the world based upon testimony. The gospel transforms hearts as the Holy Spirit moves to convict and comfort through the testimony of others. An overwhelming majority of Christians are Christians at all because of the testimony of another.

Also, the internal evidence of the gospel's grammar testifies to its truthfulness. Gospel writers' following of the Aramaic words and order, which was the spoken language, is another proof of their accurate writings of Jesus' words and deeds. A. N. Sherwin-White, an Oxford historian, studied the rate in which a legend in the ancient world replaced core historical facts, and he found it took two generations.[174] So the central truths and claims of Christianity circulating were within too short of a time to be fabricated or corrupted. Jesus also attests to the credibility of the Old Testament.

Here are a few examples:

Regarding the flood, Jesus said, "As it was in the days of Noah, so it will be at the coming of the Son of Man. For in the days before the flood, people were eating and drinking, marrying and giving in marriage, up to the day Noah entered the ark; and they knew nothing about what would happen until the flood came and took them all away. That is how it will be at the coming of the Son of Man" (Matt. 24:37–39 NIV).

Jesus also affirmed the authority of the Old Testament; when the Sadducees ridiculed the doctrine of the resurrection, Jesus argued for the truthfulness of the resurrection and pointed out they did not understand "the Scriptures or the power of God" (Mark 12:24 NIV). They had studied the law rigorously but failed to apply it properly and probe the meaning deeply and accurately. They did not understand the meaning of, "Do not think that I have come to abolish the Law or the Prophets; I have not come to abolish them but to fulfill them" (Matt. 5:17).

The Old Testament, in Exodus 3:6, affirms that the dead will be resurrected. God spoke to Moses, "I am the God . . . of Abraham, the God of Isaac and the God of Jacob." Jesus used this example to uphold the truthfulness of the Old Testament that says that God "is not the God of the dead, but of the living" (Mark 12:26–27 NIV).

When considering the historical reliability of the Bible, it's important to note that it contains many types of literature, written over a span of many centuries. There are significant differences in literary styles and intentions among the various writings. That's true for any type of literature, even today. For example, a popular song, which mentions a historical event, may communicate truth about the people involved, the culture, or even the event itself. But it is not to be understood in the same way as a newspaper or a carefully researched history book. In the same way, the Bible contains poems, songs, genealogies, letters, historical records, prophecies, parables, and other genres of writing. The Bible's historical reliability is attested to by the quantity, quality, and time span of other ancient documents affirming its historical accuracy as well.

The New Testament's historical reliability is attested to by the internal evidence of the various authors who were, for the most part, eyewitnesses, and the external evidence of historical events and other extrabiblical sources affirming the major details.

Canonization

A canon is a collection of writings that are considered complete or authoritative. "*Canon* from the Gk. *kanon* (kanw` n) and Heb. *qaneh* (hn<q;) originally meant 'straight rod, reed, stalk, cane; a rod [instrument] of measurement' (*cf.* Eze 40:5). . . . By the 2d century it came to mean 'rule of faith,' standard for revealed truth."[175] While the canon of the Old Testament was largely settled (with the exception of the Greek deuterocanonical books, which are often printed within non-Protestant and early Protestant Bibles), the New Testament canon was written between AD 50 and 100. Though over the first few centuries, church leaders came to agree on which books should be considered authoritative and canonical. While the biblical text was "central to the faith" of the early fathers, it was regarded differently than the manner that defines Protestantism. Following a more eastern Christianity, the biblical text was seen as central but was complemented by the leading of the Spirit and the tradition passed down from the apostles, which is referred to as the "rule of faith." The "rule of faith" was originally referred to as the "Old Roman Symbol" and was a predecessor to the Apostles' Creed.[176] The early-church historian Eusebius, in AD 330, was one of the first (that we have recorded) to put forward a list of texts classified as "universally

acknowledged" books, "disputed, yet familiar to most" books, "spurious" books, and "rejected" books.[177] But the reason for this was to differentiate those works that were affirmed by the vast majority of the church and expose those works by heretics under the names of the apostles (e.g. Gospel of Peter, Thomas, Matthias, Acts of Andrew, John, etc.). Luther and Calvin argued for the sixty-six books of the traditional Christian canon, whereas the Council of Trent (1545–1560) added the thirteen books (plus additions to Esther and Daniel), which are what's termed the Old Testament Apocrypha. The canon approved at the Council of Trent is the present Roman Catholic canon. Both Protestants and Catholics use the exact same New Testament canon today, which was defined by Athanasius in AD 367.

Different categories were used throughout the canonization process with the same levels of distinction. Those texts in the "spurious" category, "surfacing in and out of canonical lists and early Christian Bibles" were removed, not the "heretical" texts. In order to satisfy the requirements of canonical books, a text must met three or four criteria for New Testament canonization: apostolicity, orthodoxy, catholicity (wide usage), and traditional usage (in public worship and discipleship). Those that became the twenty-seven books of the New Testament were not disputed on grounds of orthodoxy or authority, but rather their widespread usage everywhere. Any disputes regarding the twenty-seven books of the New Testament were based on widespread usage or authorship and not orthodoxy or authority. The books joining that list were: Hebrews, James, 1 and 2 Peter, 1, 2, and 3 John, Jude and Revelation, which is not recoginzed as canonical by the Greek Orthodox Church despite the its strong grounds of orthodoxy.[178]

When considering whether a particular writing belonged in the canon of Christian Scriptures, the church fathers established four criteria:[179]

Apostolic origin: The book must be written by an apostle or under his supervision in order for it to be canonical. Non-apostolic books that are considered canonical include Luke and Acts, written under the supervision of Paul; and the Gospel of Mark under that of Peter.

Universal acceptance: One of the strongest evidences and well-attested through out the earliest centuries is the testimony of the unanimous acceptance by a vast majority of Christian churches by the end of the fourth century.

Authority of the Church: The book was regulary read, taught, and shared in early Christian churches.

Theological congruence/orthodoxy: The book is congruent with theological themes of the Old Testament and the teachings of Jesus. The agreement of the early church regarding the inspiration of certain books and their circulation and wide acceptance among the majority of churches affirmed their canonical status whereas other extra biblical books like the Shepherd of Hermas accepted by some such as, Irenaeus of Lyons, were ultimately rejected as canonical.

As mentioned earlier, the consensus of the church communities played a primary function in determining the authority of writings in the New Testament church. The prevailing understanding was that just as the Spirit had guided the Jewish communities to determine the authoritative, inspired books of the Old Testament, the Spirit would guide the Church in the same way. The authoritative, inspired quality of a book was never to be determined by one person or a small group, but the vast body, the Church, and it is a gift from God to the body.

A Pathway to Knowing God
Knowing God through His Names

There are a number of proven benefits to studying the Bible. The Bible gives us a greater understanding of other cultures and of history and an openness to the promptings and conviction of the Holy Spirit. Research indicates that when engaging with the Bible four or more times a week, we are more than twice as likely to share our faith and four times more likely to memorize Scripture. Those who study the Bible consistently are also significantly less likely to view pornography or struggle with loneliness.[180] Bible study also increases cognitive development and improves vocabulary. Yet the primary objective of studying the Bible is to know God more fully. That has been my experience over the years, and especially during my recovery.

What do we learn about God from His Word? In what ways does God reveal Himself through the Bible? An exhaustive answer to that question would fill volumes. For our purposes, we'll focus on three aspects of God's self-revelation in Scripture: the names of God, His triune nature, and metaphors used to describe God.

In speaking of knowing God, one of the essential ways is through His names. It is important to understand the significance and role of names in the ancient world to grasp the significance of God's names. A name revealed something about a person's character and purpose. To come to know God through His names, you will come to know more facets of his character and have the opportunity as you call on Him to act and as you worship Him and experience His power demonstrating that name through His actions. You can experience God through His many names. Here, we will explore the three foundational names of God and a few other compound names of God, even though there are so many more that deserve our attention. I encourage you to study more of God's names to see and experience how God works and relates to His people through His divine names. I also hope that you will be encouraged by how God has shown up in people's lives, manifesting His divine names and giving people guidance, comfort, help in difficult situations, healing, and hope. And lastly, my hope is that you will love and worship Him more through His powerful divine names. I pray that His glory will overwhelm you and so captivate your heart that your desires, affections, and pursuits reflect Jesus and you spread the fragrance of His name and the beauty of His glory through your love of others. And also that you enjoy Him.

Yahweh: The Self-Existent and Personal God

Businesses allocate millions of dollars every year in building brand identity to determine the foundational qualities of their brand and encourage costomer loyalty. Companies trademark names so that their name is protected. Names matter, and God's names matter. The most common name for God in Hebrew is YHWH and is pronounced *Yahweh*. It designates the personal, covenantal God. It occurs 6,877 times in the Old Testament.[181] Yahweh and "I AM" are derived from the same Hebrew word *hwh*, meaning "to become, be." With *hwh*'s 3,450 occurrences of the *qal* tense and 21 occurrences of the *ni* tense, it is the second-most used verb in the Old Testament.[182] The "I" of God "is used for God as the Subject who can never become an object and before whom all reality, being, happening and volition is object."[183]

"I AM" and "Yahweh" are closely related in Exodus 3:13–15. In response to Moses's question about what to say to the Israelites if they ask who sent him, God gives three answers. First, in verse 14, God says, "I AM WHO I AM," and second, He says, "I AM has sent me to you" (NIV). Third, in verse 15, God instructs Moses to say, "The LORD [the Hebrew name for Yahweh] . . . has sent me to you."

The Hebrew word *hyh* may be used in three ways: (1) the implicit, (2) the explicit (related to miracles, prophecies, legal prescriptions, and covenants), and (3) the absolute theological (referring to Yahweh).[184] In Exodus 3:14, *hyh* is used in the absolute sense without a preposition or predicate noun, "I AM WHO I AM," expressing the name that God wished to be known by his people and who He is: self-existing, sovereign, and unchangeable in His character. He is the Lord. So the Hebrew name Yahweh means He is a self-existent being and a personal God who is immutable in His character; He has and will always be the same. He is a living being with a mind, a will, and emotions and is involved in this universe and the affairs of men. Our God is personal in how He relates to all of His creation. It is also significant because He is not dependent on anything for His existence, unlike humans who are dependent on many things for our existence, such as oxygen, food, light, and all things essential to sustain life. Therefore, the usage of *hyh* in Exodus 3:14-15 affirms that God's name expresses His character and actions toward His creation as the self-existent being, who often reveals himself during difficult circumstances or trials just as He did to help Moses when he led the people to the promised land.

A few other examples of passages in the Old Testament in which God's name (YHWH) is closely related or interchangeable with "I am" are: Exodus 6:2; Deuteronomy 32:39; Isaiah 41:4; 48:12; and then in the New Testament, Jesus uses the same "I am" statements to refer to Himself, the one who is speaking, as the true and only God (Mark 14:62; John 8:18, 21, 24).

Elohim: The Creator

Another frequently used name for God in the Old Testament is Elohim, which designates God as Creator and Sustainer of the universe and Sovereign Judge over all. *Elohim, 'elohim* denotes "God, gods"; lit. "the powerful ones" or possibly "most high ones." It occurs about 2,600 times (in 2,248 vv), with varying forms (cf. Ge 1:1–2:3).[185] Many scholars conclude that elohim is derived from eloah, refering to the God of Israel which is found 57 times in the OT. About 217 times in the Old Testament, El refers to the God of Israel using compound names, such as El Shaddai or El Roi. The plural form when speaking of God functions to elevate His greatness and 'God-ness.'

God is self-sufficient and self-existent (the Almighty God), not in need of anything outside of Himself. God is pure, holy, and immutable and never changing in His infinite characteristics. The God of the Bible is not infinite in His creation, meaning all reality is divine or everything is part of an immanent God, unlike in pantheism or other new age movements, where it is believed that God and nature, or God and the whole universe, are one universal being. Therefore, if God and the universe are identical, then pantheism denies the personal and transcendent God of the Bible.

In speaking of the Almighty God, Tertullian said, "Before all things God was alone, being his own universe, location, and everything. He was alone, however, in the same sense that there was nothing external to himself."[186] So why did He create everything in the universe? Out of His love and by His grace, He created all things for His glory (Eph 1:12, 14). Isaiah 43:7 speaks of "everyone who is called by my name, whom I created for my glory, whom I formed and made (NIV). And Colossians 1:16–17 says, "For in him all things were created: things in heaven and on earth, visible and invisible, whether thrones or powers or rulers or authorities; all things have been created through him and for him. He is before all things, and in him all things hold together."

As many theologians conclude, out of the overflow of love among the Godhead, God fashions His creation. He was not lonely, for God has always had fellowship among the three persons of the Trinity, since before creation as mentioned in

Genesis 1:26: "Let us make man in our image" (NIV 1984). God did not need human fellowship, but He chose to create us out of His love. God loved us before He created us: "I have loved you with an everlasting love; I have drawn you with loving-kindness" (Jer. 31:3).

Adonai: The Lord

A third commonly used name for God is Adonai, meaning "Lord, ruler, or master"; it denotes God as Ruler himself (Gen. 15:1–2; Ex. 4:10–13; 23:17; 34:23; Judg. 6:15; Josh. 3:11, 13; Mal. 3:1). The first time that Adonai is used in the Bible is in Genesis 15:1–2 when Abram appeals to God as the ruler and Lord over all (see vv. 3, 8). In looking back to the name God used to speak to Abraham concerning His promise to Abram of a baby in Genesis 12, He gives insight into how Abraham is to reach out to God about this delay in His promise. The Lord, Yahweh, revealed to Abram personally His promise to him in Genesis 12. A decade had past and still no child, so Abram appeals to God as Adonai (Lord), the absolute ruler over all matters of his life. Essentially, Abram was saying I surrender this situation to you and only you, the Lord, who is in charge of everything, and who can bring this promise to fulfillment (because both he and his wife were very old). This humility and surrender to God opened up a path for God to move and establish His covenant with Abram.

Approaching God as Adonai, the Lord and ruler over all, can create a path of deeper communication and intimacy with God and greater revelation and movement of His plans in your life. God desires to fulfill His promises to His people but sometimes He is waiting for us to say yes to Him, His timing, and His way; and to surrender our time, desires, talents, families, dreams, treasures, and all that we have to Him.

Jehovah Rapha: The Healer

One evening in December, during a *60 Minutes* segment, a sweet eighty-three-year-old nun captured my attention. Sister Bernadette Moriau suffered from a nerve disorder that caused her to wear leg braces, a back brace, and an implant to alleviate some of the pain. One of her doctors encouraged her to journey to Lourdes, France, where more than 3 million people travel to every year for healing. She told Bill Whitaker, "I really had that feeling that the Lord was walking with us. And I heard him giving me these words: 'I see your suffering and that of your sick brothers and sisters. Just give me everything.'"[187] Upon returning home she felt revived spiritually but worse physically and experienced three days of excruciating pain. Then she found the strength to walk to the chapel and pray. While praying, she felt a heat come into her body, which relaxed her. Then she heard an inner voice instructing her, "Take all your braces off." "I didn't think twice," she explained. "And I started taking my foot brace off. And my foot that used to be crooked was straight. And I could actually put it on the ground without feeling any pain."

Her healing was referred to the Lourdes Office of Medical Observations, where doctors rigorously study every case to validate the miracles. After eight years of investigation by a group of thirty-three doctors from around the world and professors (the International Medical Committee of Lourdes), they determined that her case was the seventieth miracle.

God reveals himself in Scripture as the Healer, "the God who heals," also known as Jehovah Rapha to the Israelites when they found a river in a dry desert. The water was unfit to drink, so God cleansed the water miraculously by instructing Moses to throw wood into the water. Then God said to His people that He would be their Healer, which was a direct reference to the diseases that

He had inflicted on the Egyptians because of their rebellion. (See Exodus 15:25-27.)

Sometimes sickness is linked to sin, and then in other cases it is not the result of sin. Even Jesus' disciples questioned if a blind man's physical condition was a result of sin. In answering their question, in John 9, Jesus replied, "Neither this man nor his parents sinned, . . . but this happened so that the works of God might be displayed in him" (v. 3 NIV). Then Jesus instructed the man to do something that did not make sense humanly (like God did in his instructions to Moses in Exodus 15), and the blind man was healed.

Whether in this life or the next, we can be assured that God is our Healer. Sister Bernadette is one of seventy who experienced God's healing power at Lourdes, and I pray that more will turn their hearts to God in loving devotion and that more experience God as Healer in this lifetime. Even as I write this, I am trusting God as my Healer as I wait to hear the results of a biopsy on a mass in my right parotid gland.

El-Roi: The God Who Sees

Living in Texas for many years, one thing that I loved were the sunsets stretching across the plains as far as your eye could see. Every sunset welcomed me with open arms from the trials of the day and held my heart in its rest. It gently invited me to sit under its promise of hope of a new day. Also in Texas, I could see storms far in the distance before the threat was imminent. There are many times in my life that I wish I had that same long-range vision to see storms in my personal life before they roll in with sounds of fury or roll in quickly with popping lightning.

Have you ever had a situation like a storm spin up quickly? One situation stands out among a few. The dark clouds came in quickly, and before I knew it, I was in the fiercest part of the storm. I had thought that I was fighting one thing in the first part of the storm, but as the intensity increased, I saw clearly the core of what I was fighting. In this particular storm, the winds of fear and doubt beat against me. I called out to the Lord on the inside asking Him to help push back the winds of fear that were knocking me about, and I prayed for strength to push through. This was not a storm that God wanted me to avoid, and I sensed that He saw my need for help and heard me. God gave me clarity of thought and grounded me in the storm to speak truth. It was not easy to get the words out either as I felt like they were weighty, and I was not in a place spiritually where I was as strong or as close to God as I wanted to be, so they were almost too heavy for me.

Sometimes, we forget that truth is heavy and powerful and that it can be hard for us to bear because we are still sinners, and frankly, as humans, we are weak. But once the words came out, they brought light to the situation. I watched how truth unveiled the darkness, and God's Spirit brought a warmth and gentleness to the situation. We are in the process of becoming who we will be fully in heaven, but we still see more dimly this side of heaven.

After "the storm," the next day, I was exhausted on all levels and not sure what I had left that I could give that night from my position on the prayer team at church. I thought about not going, but God nudged me and said, "Go." As I took my seat for our prayer team meeting, our leader looked my way and said something to me that she could not have known had she not heard God's Spirit speaking to her. I was stunned. In that moment, God was saying to me, "I see you. I know how hard this weekend was for you. I was with you, and I am always with you." Through her, God gave me a big hug, and then for the next several weeks, I felt His love cover me like a blanket at night, as He wrapped me up under His wing. El Roi, one of the Hebrew names for God, means "the God who sees." Receive this encouragement: God sees you!

While I was writing this section on the divine names, a friend, whom I'd seen earlier when I was leaving the gym, sent me a text and asked if I had left a note with Scripture on one of the exercise machines at our gym. The note said, "Yet to all who did receive Him, to those who believed in His name, He gave the right to become children of God." And then underneath the Scripture was written, "Membership in God's family is by grace alone—the gift of God."

I did not write this note, but God used it to affirm to me that His names matter, that they have power, and that we come to know Him through believing in His name. This note was a sweet reminder from God that He is El-Roi, the God who sees, and that He sees what I am writing on a dark rainy night alone in my office. And He sees you right where you are. God wants you to know that you can't earn His love and that membership in His family is by grace through faith. Your plate is waiting at God's table.

Knowing God through His Triune Nature

Passages of Scripture recording God speaking in the first person affirm that the Father, Son, and Holy Spirit are distinct persons, yet all share the same essence or nature. While the three persons interact together as the Trinity, they also work in creation with one mind and one will. First, the "I am" statements of the Father and the Son as well as the Spirit's personal statements referring to the emotions of the Holy Spirit and His intellect, specifically His choosing wisdom and insight, attest to the personhood of the Father, Son, and Holy Spirit. Each person of the Trinity exists in eternal relationship, communication, and fellowship and mutually indwell one another, yet they share the same essence. The oneness or unity of essence of the three distinct persons of the Godhead transcends our understanding, and it is otherwise known, according to classical Trinitarianism, as the mystery of the Trinity.

Second, as distinct persons, each member of the Godhead enjoys genuine personal relationships among themselves. Personal relationships between the Son and the Holy Spirit with God are described in Scripture in this way: Jesus sees, hears, speaks, and does what the Father does (John 1:18; 3:11, 32; 5:19–20, 12:49). The Holy Spirit speaks what He hears and brings glory to God by sharing and making known what is from the Father and Son (John 16:13–15). Additionally, the Holy Spirit, the Counselor (John 14:16; 16:7), will convict the world regarding sin (John 16:8), testify to our relationship with God as His children (Rom. 8:16), comfort us when we are hurting (John 14:18), give us peace (John 14:27), and intercede for us when we do not know what to pray in accordance with God's will (Rom. 8:26–27).

Knowing and testifying of each other and exercising personal choice are three other important aspects of the personal relationships among the Father, Son, and Holy Spirit. John 10:15 attests to the deep relationship between the Father and Son. Jesus knows the Father deeply because He is from the Father and the one whom God has sent. And God has given the Holy Spirit alone without limit (John 3:34–36; 7:29). John 1:1 reminds us that Jesus is fully God yet is a distinct person. Jesus speaks of the mission of His life as being to make God known "in order that the love you have for me may be in them and that I myself may be in them" (John 17:26 NIV). The Spirit knows the Father and is known by the Father; for no one knows the thoughts of God except the Spirit of God (1 Cor. 2:11–13). In a similar way, the Holy Spirit is sent by the Father in Jesus' name to remind us of all that Jesus has taught (John 14:26), thus affirming the deep personal relationships among the Godhead. Both the Father and Son are involved in the sending of the Holy Spirit (John 14:26; 15:26). The Father testifies concerning the Son (John 5:36–37), the Son testifies of the Father by revealing the Father (John 3:11;

17:11) and of the Spirit's coming (John 14:16, 26; 16:7–11, 13), and the Spirit testifies of the Son and Father (John 15:26; 1 Cor. 2:11–13; Gal. 4:6). Each member of the Godhead does not relate to the others mechanically but with freedom of volition.

God has given us a visual of what a perfect man and image bearer is: Jesus Christ. In Christ, the invisible God is made visible. In Jesus' conversation with Philip, in John 14:8–9, He makes the same point: "Anyone has seen me has seen the Father" (v. 9 NIV).

At the moment of salvation, you are sealed with the Holy Spirit according to Ephesians 1:13, meaning that He has taken up permanent residence in you. The job of the Holy Spirit is to guide and teach you the ways of Christ so that you image Jesus more than you image the world. He comes bearing a gift of peace (John 14:27) for His new home in your heart like a housewarming gift, and comes with the power to help you grow and produce good fruit in your life. He outfits us with all the tools, methods, and power for your life to produce the fruit of the Spirit (Gal. 5:22–23). This peace secures our footing and grounds our faith, which will guide us in discerning direction and guard us from the tumultuous currents of hard times that try to sweep us off our feet. Peace can also help stabilize our runaway emotions when we are overwhelmed and not sure how we can handle everything. In addition, the Holy Spirit's job description is to renew the hearts of those who receive the gift of salvation (John 3:7–8) and determine which spiritual gifts to give each believer (1 Cor. 12:11). This freedom of personal choice is grounded in the nature of God, in His sovereignty. He is complete and is not constrained by anything outside of Himself, for He always acts in a way that pleases Him (Ps. 135:6; Isa. 46:10). God's actions being according to His good pleasure does not mean that He acts based on our modern definition of the word *pleasure*, which can mean "a good feeling or sentiment." But His actions stem from who He is: holy, good, and true.

In the Trinity's fellowship and functioning uniquely as persons, they defer to one another, which is modeled by their self-giving nature as their glory is displayed in their works in sustaining and redeeming the world. Jesus glorifies the Father (John 5:30; 8:29; 17:4; Phil. 2:8), the Spirit glories the Son (John 16:14), and the Father gives all that belongs to Him to the Son (John 16:15; 17:10) and glorifies the Son (John 17:5). What does it mean to glorify? It means to delight or enjoy someone to the degree that you make sacrifices to bring them joy or allow them to shine. This means that you sacrifice your own interests, desires, or happiness and choose to do what is in the best interest of the one you want to glorify. The "you" card trumps the "me" card. As a result, instead of short-term happiness, you get the gift of soul-quenching joy to see their joy. Instead of demanding and building your life around others fulfilling your needs, you place God at the center of your universe and then others after God.

What does it mean that the Father, Son, and Holy Spirit glorify one another? Loving sacrificially best describes how we are to relate to God and one another, which is modeled by the self-giving nature of the Trinity. Each person of the Trinity delights, loves, and serves one another as they mutually live and act in the world. The early Greek church used the Greek term *perichoresis* or the Latin *circumincession* to define the "reciprocal interiority" or "mutual immanence" of the three divine persons.[188] It comes from the root *perichoreo*, [which could be translated] "to dance around," referring to the mutual indwelling of each member of the Godhead.[189] From the Greek word *choresis*, our English word *choreography* is derived.

Since God is love, then each member of the Trinity is mutually self-giving to one another in their "dance around" each other. The Father gives "all that belongs to Him" to the Son (John 16:15; 17:10), the Son obeys the Father (John 5:30; 8:29; Phil. 2:8), and the Spirit brings glory to God "by taking from what is mine and making it known to you" (John 16:14 NIV 1984). Self-giving love is the currency of the Trinitarian life, meaning that each one places the other at the center of their world.

C. S. Lewis utters a beautiful mental picture of this mind-boggling and wondrous relationship of the Godhead and the life- and world-transformative implications of love as a currency:

> In Christianity God is not an impersonal thing or a static thing—not even just one person—but a dynamic pulsating activity, a kind of drama, almost, if you will not think me irreverent, a kind of dance. . .[The] pattern of this three-personal life is . . . the great fountain of energy and beauty spurting up at the very center of reality.[190]

Self-giving love—love that says, "I place your needs above mine"—is the currency of the fullness of life and life eternal. The self-giving nature of each person of the Trinity is the model for man to reflect the image of God. In sacrificially loving humans, we imitate the Trinity.

What Matters Most

His Glory

A biblical understanding of the image of God leads us away from a needs-based understanding toward focusing on God, who is the model of how man is to live before God and one another. What we chiefly see about God in the Bible is that He is glorious, and His goal is glory. God's glory is revealed in creation and through "the law" of the Lord. The beauty of God is revealed in the Old Testament in forms of light and radiance and in the manner in which He radiates joy (His glory). Just as natural light needs nothing to manifest itself as light in darkness, the glory of God "is worth which God himself creates for Himself . . . simply by revealing himself."[191] Divine beauty refers to "the form and manner" [192] in which God's glory is expressed. "God's glory is the indwelling joy of His divine being, which as such shines out from Him, which overflows in its richness, which in its super-abundance is not satisfied with itself but communicates itself."[193] God's glory shines forth as light because the Lord is the light, and light is the luminous presence of God. "God is light; in him there is no darkness at all" (1 John 1:5 NIV). Jesus says, "I am the light of the world. Whoever follows me will never walk in darkness, but will have the light of life" (John 8:12). The psalmist compares the glory of the Lord to mountains: "You are radiant with light, more majestic than mountains rich with game" (Ps. 76:4). According to Revelation 21:23 and 22:5, the light of the sun, moon, and stars will no longer be needed for illumination in New Jerusalem, for "the LORD will be your everlasting light" (Isa. 60:20).

The Hebrew term *kabod* for the English *glory* means "weight,"[194] "heaviness, glory, and splendor,"[195] communicating the immensity of God's worth. His glory refers to God's self-revelation in manifestations of light,[196] visible manifestations of His holiness, and His manifestations in His actions of intimate involvement with people. God's glory is described in His dealings with Israel, as their King, Leader, Ruler, and then in the New Testament as the Savior of the world.[197] The "glory" of God dwelled on Sinai

(Ex. 24:16), in the cloud that goes before the people (Ex. 16:10; Num 14:22; Ps. 97:6; Isa. 60:2, 66:18), in the tent of meeting and tabernacle (Ex. 33:13–18, 22; 40:34–35), in the temple (Ex. 40:34; 1 Kings 8:11), in the promised land (Ps. 85:10; Isa. 35:2; 58:8; 60:1–2; Ezek. 43:2), and at Jesus' birth (Luke 2:9). God dwells with men, to have His reality and His splendor known to them.[198]

The glory guides His people through impossible circumstances. Not only does He go before us illuminating the way, but He also instructs and protects us from behind. When you are moving forward, it is hard to watch your back. God says, "I got your back." How does this change your perspective of God, knowing that He has your back? How has God had "your back" recently? Once the Egyptians knew that God was fighting for the Israelites, they wanted to get away. They knew that fighting God was a losing battle. ("If God is for us, who can be against us?" [Rom. 8:31 NIV].) The Israelites did not burst out into song in Exodus 15 because their longings were met but because the Lord was glorious, holy, and wondrous—the true God who has no rival and defeated the Egyptians gods. With one simple outstretched right hand, God released His wondrous power, and the sea swallowed up the Israelites' enemies.

Chief among the terms describing God is also His holiness. The Most Holy Place was always where His presence dwelled. Orthodox Christian theology of God is rooted in His self-existence and otherness; therefore, God is innately glorious and holy.

The Glorious Light

An understanding of the divine names of God and the characteristics that proceed from His divine essence related to those names will inform your view of God as holy, light, and righteous, to name just a few of His characteristics. Jesus uses a metaphor to help people understand who He is by describing Himself as "the light of the world" in John 8:12. John also testifies to God as "light" (1 John 1:5), and "in him was life, and that life was the light of men" (John 1:3–4 NIV 1984). It means that God is fully all that light encompasses and perfect in His holiness, righteousness, and truth. This light that shines forth and pierces darkness is the light of the gospel of the glory of Christ. "For God, who said, 'Let light shine out of darkness,' made his light shine in our hearts to give us the light of the knowledge of the glory of God in the face of Christ" (2 Cor. 4:4–6). Christ is the archetype of beautiful light, as "the Son is the radiance of God's glory and the exact representation of his being, sustaining all things by his powerful word" (Heb. 1:3).

Knowing God and experiencing His presence in your life cannot be grasped or ascertained through reason alone but through illumination by faith.

> The kind of knowledge associated with this illumination is neither the scientia that results from knowing causes better than effects (scire), nor a kind of intuited understanding (intellegere). Rather it is a willing opening of oneself to the otherness of form, that is to say, a will to becoming in-formed by the object (cognosscere)."[199]

Aquinas uses the term "form" above in reference to Christ, the source and archetype of all forms. To be "in-formed" as Aquinas describes above means something entirely different than our twenty-first-century understanding of the world. "Informed" by Christ does not mean that you know more information about Him. Often, we are informed about a situation or event, but this does not mean that this new knowledge changes our actions or thoughts. However, to be "in-formed" by Christ is to be formed by Him in a whole new way in the receiving of our new nature that changes how we live. "To be formed" by Christ is to be "a new creation" (see 2 Cor. 5:17). He is referring to the process of the Spirit now forming who we are instead of the sinful nature (Rom. 8:5–8). This new nature of God's light reforms us on the inside, helps us to turn away from darkness in our life, and increases our desires and affections to walk in stride with Him in the light. Walking in stride with Him means to walk in fellowship with Him, and when we walk with God, we share His light with the world.

The Gift

The Bible describes this illumination of faith that Christ gives us as a gift. All religions except Christianity say that you must do things to gain God's love and acceptance, while Christianity says you are already loved and forgiven through the blood of Jesus Christ, and all you have to do is to receive this free gift of salvation by grace through faith. The Bible clearly emphasizes the need for cleansing and renewal of the human heart. In the Old Testament the Hebrew words for "heart," *leb* or *lehab*, occur 850 times. In the Bible the word "'heart' became the richest biblical term for the totality of man's inner or immaterial nature."[200] According to *Strong's Hebrew Bible Dictionary*, the Hebrew word for "heart" means inner man, mind, will, or heart.[201] The inner man refers to all that constitutes his inner person: mind, soul, spirit, and self. The heart is "the source of the life of the inner person in various aspects, with a focus on feelings, thoughts, volition, and other areas of inner life."[202] (See Deut. 2:30; Isa. 57:15; Eccles. 2:1.) Ephesians 2:8–9 says, "For it is by grace you have been saved, through faith—and this not from yourselves, it is the gift of God—not by works, so that no one can boast" (NIV). And Romans 6:23 says, "For the wages of sin is death, but the gift of God is eternal life in Christ Jesus our Lord." So becoming a Christian is not about receiving a list of do's and do not's but receiving the ultimate gift, a relationship with the Creator of the universe through the sacrificial blood of Christ.

This gift of salvation was costly, as it cost Jesus His life. The best-known passages of Jesus' agony, of what He went through for us in becoming the sin offering, are found in Matthew 26:38–39 and John 12:27–28. We often think of sin as the bad things we do, and yes, that is true, but the Bible speaks of sin as having dominion, as reigning. More than the bad things that you do, sin is a power in your life. Sin exercises authority. "For if by the trespass of one man, death reigned through that one man, how much more will those who receive God's abundant provision of grace and of the gift of righteousness reign in life through the one man, Jesus Christ." (Rom. 5:17 NIV). The sin nature exercised dominion and had a power in your life before you became a Christian, and now, you still sin, but because you are in Christ, you have the power of the Spirit living in you to resist sin, and you have God's presence living in you, changing your desires and affections as He is making you more into the image of His Son.

The Bible refers to this new relationship that we have with Christ, through faith by the Holy Spirit, by using the phrase "in Christ" (1 Cor. 1:30; Gal. 3:26; Eph. 1:3-6). Humans were created from the beginning to fellowship and commune with God, but sin destroyed this fellowship between God and man, who then became guilty and deserving of death. Believers are united in a way that is eternally binding, extending throughout all of time, meaning that Christ's death accomplished salvation for all your sins, past, present, and future (Rom. 6:3–7). And now, our position before God is at His table, as God "seated us with him in the heavenly realms in Christ Jesus" (Eph. 2:6 NIV). You now have an eternal, secure place at God's table.

Thomas Aquinas, medieval theologian, describes the gift of salvation through Jesus as a divine illumination that exceeds the intellect's ability to understand; therefore, divine revelation or light is necessary for human understanding.[203] It is important to note that this union with Christ is mystical, meaning that this revealed mystery in Christ's death and resurrection (Col. 1:26–27) is not at odds with reason, but the full understanding of this mystery is beyond human comprehension (1 Cor. 2:9). Christ dwelling "in your hearts" means to have His Spirit living in you. (Eph. 3:16–17). This union with Christ is life-giving and by which we become a new creation (2 Cor. 5:17), and this union is permanent.

The infinite excellency of God's essence is the grounds of true love expressed in our affections toward God and others. Through our union with Christ, we are purged of sin, and our affections are in the process of transformation in this world and will reach fulfillment in heaven. His life for your life, that you might live to please Him. Being filled "with the knowledge of his will through all spiritual wisdom and understanding" (Col. 1:9 NIV 1984). Those true and holy affections overflow with love and thanksgiving for the gospel, whereas false affections elevate the greatness of spiritual discoveries without giving glory to Christ, and they are laden with pride.

The medieval understanding of the form and purpose of art can help us understand how humans are formed by the gospel and reflect more the image of God. Following the medieval theory of art, Aquinas believed that art was not self-expression but rather a "science" of constructing forms based on theories and laws and its proportionate correspondence to the source. So what does this mean practically? An architect drafts a building plan according to the concept in His mind. He constructs a magnificent house with intricate detail and ornamentation. What makes the house beautiful? Is it exterior beauty, or is it something more? According to a medieval philosopher, the house would be considered beautiful according to its likeness to the plan of the creator, and the creator would be God.

The Great Reconciliation

Understanding that the Abrahamic covenant, or old covenant, depends only on God's fulfilling His part is key to understanding God's purpose for Israel and for the nations, as well as His relationship with humanity and the basis of the new covenant. The old covenant makes clear that all people throughout history can experience a restored relationship with God through the saving work of Jesus, which was applied to Old Testament believers. So salvation under the old covenant was by believing that God would fulfill His promise in the future of sending the Messiah. Jesus' fulfillment of that promise, through His death and resurrection, was applied to Old Testament believers ahead of time, prior to Jesus' incarnation and death and resurrection in history.

The foundation of the Mosaic covenant and all other covenants to follow is grace through faith. Throughout the Old Testament, rebellion against the covenants traces back to unbelief (Deut. 1:32; 9:23; 2 Kings 17:14; 2 Chron. 20:20; Ps. 106:24). Obedience to the Ten Commandments or any other laws was never intended as a means to salvation. Instead, Israel's obedience to the law was a response of faith to the grace of God, who chose to make an everlasting covenant with Abraham and his descendants (Gen. 12:1–4). According to Genesis 15:6, God credited righteousness to Abraham in response to Abraham's faith. In this ceremonial expression of the covenant, God did not follow the traditional protocol to ratify a covenant, where both parties would arrange and walk together between the animal halves, symbolizing their commitment to uphold the contract. Instead, God caused

Abraham to fall into a deep sleep so that He was the only one to walk through, thus ratifying the covenant alone. Since God never breaks His promises, this covenant is eternal.

Justifying faith or belief in God is not something that anyone can do for themselves or anything that they had a part of. It is God's initiative and actions only that accomplish salvation, which is both judicial in our eternal standing before God and relational in our restored relationship with God. Paul sums up the love and justice of God that causes our cognitive dissonance of "how can this be," in this explanation that the shedding of Jesus' blood made it possible for God to be both just and "the justifier of" those who believe in Jesus (Rom. 3:26 KJV).

Consider Exodus 14, when the Israelites faced a dire situation—Pharaoh's army, including six hundred of his best chariots, were pursing them, leaving them with nowhere to escape. The Israelites' obedience to God's laws did not save them, but their belief in God's promise that He would guide them safely to the other side of the Red Sea did. Trusting in God's grace through faith saved the Israelites. The Exodus was a signpost intended for them to look back to for encouragement that God is for His people and works for their good, if they will put their faith in Him and trust in Him and not in their ability to please Him through their own good works.

Remember, the Ten Commandments began with a call to remembrance of how God had demonstrated his love for His people, by recalling His gracious saving acts on their behalf. The structure of the Decalogue reflects the structure of a royal treaty. God, as the King of Israel, sets forth His covenant laws for His people. Out of gratitude for God's mercy and love for Israel and His continued care for Israel as their Sovereign Lord, is birthed Israel's obedience and submission to God's laws. Obedience to the law is an outward sign of an inward commitment of trusting in God through grace by faith and an expression of love. The obedience to law was never meant to be a burden to follow perfectly as a means to salvation but was to be a response of gratitude for God's saving grace.

Faith in God has always been about a matter of internal transformation of the heart and not about external obedience to the laws under the sacrificial system. The Bible speaks of this internal transformation as a circumcised heart (Lev. 26:41; Deut. 30:6–10), a new heart (Jer. 24:7; 32:39), the gift of His Spirit within them (Ezek. 11:9; 36:2; John 14:16–17; 16:7–15), and the writing of the law of God on their hearts (Jer. 31:32). The sacrificial system provided a way of forgiveness and communion with God and pointed to the fulfillment of the law in the ultimate sacrifice of the spotless lamb, Jesus Christ. The book of Hebrews testifies to the inadequacy of the Levitical sacrifices for the sins of the people and the sufficiency of Christ's sacrifice.

Keeping the commands perfectly under the covenant is not a means to salvation, as God knows we can't do it; salvation comes by grace through faith. The law of the Lord is a light, illuminating how God desires His people to live, and it exposes our darkness due to the effects of sin on mankind. "Therefore no one will be declared righteous in God's sight by the works of the law; rather, through the law we become conscious of our sin" (Rom. 3:20 NIV). First, the law makes us conscious of sin in the sense that we can't fulfill the requirements of the law apart from God's help. To inherit the blessings under all the covenants, "the only thing that counts is faith expressing itself through love" (Gal. 5:6). Though for centuries, the Israelites tried to fulfill the law by works, Paul makes it clear in Romans 9:30–32 that the law is based on faith in God's promises and not on striving to earn salvation through good works.

Second, the law of the Lord enlightens our eyes, adjusting our vision to see with eyes of faith. His light sheds light in our hearts, giving wisdom and instruction. The metaphorical usage of the word *light* relates light to instruction of the Word of God and a parent's teaching (Prov. 6:23). "The unfolding of your words gives light; it gives understanding to the simple" (Ps. 119:130 NIV). A lamp illuminates the way, and the Word of God "is a lamp for my feet and a light on my path" (Ps. 119:105).

Psalm 19 illuminates the life-giving effects of the law of the Lord: "The law of the LORD is perfect, refreshing the soul. The statutes of the LORD are trustworthy, making wise the simple. The precepts of the LORD are right, giving joy to the heart. The commands of the LORD are radiant, giving light to the eyes" (vv. 7–8 NIV).

Many of us consider God's law as a list of do's and don'ts. God designed His laws for our good, safety, and joy. The law describes what faith looks like in daily living. At the heart of the law is God's love. The whole law is boiled down to this one thing—love. "Love your neighbor as yourself" (Lev. 19:18 NIV), which is known as the law of love or the "royal" law. Paul sums it up for us in Romans 13:8–10:

> Let no debt remain outstanding, except the continuing debt to love one another, for whoever loves others has fulfilled the law. The commandments, "You shall not commit adultery," "You shall not murder," "You shall not steal," "You shall not covet," and whatever other command there may be, are summed up in this one command: "Love your neighbor as yourself." Love does no harm to a neighbor. Therefore love is the fulfillment of the law. (NIV)

Jesus said it this way in Matthew 7:12, "So in everything, do to others what you would have them do to you, for this sums up the Law and the Prophets" (NIV).

The goal of the law is to make us more loving people. How has obeying God's laws (or following Jesus) made you a more loving person? We love because He loved us first (1 John 4:19). We obey because we love God; therefore, love fulfills the law. Love is not a work to earn God's favor but is the fruit of faith. "Love comes from God" (1 John 4:7 NIV). Love is a fruit of Spirit, meaning that love is produced by God through the work of the Holy Spirit (Gal. 3:5; 5:22). Like a light, love dispels the darkness and weightiness of sin and glorifies God. Remember the word *glory* means "weight, heaviness, splendor," and the word *matter* is the best equivalent in English. His glory is so powerful and weighty because He is the Sovereign Lord. Therefore, the Almighty God, who is the one who matters most, displays His glory in love, and love's power is rooted in His glory. Love is glorious because love comes from God who is Love, full of glory and truth. Jesus' greatest commandments and the sum of how to live as a follower of Jesus are, "'Love the Lord your God with all your heart and with all your soul and with all your mind.' This is the first and greatest commandment. And the second is like it: 'Love your neighbor as yourself.' All the Law and the Prophets hang on these two commandments" (Matt. 22:37–40).

In 1 Corinthians 13:12, Paul illustrates our partial vision of seeing and experiencing God in this world by using the comparison of seeing an image in a mirror versus seeing someone face-to-face. This would have been a comparison that Paul's audience would have understood since Corinth was famous for making mirrors. Upon Jesus' return and when He establishes His kingdom on Earth, we will see him face-to-face (Rev. 22:3–4). While our vision is indirect, we see with clarity the glory of God in Jesus, and we see Jesus in the Bible through the revelation of the Holy Spirit, and we are in the process of being transformed to image God (2 Cor. 3:17–18).

Jesus modeled love by seeing the numerous interruptions in His day as opportunities to fulfill God's purpose of loving care for His people and the world. J. R. R. Tolkien's short story, *Leaf by Niggle* illustrates this struggle to see distractions as opportunities to glorify God. This short story centers around the protagonist, Niggle, wanting to make a difference in the world through his painting. Throughout the painting of his art piece, he experiences frequent interruptions, which cause much frustration. I identify with Niggle as you might as well. Many of us, like Niggle, have a vision of how we want to be remembered, but like him, we have lost sight of what really matters most while we are pursuing good things. God continues to interrupt Niggle to show him that small acts of love are far more important than his good endeavors. God wants all of us to follow Jesus' model of seeing distractions as opportunities and invitations to live on purpose and enjoy and share the beautiful, transforming power of God's love.

Tim Keller speaks to the goodness of work accordingly: "Every good endeavor, even the simplest ones, pursued in response to God's calling, can matter forever."[204] Things that we are asked to help with that might seem meanly or ordinary are not distractions to fulfilling your purpose, but instead they are seeds of love sown into the garden of man's and woman's hearts—acts of culture care. Believers have this great hope that our dwelling with God upon Jesus' return is a place where there will be no more death, suffering, or pain (Rev. 21:3–4). The Bible says: "He will wipe every tear from their eyes" (v. 4 NIV). Heaven is a place of fullness of redemption, restoration, and resurrection.

Imaging the Glorious Light

While all of creation speaks to the glory of God, Jesus, who is the exact representation of God in bodily form, is the image of God's glory (Heb. 1:3). "For in him all things were created: things in heaven and on earth, visible and invisible, whether thrones or powers or rulers or authorities; all things have been created through him and for him" (Col. 1:16 NIV). The deepest desire of Jesus is God's glory, as He prayed, "Father, glorify your name" (John 12:28), and He desired that the Father would glorify the Son (John 17). God's glory is expressed in His love, mercy, and justice, reconciling sinners to God. Second Peter 3:9 expresses God's great mercy as He delays the final judgment because He doesn't want anyone to perish. While He is loving and compassionate, He is just and will not allow sin to go unpunished (Ex. 34:6).

Humans made in the image of God are created to be partakers in the fellowship and community of the Trinity through the indwelling presence of God given to every person at salvation. Upon becoming a Christian, man is brought into relationship with God, the most significant relationship of his lifetime. Also, the abiding presence of the Holy Spirit, the Spirit of Truth, indwells a believer, convicting the world of sin (John 16:8–9), and guiding belivers in all truth, giving them the capacity to love, obey, and serve God.

As a result of the Fall, the image of God was marred or corrupted in us, meaning that our ability to reflect and know God was corrupted by sin. Though we do not know the degree to which the image of God was corrupted or distorted in mankind, we do know that the image of God was so disfigured that sin alienated man from God, from himself, and from others. Based on the transmission of Adam's image and likeness to his son in Genesis 5:3 and 9:6, the Bible makes clear that man still retains the image of God even after the fall, but it is now corrupted. In James 3:9, the Greek tense of the verb *ginomai*, which is translated as "have been made" (NIV), is significant in speaking of man formed in the image of God. The perfect tense describes a past action with continuing results. Therefore, according to James 3:9, man has been made in the image of God and still bears His image and likeness. Sin has corrupted man's nature to the degree that he has become spiritually dead. The wages (or effects) of sin... of sin was death, and only through Christ's blood can we be justified or placed in right standing before God. "For all have sinned and fall short of the glory of God, and all are justified freely by his grace through the redemption that came by Christ Jesus" (Rom. 3:23–24). Yes, you still sin, but the reigning of sin and the condemnation for your sins were paid for by Jesus Christ's shed blood. Fallen man still reflects the image of God, though imperfectly, and the Spirit's abiding presence is continually working to restore the beauty of God's image in man.

God's presence that indwells Christians does not mean that humans become divine (unlike pantheism, spiritism, or New Age beliefs), but we are indwelt by God through the Holy Spirit. Humans are made "partakers of the divine nature" (2 Pet. 1:4 ESV), meaning that we are filled with God's presence. Describing a believer as godly, Christlike, or spiritual comes from a believer's infilling of the Holy Spirit. First, the Holy Spirit, the Counselor (*Paracletos*) will be "with" and be "in" believers (John 14:17). Second, indwelt by God means the Son will indwell believers. The Son is in the Father, and the Father is in the Son (John 14:11), and Jesus said, "You are in me, and I am in you" (John 14:20 NIV). Third, all three persons of the Godhead, Father, Son, and Holy Spirit, make their home with believers (John 14:23). The Spirit primarily indwells us; however, since all three members of the Godhead indwell the other, we experience the presence of the Father and Son in the abiding presence of the Holy Spirit in us.

Our chief aim is to reflect the image of God by glorifying God; in other words, to imitate the self-giving love of God to the world rather than imaging the self-centeredness of the world.

The currency of God's love gives life, while the currency of the world is greed, which is a deceiver that never satisfies and is also a thief of joy and peace.

The Westminster Catechism begins by telling us that the purpose of man is to glorify God and enjoy Him forever. In the aftermath of England's civil war in the seventeenth century, a national assembly of clergy gathered to define the central truths of Scripture, to form the core doctrines, and to clear up errors and divisions within the church. Still almost four hundred years later, Presbyterians and many other denominations look to this comprehensive document to define Christianity's core belief by reciting the Westminster Confession as a church; this teaches and reaffirms the principles of their faith. Additionally, it is important to note that in writing the confession of faith, the assembly was committed to Scripture alone as the final authority on faith, and the catechism serves as a doctrinal anchor for the church to teach the people in matters of faith and to build unity. So my central question no longer becomes *How can I get my needs met?* but *How can I glorify God?* Another way of saying this is *How can I give more of my attention or energy toward knowing God and making Him known?* In other words, *How am I living like Jesus?* matters more than anyone or anything in my life. Jesus is more worthy of your attention, affections, and time than anyone in this world. Americans spend millions of dollars every year trying to look like celebrities, purchasing the latest beauty creams, beauty tools, trendy purses or shoes, and more. The Bible is saying that the way to look like God is to shift what matters most in your life to imaging God rather than imaging the world. Is Jesus the one you spend most of your time trying to look like? What does your credit card statement or Amazon account say about who you want to look like? When you give God glory, you are giving Him the weight in your life that He deserves. The best way that we glorify God is by following Jesus' example of first loving God and then loving others. Christians' portrait of love for all to emulate is found in 1 Corinthians 13:4–7:

> Love is patient, love is kind. It does not envy, it does not boast, it is not proud. It does not dishonor others, it is not self-seeking, it is not easily angered, it keeps no record of wrongs. Love does not delight in evil but rejoices with the truth. It always protects, always trusts, always hopes, always perseveres.

Since all people are created in the image of God, all people have dignity and worth. This foundational doctrine informs our ethics, so even the people you disagree with or who infuriate you are to be treated as image bearers of God. Through Christ, a civil discourse is possible with those who share differing worldviews.

Pathways to Life Transformation

A Pathway to Growing in Family Resemblance

Has someone ever today you that you look just like your mother? Maybe it is your eyes, voice, or your smile that reminds them of her. When I was a teenager, people would ask, "Who is the mother, and who is the daughter?" My mother and I would smile and laugh. Now that I'm older than mom was at that age, I imagine that made her feel good, especially when she was exhausted as a single mom who was working hard and trying to keep up with two teens. Sometimes, we do not like our family resemblances, so we might bristle at these comments or offer a forced smile. Other times, we might say, "I do not see that." Whatever the case, there are always some family traits we would have rather skipped our generation. Maybe you do not like your nose or moles on your body? Or you have curly hair when you wish that you had straight hair? Or you are quick tempered? Or you have a heart problem or high blood pressure like some of your relatives? The good news with God is that we only inherit good characteristics from Him because God is full only of goodness, truth, and love. He is perfect and without any sin qualities. Through studying Romans 8, Ephesians 1:3–6, and John 1:12–13, we learn that through faith in Jesus we become children of God, sons and daughters. He has given us the Holy Spirit who lives within believers to teach us God's family values, to help us grow in resemblance in our thoughts and actions to our Heavenly Father, and to be there as a Comforter and Counselor because God knows life is hard and that we struggle with sin. This process of growing in family resemblance is progressive by nature and described by "the renewing of your mind" (Rom. 12:2 NIV). This means to grow in our love and affections toward our Heavenly Father and to learn and follow His teaching and example of living in a broken and fallen world.

One of the family values of a follower of Jesus is to "honor your father and your mother" (Ex. 20:12), which comes from the Ten Commandments (vv.1–17). This can be very challenging to follow when one parent makes very mean comments and is consistently never satisfied with the good care he or she is receiving. One of my close friends really struggles with this verse relative to her aging parent. The day after my friend had spent at least eight hours helping her dad by buying groceries, going to the pharmacy, paying his bills, bringing lunch to him, visiting him, and taking care of other things around the house, her dad said that she did not love him, because if she did, she would be at his house more. My friend spends all day and part of the evening with him a few days a week, and her dad has a couple of sitters who have stayed with the family for years now and one for over a decade, so he has twenty-four-hour care. Instead of losing her temper, God is helping her to honor her dad; she reassures her dad that she loves him and understands that he is frustrated by his situation since he is very limited by what he can do for himself. Then she tries to get her dad talking about old stories from his past that make him happy. That is love—listening to the same story once you have heard it a handful of times.

The Holy Spirit has helped my friend not to take it personally when her dad says mean things to her, but instead to counter this anger and frustration with his situation by reassuring him that he is loved. She knows that this parent has struggled with misplaced anger for years. When she is especially getting weary and feeling the weight of all the complaining, she reaches out to a few close friends to pray for her dad to experience more contentment and see some things to be thankful for, and for her to continue to love, care, and provide for him when she feels like she is not appreciated and that nothing is good enough. Continuing to honor a difficult parent resembles God's family values.

Fight your Battles with the Word of God

Remember that the Bible is a collection of books inspired by God and written by human authors by the inspiration of God's Spirit. It contains different types of literature, which date back to about the second century BC, with some of the oldest Hebrew manuscripts being the Dead Sea Scrolls. There are sixty-six books in total with two sections: the Old Testament (thirty-nine books) and the New Testament (twenty-seven books). It is a story of creation, fall, redemption, and restoration. The Bible tells of God's plan to save the world and the people He loves. He gave us the Bible so that we can grow to love Him through loving His Word and so that it can change us into people who live its message. The Bible testifies to the words of God written in the Bible as living power that perceive the deepest thoughts of man, and the intentions, affections, and desires of the heart (Heb. 4:12).

The "word" of God (*logos* in Greek) comprehensively refers to Jesus who embodies the gospel (John 1:14). Because of this, we must make hearing the Word of God a priority in our life. This can mean listening to the Word of God, reading the Word of God, gathering with other believers in church to worship, studying the Word of God individually and in a small group, and listening to and reading other resources, such as podcasts or books. Then through the power of the Holy Spirit in giving us understanding of God's Word, the words of the Bible can judge and convict the thoughts and attitudes of the heart and teach us how to live as followers of Jesus.

The question is: Does how we live out our beliefs line up with Scripture? The Word of God has the ability to realign our hearts and retune our daily life rhythms to God's beat. He can retune strings of deception and remove bad strings to inspire new, life-giving tunes of the heart, which beat to the songs of heaven and the promises of God. We must be careful to pay attention and guard the attentions of our hearts by being intentional with the focus of our eyes and invite God's eyes of light and life into our inner life. Unbelief and the deceitfulness of sin keep our hearts hard (Heb. 3:12) and entangled in darkness, which always promises future happiness but instead delivers pain and regret.

In order to fight your battles with God's Word, you must first believe in God's promises, then repent, turn from following the deceptive promises of sin, and trust in God's promises that bring the good life and life eternal. God promises through the prophet Isaiah, "My word . . . will not return to me empty, but will accomplish what I desire and achieve the purpose for which I sent it" (Isa. 55:11 NIV). Any time spent in God's Word is useful, even in the routine hearing the Word on Sundays at church or in a small group when you may not feel like you learned something different. Ordinary daily time in God's Word builds up your savings account.

Lots of daily deposits of God's Word build the kind of spiritual strength that will help you endure hard times. We have become too accustomed to quick, snappy soundbites for our spiritual diet, which, while of some benefit, will not build strong, lean spiritual muscles. Keep building the small daily deposits because, over time, all the small promises deposited and then applied to your life will transform your life's portfolio. There is no problem or life situation for which you cannot find help from the Bible. Here are some examples:

- When you struggle with pride or difficult family relationships, read about Joseph.
- When you feel impatient and frustrated with God about the difficult circumstances of your life, read about Job.
- If you need courage, read about Esther, Elijah, Paul, and Jesus.
- If you are struggling with an unfulfilled longing, pray the Psalms and read about Hannah (1 Sam. 1–2).
- When you can't see the way out of a bad situation, read about Paul.
- When you feel ashamed, read about David's confession in Psalm 51:1-7.
- If you are struggling with moral issues, read 1 Corinthians or Ephesians.
- If you are struggling with sin, read Jesus' temptation story in Matthew 4:1–11.
- If your heart feels distant from God, read about John.
- If you want to understand the gospel message of forgiveness for all who call out in repentance to God through a short story, read Jonah.
- If you are losing hope for a future in which God will rule, read Revelation.
- If you need perseverance, read James.

- If you are unsure about who Jesus is and feel distant from God, then read one of the Gospels: Matthew, Mark, Luke, or John.
- If you need wisdom, read Proverbs.
- If you need comfort and hope, read Psalms.

A Pathway to Forgiveness

Forgiveness is one of the main battles that our hearts face. Forgiveness blooms in muddy waters. One story from Scripture that has helped me fight some of my battles with trusting God's promises and tuning my heart's beat to forgiveness, begins with two brothers. One brother takes his inheritance and squanders it all on wild living; the older brother remains at home and responsibly works to preserve the family business. During the time the younger brother is living a self-serving and licentious lifestyle, the older brother becomes resentful of his young brother since he himself has stayed and sacrificed each day to honor his father's work and preserve his legacy through the business. While steeped in mud, feeding pigs for work just to get by, the young son feels the weight of his sin in abandoning his family and squandering his inheritance; he decides to leave this life and return home to ask his father to forgive him. Much to his surprise, when he is at a distance and expecting coldness or a lecture on his bad choices, his father is filled with compassion and runs to him, throwing his arms around him and kissing him.

Perhaps while the son was in his father's embrace, his request for forgiveness was released like the waters through an open dam. It filled the hole in the father's heart. His father had been missing his son for all that time, so in celebration of his son's return, he threw a party, filled with singing and dancing. The father said to all, "This son of mine was dead and is alive again; he was lost and is found" (Luke 15:24 NIV).

The older brother's heart had become muddy with resentment toward his brother, so he refused to join in the celebration. The father listened to the older brother's anger and lovingly reassured him that he is very loved and all that he has is also his. The older brother missed the heart of the father, which is forgiveness and restoration. Also, he failed to understand that his brother's restoration would in no way jeopardize his own inheritance. This story might be familiar to some of you as it is the story of the prodigal son in Luke 15.

When I have felt like I blew it or followed the ways of the world in living to please my own needs or desires, this story reminds me that God's arms are open wide, and He is so excited that I have come back home to Him. His first words are not, "I told you so," but, "I love you, and I am happy to see you." Sometimes I think that we see the Bible as a rule book, and we forgot it is about God's story and contains instructions on how to help us know God and develop a strong relationship with Him. We forgot that Christianity is about having a relationship with a personal God. Also, perhaps you have had a broken relationship where one or both of you parted ways for the high life. One of the greatest joys of my life was the restoration of friendship with a sweet friend who is like a sister. For years, I wanted to be close again, and asking for forgiveness felt like a homecoming. Just like muddy waters when the mountain snows melt, soon the spring sunshine will clear the waters. Forgiveness heals one of the greatest gifts of God, relationships.

Through studying the Bible, you will come to know God, come to love Him, and be transformed to be grace-filled and faith-filled and to be a faithful follower of Jesus. It will also help you to understand His plans and purposes, fill you with gratitude for the gift of salvation, and give you hope that you are never alone because the Holy Spirit dwells in all Christians. Studying the Bible will also help you understand God's redemptive plans for individuals and the world and how you can join His redemptive work in the world.

Paul, the writer of many of the New Testament books, was less concerned with teaching his congregations what to do than he was with teaching them how to think. The essence of Paul, and I would argue the essence of how we are to approach Scripture for our instruction and ethical formation, is not simply to extract moral platitudes from their context and apply them to our lives. Instead, it is to enter into the approach of Paul: examine Scripture together, under the leading of the Holy Spirit, to see how our life choices impact the lives of those around us (the unity of the church and its witness in the world) as well as how they fit in the grand scheme of God's unfolding redemptive plan in creation.

God created not only individuals but also the local church to reflect the self-giving nature of the Trinity. The nature of God is best reflected in our unity and fellowship with God and with the community of believers, the local church. Jesus prays for this unity among believers in the church, so that the world will know God's love for Christ and all people (John 17:20–23). Just as the Spirit unites a believer to God, the Spirit unites believers in Christ to one another. The indwelling of the Spirit in believers mirrors the communal nature of the Trinity, though the divine perichoresis is distinctive to the Godhead. What we learn is that God's being is understood by the eternal personal relatedness of the Trinity, and the Christian community is to reflect the communal nature of the Trinity. The greatest expression of community to the world is the church filled with diverse people united in Christ. All of Scripture and its thematic elements testify to the nature of God's redemptive mission to reconcile all of creation, chiefly humanity, unto Himself.

The Importance of Corporate and Personal Study

Why is it important to study the Bible in groups or church in addition to personal study?

Few individuals in the Roman world had the capability to read and to write. Throughout most of human history, this has been the case. People engaged with Scripture as it was read aloud to them in their Sunday gatherings. González, in his work on Christian history until the Reformation, notes how early Christian gatherings would have resembled something of a potluck (my words, not his), in which believers would have brought food together to share in a common meal. The eucharistic bread would have been blessed at the beginning and the wine at the end of the meal. Somewhere within those gatherings would have been the public reading of Scripture, the singing of hymns, and further fellowship.[205] As Christianity became institutionalized, so too its liturgy became formalized. Any cursory reading of the Book of Common Prayer or the equivalent prayer books of other traditions reveals a tremendous integration of Scripture within the liturgy itself, which would be corporately recited in the assembly.

The influence of the Reformation era's prioritization for people in the West to have access to the Scriptures in their own language, gave rise to an increased priority of the sermon as a focal point in Protestant assemblies. While there are notable exceptions, for Protestants it is typically the pulpit, not the eucharistic table, that is the focal point of the service, signifying an elevated prioritization of the public exposition of the Word. That said, it is worth noting, as James Stamoolis does in his work on Eastern Orthodox missionary history, that the insistence upon a unified language for the liturgy and a resistance to individual accessibility to Scripture was a decidedly *Western* phenomenon before the Reformation. Deeply woven into the Orthodox missional ethos was the belief that the Scriptures and the liturgy be translated and made available to people in their heart language. Centuries before Wycliffe Bible translators and others began to prioritize Bible translation in their missionary work, the Orthodox were doing it in the East.[206]

Prioritization of individual reading of Scripture came about in parallel with the rise of global literacy in the nineteenth century. In Europe, the nineteenth century generated the first mass education movement in the world as a shared responsibility between religious institutions and governments.[207] While the printing press was invented in 1440, it was not until the nineteenth century when the steam-powered rotary press replaced the hand-operated printing press that the production of books took off. By 1800, the number of books printed in English per decade had grown to seven thousand, more than twice what it was a hundred years earlier.[208] There was astounding power in the printing press to end global illiteracy, yet parts of the world that maintain incredulous levels would have been unfathomable to those in the nineteenth century. Grant Lovejoy estimates that there are approximately 5.7 billion adults in the world today who are primarily oral communicators "because they are illiterate, or their reading comprehension is inadequate."[209] While Lovejoy is certainly right about the dominance of oral communication, his conclusion that it is a matter of illiteracy or poor reading comprehension is potentially not absolute. Many cultures *prefer* oral communication to written communication.

Dr. Vicki Elgi (DIS, Fuller Theological Seminary) works in the field of oral Bible translation among oral people groups in Cameroon. She has remarked frequently about how, in her work, which involves a translation process whereby biblical narratives are recorded and distributed among tribes via mp3 players and other audio devices, many who receive the work she does prefer the orality because of the broader cultural implications of receiving that information. People gather around the recording device to listen together and then, as a group, discuss the story they have learned, usually a story with a missionary involved. For them, it is a community enterprise because (as most collectivist cultures operate) understanding can only come through the consensus of the community—for an individual to engage in that enterprise alone is arrogance. Also, remember that Jesus modeled the importance of growing in faith, fellowship, and ministry in community by choosing twelve disciples to teach and train and to minister alongside Him as they traveled about sharing the good news of salvation and meeting the needs of people.

While it is true that orality is some people's *only* choice, we must consider the implications of written storytelling and its impact on culture, especially when it coincides with an insistence that such reading be consumed privately. I am not suggesting that a personal discipline of Bible study is not beneficial. It is, indeed. But it is worth asking ourselves how much our value of personal study is overvalued in light of the more biblically faithful practice of communal study.

Bible Study Methods

Missiological Hermeneutics[210]

Four Questions of a Missiological Hermeneutic

1. What is going on in the text? What did it mean for the people involved?
2. What is the meaning and intent of God's mission in the text?
3. How does the text inform my participation in God's mission?
4. What does the text mean for mission in the twenty-first century?

10-Step Exegesis of a Paragraph[211]

1. Determine the beginning and the end of the paragraph. Identify signals of beginning and ending.
2. Review the place this paragraph has in the scheme of the book as a whole.
3. Read the paragraph several times. Notice any textual variants (if your Bible has notes of that kind), literary features, major emphases.
4. Review the cross-references, especially of another book of the Bible that relates to the same church, places that relate to the same historical event, texts that relate to the same persons featured in your paragraph, and so on.
5. Identify the historical, cultural, geographic setting of the paragraph, using a Bible dictionary or Bible atlas.
6. Identify the salient grammatical points, sentences, major grammatical divisions of the paragraph; notice changes in tense, person, number, etc.
7. Write the major theme of the paragraph in one sentence.
8. Outline the major points of the paragraph as sub-ideas under the main theme.
9. Identify the people featured in your paragraph, and determine their interrelationships, both in the paragraph and in the larger context of the book.
10. Identify the main theological (and missiological) concepts or "big words" found in your paragraph, and determine how they fit and what they mean in the context of the theme of your paragraph, as well as in relation to the main themes of the book.

Seven Pathways Study Plans for the Books of the Bible

1. **Thanksgiving**: Think of five things that you are thankful for. What are your five?
2. **Silence**: Quiet your surroundings and yourself before God and ask Him to speak to you.
3. **Confession**: Spend some time confessing your sins to God and thank Him for His faithfulness to forgive; also spend some time confessing who God is.
4. **Song**: Connect with God through listening and singing one or two worship songs from wherever you stream music.
5. **Pray**: Follow the daily structured prayer plan to guide whom you pray for.
6. **Bible Study**: (1) Listen to or read one chapter of the Bible. (2) Read the Seven Pathways Scripture reflection on those Scriptures and answer a few application questions. (3) Pray a guided prayer.
7. **Scripture Meditation**: Follow the Seven Pathways Scripture memorization method outlined in the next chapter.

See the Appendix for one sample day of the Seven Pathways Journey through John on our website at www.sevenpathway.com.

Practical Resources for Bible Study

Thousands of resources are available for studying the Bible. This list is by no means exhaustive, but it will provide a starting point for understanding and exploring the basic types of resources for studying the Bible.

- Online resources

- Hendrick Center at Dallas Theological Seminary library of biblical resources and online events and The Table Podcast[212]
- Dallas Theological Seminary—Free Online courses[213]
- Taylor University's Center for Scripture Engagement Resource Page[214]
- The Assemblies of God's Bible Engagement Project[215]
- The How to Read the Bible Series from The Bible Project[216]

  Note: The Bible Project also has an expanding collection of exceptionally well-done videos on word studies, themes, and books of the Bible.

• Basic principles of Bible study (hermeneutics)

- *How to Read the Bible for All Its Worth*, by Gordon Fee and Douglas Stuart
- *Grasping God's Word*, by J. Scott Duvall and J. Daniel Hays
- *How to read the Bible Book by Book*, by Gordon Fee and Douglas Stuart
- *Literary Approaches to the Bible*, by Douglas Magnum and Douglas Estes

• Understanding the language and culture of the Bible

- *Ministering in Patronage Cultures* and *Ministering in Honor-Shame Cultures*, by Jayson Georges
- *History of Christianity: Volume 1-111,* by Justo L. Gonzalez
- *Transforming Worldviews*, by Paul Hiebert
- *Understanding Folk Rel*igion, by Daniel Shaw, Paul Hiebert and Tite Tienou
- *Contextualizing the Faith*, by Scott Moreau
- *The IVP Bible Background Commentary*
- *The Bible Knowledge Commentary: Old and New Testament, Two Volumes*

  - *The 3D Gospel*, by Jayson Georges
- Study Bibles
  - A study Bible is a copy of the Bible that includes Bible studies along with the biblical text. Many people find this convenient and helpful.
  - I have used the NIV Study Bible and the NET Bible for years.
  - Key Word Study Bible, New International Version, AMG Publishers
- Concordance
  - *Strong's Concordance*
- Bible Dictionary
  - *Holman Bible Dictionary*
- Logos Bible Software- Bible Study Library
- Commentaries
  - Commentaries are books by Bible scholars and theologians that explain the biblical text. There are thousands available, written from various theological perspectives. Some are devoted to only one book of the Bible. Others comment on the entire Bible. Some are academic in nature; others are devotional or pastoral. BestCommentaries.com is a forum by which a person can search for the highest-rated commentary and determine which one best suits their needs.
  - The Pillar New Testament Commentaries are very good as well as The Anchor Yale Bible Commentaries.
  - Following advice from Old Testament scholar Michael Heiser, I also recommend that people invest in commentaries instead of using older online commentaries that are in the public domain.

Biblical studies is not a static, unchanging field. It rapidly develops as we learn more about ancient cultures and languages and discover new archaeological finds. Most public domain resources are extremely old—some (e.g. The Matthew Henry Commentaries) predate the finding of the Dead Sea Scrolls.

PATHWAY 7

Biblical Meditation

Visit many good books, but live in the Bible.
—Charles H. Spurgeon

I remember the days of long ago; I meditate on all your works and consider what your hands have done.
—Psalm 143:5 NIV

Meditation is one of the most basic spiritual disciplines. It is so simple and useful that it is practiced in some form by people of nearly all religions. The word itself conjures images of an Indian yogi sitting cross-legged, eyes closed, in perfect stillness, or of an orange-clad Buddhist monk in an incense-filled temple. Because Christians often associate meditation with Eastern religions, many are skeptical of the practice and surprised to learn that it has deep roots not only in the Christian community but also in Scripture. As we'll see, the Bible refers or alludes to this practice quite often.

Even so, the entire concept seems foreign to Western spirituality. Our minds are geared for action. We want to do something, like pray, study the Bible, or some other activity that we can quantify. To sit still and empty one's mind seems awkward and pointless, and very nearly impossible amid the frenetic pace of our lives.

Yet I assure you that entering into the practice of biblical meditation is both possible and highly valuable. And while there is some overlap in the way Christians practice meditation with that of other religions, biblical meditation is a uniquely Christian practice and one that brings a host of benefits, physically and psychologically as well as spiritually.

According to the *Journal of Behavioral Medicine*, research findings suggest that meditation can change the brain and immune function in positive ways. According to a 2017 US survey, the number of adults who practiced some form of mindfulness meditation or spiritual meditation in the previous twelve months more than tripled between 2012 to 2017, from 4.1 percent to 14.2 percent.[217] In the *Journal of Personality and Social Psychology*, researchers found that meditation practiced over time increased positive emotions, purpose in life, and social support, while decreasing illness symptoms.[218] Due to the growing number of adults, especially older adults, struggling with some form of sleep problems, meditation might help improve sleep and reduce sleep-related impairment during the day.[219] Additionally, those who struggle with a chronic condition like asthma benefit from improved symptoms when meditation is combined with standard care.[220] Mindfulness-based practices reduced psychological distress from physical symptoms for breast cancer survivors,[221] chronic pain,[222] and increased quality of life.[223]

Biblical meditation is our Seventh Pathway to building a deeper relationship with God. Briefly defined, this is meditation on Scripture. The practice can improve our overall health, boost cognition and perseverance, strengthen our faith, and empower us as it builds spiritual strength and increases our reserves. In this chapter, you'll discover what biblical meditation is and what it isn't. You'll understand how this ancient and trusted practice leads you closer to God. You'll also gain some insight into the practice of Scripture memorization, which is an invaluable aid to biblical meditation, and you'll discover practical resources for starting down this Pathway yourself.

What is Biblical Meditation?

Biblical meditation is the practice of emptying your mind of other thoughts in order to focus on God so that you may hear His voice. What makes biblical meditation different from other forms of meditation is that in the Seven Pathways practice, we focus our minds on a particular portion of Scripture as the starting point for meditation. In other words, we do not simply empty our minds or even focus on God in some abstract sense. Instead, we drive out stray thoughts and distractions so that we may know God through a portion of His word, the Bible.

This practice originated in Scripture itself. We see references to the concept in both the Old and New Testaments. In both cases, it is strongly tied to the concept of remembering what we know about God through the Scriptures. This is very different from the Eastern concept of meditation. Anglican historian and theologian Rev. Dr. Peter Toon highlights the difference this way:

> The simplest way to highlight the difference is to say that for the one meditation is an inner journey to find the center of one's being, while for the other it is the concentration of the mind/heart upon an external Revelation. For the one revelation/insight/illumination occurs when the inmost self (which is also the ultimate Self, the one final Reality) is reached by the journey into the soul, while for the other it comes as a result of encounter with God in and through his objective Revelation to which Holy Scripture witnesses.[224]

Bible.org defines meditation as "the act of focusing one's thoughts: to ponder, think on, muse." The site goes on to explain that "meditation consists of reflective thinking or contemplation, usually on a specific subject to discern its meaning or significance or a plan of action."[225] It is used synonymously with contemplation, reflection, rumination, deep thinking, or remembering.

Eastern (also New Age) practices of meditation (such as TM, or transcendental meditation) place a focus on emptying one's mind in order to detach from the world. Many Eastern forms of thought view escaping the world in order to enter into a higher plane of cognitive and spiritual existence to be a primary objective in meditation. By contrast, biblical meditation empties the mind of the wrong things and refocuses on the things of God (Phil. 4:8). This is at the root of the key differences between Eastern and biblical approaches to meditation. Biblical meditation has an object in view, whereas

Eastern meditation seeks to do precisely the opposite of that. Bible.org affixes the objects of meditation to be worship (Ps. 27:4), instruction (Ps. 49:3), motivation (Josh. 1:7–8), and transformation (Ps. 4:4).[226]

Meditation in the Old Testament

Biblical meditation is seen in a number of places in the Old Testament, which shows its place in both ancient Judaism and in Christianity. Here are a few passages that demonstrate the concept most clearly.

Psalm 19:14: This is an introduction to the concept of meditation as musing or even speaking out one's internal dialogue before God. Here David writes, "May these words of my mouth and this meditation of my heart be pleasing in your sight, LORD, my Rock and my Redeemer." The word here translated as meditation is *higāyôn*.[227] It refers to a murmuring sound, musically to indicate a solemnity of movement (*Ital affettuoso* in music). It appears to be connected with contemplative thought and reflection. Alternate Scriptures where *higāyôn* is used include Psalm 9:16 (used outright, seemingly as a command, like *selah*); 92:3 (as playing the harp with "solemn sound"); and Lamentations 3:62 (as "murmuring sound" used as a device).

The wider context of Psalm 19 demonstrates that this musing is not merely the inner small talk that we carry on with ourselves throughout the day. This meditation is occasioned by some specific content, namely creation and Scripture. Verse 1 begins the song: "The heavens declare the glory of God; the skies proclaim the work of his hands." This is a reference to general revelation, what we may know about God simply by observing the world He has created. As we observe nature, especially the grandeur of the heavens, we are prompted to think about the God who stands behind it.

In verse 7 David moves from the more general revelation of creation to the specific revelation found in Scripture, particularly in the books of the law. "The law of the LORD is perfect, refreshing the soul." We meditate on God based on what He has revealed about Himself. Both creation and Scripture may be source material for this. In either case, David's goal is seen in the concluding verse of the psalm as he prays that his thoughts and God's thoughts may be aligned.

Psalm 119:15–16 describes the action of meditation as a loving rehearsal or going over in one's mind. The Hebrew word for "meditate" is *siyach*. In contrast to *hâgâh*, *siyach* can be either spoken out loud or in one's heart.[228] Alternate Scriptures where the Hebrew word *siyach*[229] refers to a contemplation, complaint, meditation, prayer, or conversation include Judges 5:10; 1 Chronicles 16:9; Job 7:11; Psalm 55:17; 69:12; 77:3, 6, 12; 105:2; 119:5, 23, 27, 48, 78, 148; 143:5; 145:5; Proverbs 6:22.

Joshua 1:8 expounds on the meaning of *meditation* as meaning to speak what you have been pondering or reflecting upon. The Hebrew word for "meditate" used here is *hâgâh* (and elsewhere, e.g. Ps. 1:2). It implies something more than silent reflection. It means "to whisper or murmur" (likely connected to the cultural practice of reading Scripture aloud).[230] Outside of its rendering as "meditate," *hâgâh*[231] is rendered most commonly as "mourn," "speak," and "imagine."

Alternate Scriptures where *hâgâh* is used are Job 27:4; Psalm 1:2; 2:1; 35:28; 37:30; 38:12; 63:6; 71:24; 77:12; 115:7; 143:5; Proverbs 8:7; 15:28; 24:2; Isaiah 8:19; 16:7; 31:4; 33:18; 38:14; 59:3, 11, 13; and Jeremiah 48:31.

It is worth noting that both the Hebrew and Greek often have wide and varied meanings to their words (e.g. the Greek *agape* isn't always the word used to describe God's love), and the connection between pondering and speech is interesting here. In nearly every usage the verbal utterance derives from a state of pondering—it is not flippant speech but a "Freudian slip" of sorts—speech that reveals the deep recesses of the heart.

Meditation in the New Testament

Philippians 4:8: The Greek word here for "think" is *logizomai*. It is used about forty times in the New Testament and means to "consider, ponder, let one's mind dwell on."[232] Bill Mounce defines it as enumerating, to set as a matter of account, to impute.[233] This term has a more cerebral connotation to it, but too much should not be read into that, as this is indicative of broader contrasted features between Hebrew and Greek culture that the linguistic differences simply represent.

Luke 2:19: The word for Mary's pondering here is *symballō* and means to "revolve in the mind."[234] Elsewhere it refers to throwing or bringing together, to meet, or to converse.

The Ultimate Focus of Meditation

While Scripture is the starting point for biblical meditation, it is not the object or end. In other words, we don't meditate on Scripture so we may know the Bible more deeply. We meditate on Scripture as a pathway to knowing God. OurDailyBread.org defines biblical meditation as the act of "pondering the words of Scripture with a receptive heart, trusting the Holy Spirit to work in you through those words."[235] While it is true that biblical meditation involves pondering on Scripture, this definition would be better widened to also include the One to whom Scripture bears testimony. There is a real dynamic to biblical meditation that is simply the silent adoration of Jesus Himself, not Holy Scripture alone.

Ties of meditation, biblically speaking, with the acts of remembering, pondering, etc., are virtually synonymous. But there is an intentionality to the practice as an act of remembering. Meditation and contemplative prayer are effectively one and the same. It is setting aside intentional time to quiet our hearts, remove as much as we can in the way of noise pollution and distraction, and allow God to speak over us and to call to mind His past faithfulness, the truths of the Bible, and Scriptures we have memorized. It is to create space for the Spirit to speak to us in the silence, not the striving to achieve a higher cognitive plane as with TM.

Pondering on Scripture, in particular, refers to "weighing in the mind."[236] When we meditate or memorize Scripture, we are giving weight or importance to it in our life, thereby enabling the Spirit to allow those words to transform us. An American idiom would be to "chew on it." We cannot remember or ponder by accident. Remembering and pondering and preaching God's truth to ourselves are intentional actions undertaken during the act of meditation.

In Deuteronomy 6:5–9, we see a picture of the practice of biblical meditation. The passage describes the wholistic scope of meditation in this way:

> Love the LORD your God with all your heart and with all your soul and with all your strength. These commandments that I give you today are to be on your hearts. Impress them on your children. Talk about them when you sit at home and when you walk along the road, when you lie down and when you get up. Tie them as symbols on your hands and bind them on your foreheads. Write them on the doorframes of your houses and on your gates. (NIV)

This illustrates the consistent habit that the Israelites had of keeping God's word in their mind, in their hearts, on their lips, in all circumstances and with all people.

The Value of Biblical Meditation

When you feel overwhelmed or exhausted or are experiencing a difficult season in your life, having Scripture memorized is invaluable. One of the passages God brought to mind during my recovery was Matthew 11:28–30. "Come to me, all you who are weary and burdened, and I will give you rest. Take my yoke upon you and learn from me, for I am gentle and humble in heart, and you will find rest for your souls. For my yoke is easy and my burden is light" (NIV). These were some of the verses I memorized as a teen and recalled often because they brought me peace knowing that God is someone I could trust and that I could rest and have peace even in my physical pain and in the longing for the hard part of this season to end.

Writing down two or three verses a week to meditate on was very helpful to focus my thoughts on God rather than on my situation. I noticed that I was less focused on what I was missing and more engaged in growing and trusting God in my current situation. Biblical meditation directs your thoughts from being self-focused to becoming God-focused. It lightens your burdens and makes you more thankful even in hard times. Meditating on Scripture helps you stand on the promises of God and trust Him in hard times.

It Renews the Mind and Heart

Meditating on the Bible renews and restores our mind and heart from the junk food that we consume in our gluttonous culture, which tells us, "More is better" and "Do whatever you feel is right." The idea is that the renewing of the mind, described in Romans 12:1–2, would be reflected in our thoughts and actions, our worship of God together, and our fellowship and service in the church and community. The point is established throughout Romans that the sinful human nature distorts the truth and shapes a self-absorbed worldview; therefore all people are in need of a reframing and reorientation of the mind and heart by the Holy Spirit. We are all in need of spiritual food from God, which Alan Noble speaks of in his book *Disruptive Witness*. He compares our mind amid distraction and information overload to a stomach gorged on gluttonous indulgence with food. The body needs time to digest food. There are even scores of people who lose tons of weight through "intermittent fasting" (i.e., allowing the body to fully digest what is taken in). People who fast intermittently often find that their glucose levels regulate, they have increased energy, and they lose weight—all because they allow their digestive system to fully do what it was made to do. Our minds are seldom actually allowed to rest and "digest" the huge amount of information we receive. The acts of praying, reading the Bible, and meditating on Scripture center our attention on God, remove the distractions of the world, and welcome the Spirit to renew our minds through the living and powerful Word of God (Heb. 4:12).

Meditating on Scripture is like talking to oneself and reasoning with your heart and mind to dismantle fear and doubt and reclaim the mantles of faith and trust in your heart. Remember that "our struggle is not against flesh and blood, but against the rulers, against the authorities, against the powers of this dark world and against the spiritual forces of evil in the heavenly realms" (Eph. 6:12 NIV). Recently, while editing this book, I had a biopsy for a mass in my right parotid, a salivary gland in front of the ears. A few days before the biopsy, I reached out to my inner circle of prayer warriors. One of the verses that my friend prayed over me stuck in my heart. (Remember the Lionel Richie song "Stuck on You," where he talks about how he has got a feeling that he just can't lose and is finally coming home to stay?) Just like love binds us to one another, a Scripture verse can capture our hearts in the same way and bind us to the Lover of our souls, God, who loves and knows us better than anyone.

Having suffered with pain in my head and neck for almost five years now (though so much better than it was at first), I get weary sometimes from the fight for my health as I work hard to get well and wonder if this chapter in my life will come to an end. Now that I have a mass that can be serious, I need more encouragement. I need to trust and not be afraid, and I need to remember this: "And the God of all grace, who called you to his eternal glory in Christ, after you have suffered a little while, will himself restore you and make you strong, firm and steadfast" (1 Pet. 5:10 NIV). Though five years seem like a long time, this verse comforts me that God says that restoration is coming after a while. In some way, I believe, God will use this suffering to make me even stronger. First Peter 5:10 echoes in my ears every day as I sing this to my heart. I pray this verse over my heart, fix it in my memory bank, and recall it every day in my prayers. This verse renews my heart with strength like oxygen filling my lungs, and I breathe in peace. Each day that I recall it I am making another deposit. Then other moments in the day, I draw out this strength, especially as I wait to hear the medical reports and the next steps. Depositing the Word of God builds up my savings so that during hard times, I can draw from the reserve.

It Expels Darkness and Illuminates

Meditating on the Bible expels sin or darkness in our hearts as the Holy Spirit brings to light our sin so that we might confess it. Through confession and then repentance, we experience freedom. Meditation calms the distracting noises of the world, and the truths of the Bible applied to your life will clean the noisy pollution that has infiltrated your heart and mind. Our adversary majors in several things: noise, hurriedness, and anger. Richard

Foster cites Carl Jung as saying, "Hurry is not *of* the Devil; it *is* the Devil."[237] He says that biblical meditation involves listening to God's Word, reflecting on God's works, rehearsing God's deeds, and ruminating on God's law.[238] Meditation creates the landscape where we can slow down and seek God before reacting to a situation. Changed behavior is a result of our encounter with the living God through meditation. When illumination from God's Word expels, we can better hear God's voice and obey His Word.

Everywhere we look, most people are plugged into their devices. This constant connectivity is training people to hear much but listen less (attentively and wisely). Listening can be one of the most challenging tasks in a noisy culture. Our soundscape burgeons with fine-tuned messaging that is making us more distracted. We are overwhelmed by the constant reel of bite-sized information that has little context and gives us no time to process, which is causing responses that are more reactive than wise. Unfortunately, we are more prone to accept the soundbite menu than to take the time to determine if we are being fed junk, bite-sized morsels full of preservatives. We are hearing but not listening. Our ability to listen has been muffled by all the noise. Listening involves weighing and discerning the truthfulness, looking at the facts, investigating, and thinking through a thoughtful response. Just because someone yells the loudest in our culture or delivers a well-planned message does not mean they are right. Nor does a conflict in point of view or even the facts mean that one party has the right to hate another party or even retaliate. The Bible speaks of wisdom as being "quick to listen, slow to speak" (James 1:19 NIV). Noise ignites reaction whereas meditation breeds wisdom.

Exercising this kind of wisdom that the Bible speaks of has been very challenging at times in my work. Perhaps you can identify with me. A few months into one of my jobs, a coworker on my team started trying to undermine my work and make me look bad.

That biblical principal of being slow to speak was greatly tested when I had to listen to my boss talk with me about this coworker's latest scheme. I had to maintain my composure and listen without becoming defensive. On the inside, I was thinking that this is the most ridiculous thing, and I wanted to go talk to that guy and give him a piece of my mind.

Later that night, I spoke to my mom and stepfather (who have dealt with similar situations and whom I have a lot of respect for in their professional, personal, and spiritual lives). They both reminded me of the verses in Luke 6:27–28: "Love your enemies, do good to those who hate you, bless those who curse you, pray for those who mistreat you" (NIV). I had the choice to allow the anger to fester, affecting my attitude at work, or I could go back to work and show that person kindness.

I think he knew that our boss spoke with me, so he was expecting me to have an edge of unfriendliness. Instead, I treated him with kindness and continued throughout the weeks. It was hard at times to be kind because he was disrupting the big plans and hopes that I had for this job and my future growth opportunities at the company.

It was very hard for me to swallow that even when I defended myself, I could not make the situation better. Over time, I came to understand this person's family life more and understood what might have led him to try to undermine my work. A few days before I left that job, he apologized to me and explained why he did what he did. I told him that I forgave him. I left my job genuinely wishing him the best, a feeling that only could be from God.

Not all situations have ended so well for me nor have your situations either, I bet. It was a gift from God to experience the love of God, which had led him to apologize to me, and which helped me to be kind to him and forgive him. What also made it easier to forgive him was that I know my job as a believer is to extend the same kind of forgiveness that God gives to me, and I also knew that God is in the business of working even bad situations for my good. The Bible is full of biblical life-application teachings like those of Jesus that instruct and form us into His followers. What would it look like if more people followed this biblical principle of doing good to your enemies?

It Transforms How We See God, Ourselves, and the World

Meditation transforms our relationships, how we see ourselves and the world. Through meditation, we invite Jesus into the rooms of our hearts and enjoy conversation with Him. There He makes His home to feast and fellowship with us, and as our good Teacher, the Lord will restore our hearts with righteousness, peace, and joy (Rom. 14:17). He will transform how we engage in the world, not as consumers, but instead as people using our gifts and talents to make a positive impact on the world. Citing Thomas à Kempis, Foster calls meditation's ultimate purpose "friendship with Jesus," adding, "'he walks with me and he talks with me' ceases to be pious jargon and instead becomes a straightforward description of daily life."[239]

Pastor Ken Shigematsu shares the intimate and transformative experience of his own Scripture meditation practices:

> My own practice of meditating on the Word is simple. In the morning, over a bowl of cereal, I put on my headphones, turn on my iPhone, and begin to listen to a selection of Scripture. In the summer I walk up Little Mountain, a hill not far from our home, or go to a nearby beach and listen to the Psalms or a passage in the Gospels. If something speaks to me, I'll pause the Scripture on my iPhone, scroll the text back, and replay it a few times. I will reflect on it and pray over it. Recently, I was listening to

> Psalm 90. It begins with the words: LORD, *you have been our dwelling place throughout all generations* [NIV].
>
> As I hear these words I think about my grandmother, my only living grandparent, who is now ninety-four. She is experiencing memory loss and some of the first signs of dementia, and I am not sure how much longer she will live. I think about how when she dies a whole generation of my family will have passed away. I become conscious of how quickly our lives fly away.
>
> Then I am struck by the words of the psalmist: *Teach us to number our days, that we may gain a heart of wisdom* (v. 12).
>
> I play these words over and over again. They echo through my soul. I grow conscious of how brief our days on earth are, and I start praying for God to give me a heart of wisdom—to not pursue something just because it brings me honor but because it is pleasing to God's heart. Later that morning while swimming laps at the pool, the words *give me a heart of wisdom* come to mind and I offer a brief prayer that God would fill me with his wisdom. As I walk to work, they return to mind yet again. One of the gifts of prayerfully listening to Scripture is that the Word becomes part of who we are; it lodges in the heart and becomes available as food for our journey.[240]

Meditating on Scripture helped Shigematsu to see that pursuing God's wisdom rather than what makes him look good pleases God's heart. The simple practice of listening to Scripture in the morning sets a good example for us. Start your day by listening to a psalm while you eat breakfast. This quick, simple practice will realign your thoughts toward God. Replaying Scripture is important to understand the meaning, and the repetition works it into your thoughts for the day, highlighting it for the day in your memory bank. Like Ken, when I have meditated on a Scripture in the morning, later on that day God, has reminded me of that Scripture. With a constant reel of information each day pulling our attention, it is more important than ever to focus and guard our attention by placing the wisdom in our memory bank every day so that we draw from it throughout the day.

It Helps You Understand the Bible and Its Purposes More

Meditation and prayer carve a channel of grace for you to hear God's voice and to get still so that you can allow the Holy Spirit to reshape your thoughts, direct and guide your life decisions, and give you perspective on how you can be a part of God's purposes in your life. Meditation's capacity to help us understand the Bible more is straightforward but overlooked. It allows us the capacity to savor the unfathomable richness of Scripture when our knee-jerk impulse is to guzzle it down and move on. Our culture drinks through content like a firehose. Just in our first social media scroll in the morning, our brains take in dozens of different headlines, topics, current events, tragedies, celebrations, and more. We have grown accustomed to throwing back content like we're downing a glass of water on our way out the door. Just like handmade chocolate, Scripture, when consumed slowly and savored as long as possible, utterly transforms the experience of the one who engages with it. It allows the human mind to more fully grasp its heights and depths and, therefore, more fully transform the inner woman or man.

During my recovery I have savored verses of Scripture that have sweetened my days with joy as a strength. When achieving undisturbed, sustained sleep throughout the night was challenging because the pain would keep me up or wake me up, I imagined myself in God's hospital. God reminded and encouraged me with this verse: "The Lord will sustain him on his sickbed and restore him from his bed of illness" (Ps. 41:3 NIV 1984). The hospital I imagined was large with lots of patients, and each night, while we were sleeping, God watched over us and attended to all our needs.

This image and verse also helped me to accept where I was, meaning not to be angry about my circumstances or try to act like everything was great and keep up with all the social pressures. I needed to think and act like a patient. That meant that I needed to limit my activities and prioritize sleep, eating, and those things that would nourish me physically, emotionally, and spiritually. I reached out to close friends, family, church prayer-room workers, and other networks to pray for me. Verses of Scripture and biblical principles that I heard through music were like medicine to my soul. Being a patient did not mean that I have license to complain, but I have been given the opportunity to grow. Instead of focusing on my limitations or old life, I focused on what I could do, and I found joy in taking small steps, celebrating progress, praying for others, and in spending meaningful time with God like I used to prioritize.

What sustained my joy was God reordering the affections of my heart. My affections and "sense of the loveliness and beauty of that holiness and grace"[241] had dimmed over the years, as I had not been investing in our relationship as much. My heart was lonely and impatient as I pursued comfort through other means and stoking fires of affections in worldly pursuits. During my recovery, I received something Jonathan Edwards described as a restored greatness of God who desires our highest affections and reordered affections of the heart.[242] Finding my chief joy in God has given me strength to persevere in faith without blaming God and helped me to start and complete this book when I felt weak and not at my best. The joy of the Lord has given me strength (Neh. 8:10) to endure pain and to fight for my recovery, and it has given me hope that God has good purposes for this; He never wastes a hurt.

This joy has caused me to laugh more and enjoy the bumpy climbs and bruises when I would fall on the steep climb of recovery. Just like a child, I would look at the bruises, believe that they would heal, and then continue to get back out and play. Each day I get back up and engage in life knowing that God is my Sustainer, and He will restore me as Psalm 41:3 speaks of. Making God your chief priority will give you joy that will be your strength to face the challenges of life and joy that also initiates laughter and still finds time to play. Meditating and studying the Bible will increase your spiritual savings, so that you can draw from the previously stored truths and resources during the hard times.

Also, meditating on Scripture has helped me understand that suffering is a normal part of the human experience. We have all experienced suffering personally or have been torn apart by watching a loved one suffer physically, endured hardships in family or job situations, or have suffered the loss of a friend, family member, or child. What trips us up is our misunderstanding of suffering, as most of us do not really believe that suffering is a normal part of the Christian life. Just as Christ suffered for you "so that by his wounds you have been healed" (1 Pet. 2:24 NIV), you are also called to follow His example of patience and endurance of suffering (1 Pet. 2:21).

At first it was hard for me to swallow the realization that this season of suffering was more like a marathon than a sprint. "Dear friends, do not be surprised at the painful trial you are suffering, as though something strange were happening to you. But rejoice that you participate in the sufferings of Christ, so that you may be overjoyed when his glory is revealed" (1 Pet. 4:12–13 NIV 1984). This passage encouraged me to know that it was not strange to suffer and that in some way God uses our suffering to display His glory, and through it we can experience joy that cannot be humanly fabricated. Only God can raise joy in and through our sufferings. Our weakness and sufferings display the beauty of the resurrection life—in our weakness and sufferings God reveals His total sufficiency. Our sufferings validate our faith, for just as Christ suffered you will suffer. And since we are God's children and His heirs, then as we share in His sufferings on this earth, we will also share in our future inheritance which is the resurrected life (Rom. 8:17).

Some of you may suffer from an emotional hardship or a physical disability that may or may not result in physical pain. I have heard a few stories of women suffering from a stroke or breast cancer that just melt my heart. One woman experienced a stroke in her late twenties, leaving her with a speech impediment and affecting her hearing. She could very easily be angry at God for allowing her body to be disabled. Instead, she speaks with a deep understanding that everyone suffers in some way, and this is her way of suffering. Listening to her reminded me that contentment, joy, and love for Jesus are possible in hardships and even grow deeper. Another woman felt like part of her was taken away in the removal of her breast, and she struggled to feel beautiful with the reconstructed breasts. It is so hard for a woman to lose her breasts, as they are so tied to femininity. Being thankful that she does not have cancer helped diminish the loss, for thankfulness diffuses anger and pumps love into the heart. A diet of thankfulness produces a healthy heart. Many of you may suffer from an illness or disability that is not visible and may be something that you do not share often. You know how real the struggle is to choose thankfulness instead of anger and resentment. Negative self-talk hinders the healing power of contentment while you are contending for healing and thankfulness.

It Welcomes Peace

Meditation welcomes peace into your heart from the inner and outward noises. In essence, *shalom* refers to wholeness as God intends it to be, inwardly for the individual, interpersonally between human beings, within broader human communities, with creation, and ultimately with Him. It is nothing broken, nothing lacking, all things restored. While meditation alone does not come close to accomplishing *shalom* in creation (only God's redemptive mission through his church accomplishes this), it can do tremendous good toward creating space for the Spirit of God to cultivate that *shalom* in us as the Bible speaks of in Philippians 4:7: "The peace of God, which transcends all understanding" (NIV). Through meditation, we will experience God giving us peace as we give our worries to Him and trust Him in difficult situations. Also, this peace will position us to be a force of *shalom* in the relationships and communities around us.

This summer a friend noticed some bruising on her body, but she chalked it up to helping someone move. Just to be sure, though, before leaving on a trip, she called her doctor to do some blood work. A few hours later, after getting her hair done, she got a call that she needed to drive to the emergency room right away and to drive carefully because her blood levels were dangerously low. She was told that she had a rare form of leukemia. Instead of focusing on herself and on the negative things, she decided to start each day filling her head with good things, positive things, and things that gave her hope. (I can totally relate, as I also made a decision early on to focus on the positive things that I do have rather than what I do not have or what I am missing out on.)

After starting each day with music, my friend focuses on a Bible verse. She made a paper chain, counting each day she was in the hospital. She and her daughter wrote the day and date on one side and the verse for that day on the back. One of her favorites is John 11:4: "But when Jesus heard it, he said, 'this illness does not lead to death. It is for the glory of God, so that the Son of God may be glorified through it'" (ESV). What wonderful news, as this takes the focus off her and leukemia and puts it back on God. She said, "I need to get my eyes off myself and all the things that are currently wrong and turn my eyes upon Jesus, and like the song says, when we 'turn our eyes upon Jesus, the things of this world (sickness, pain, depression) will grow strangely dim in the light of His glory and grace. That is a much better place to be."

Bible Memorization Aids Meditation

Scripture is the starting point for biblical meditation. However, the Bible is a vast and diverse collection of writings. Some passages reveal the character of God more directly than others. So it is helpful to identify some passages of Scripture that particularly speak to you about the nature of God and use them in meditation. You could create a simple list or even underline meaningful passages in a Bible. Yet perhaps the best technique for assembling a variety of Bible passages on which to meditate is to memorize them. Bible memorization is an invaluable aid to biblical meditation.

Scripture memorization has been prioritized by great Christian writers and theologians throughout the centuries as a way to help people grow spiritually and to engage in spiritual warfare as Jesus did. Martin Luther was self-described as having nearly all of Scripture memorized: "I had then already read and taught the sacred Scriptures most diligently privately and publicly for seven years, so that I knew them nearly all by memory."[243] While not able to uncover the way of Luther's *own* Scripture memorization habits, there is much to be said about his professional contribution to the Scripture memorization of others. His German translation of the Bible made several noteworthy contributions that we Protestants tend to take for granted today. Luther aimed for a text that provided readability while not sacrificing reliability of translation. Luther also grouped the apocryphal texts at the end of the Old Testament instead of interspersing them with the canonical books, helping readers better distinguish between canonical and apocryphal.

Fanny Crosby is alleged to have memorized five chapters of the Bible each week, beginning at age ten, with the help of both her grandmother and a landlady. Because Fanny was blind and could not learn the way other children did, Fanny's grandmother helped her see in her mind's eye through describing the world and reading to her. Mrs. Hawley, a landlady, helped Fanny memorize chapters of the Bible. She memorized the Pentateuch, the Gospels, Proverbs, the Song of Solomon, and many psalms. Not focusing on her limitations and building on her strengths taught Fanny that her blindness aided her in developing her power of memorization and concentration.

Jesus quoted from memory when he was tempted in the desert by the devil. He said, "It is written: 'Man shall not live on bread alone, but on every word that comes from the mouth of God" (Matt. 4:4 NIV, from Deut. 8:3). The devil had hurled words at Him to tempt Him to doubt His Sonship and the goodness of God's plans, and he tempted Jesus to use His supernatural powers to satisfy His needs, apart from God and averting God's plans. But Jesus quoted another passage from Deuteronomy: "Do not put the LORD your God to the test" (6:16; Matt. 4:7).

Remember that the verses in the Bible can function like a sword to use when fighting your flesh or the devil (Eph. 6:16–17). So the more that you meditate and memorize it, the more that you will be able to fight, with the Word as your weapon: "All Scripture is God-breathed and is useful for teaching, rebuking, correcting and training in righteousness" (2 Tim. 3:16 NIV). Memorizing Scripture cultivates wisdom and plants God's truth in the soil of our minds and hearts, producing a renewed mind and heart. At a leadership training, a Christian lady who had formerly been imprisoned for her faith handed her Bible to another participant because there were not enough Bibles to go around and she knew the chapter from memory. Many persecuted Christians memorize sections and pages of the Bible because they never know when it might be taken from them. What you memorize cannot be taken away by outside persecution, so strengthen your faith by hiding the Word in your heart (Ps. 119:11).

Memorizing Scripture, to me, is like lifting weights—the more you do it, the stronger you become. I mentioned this throughout the previous chapters, but I cannot repeat it enough: I have placed a high priority on recalling Scripture and on God reminding me of Scripture during my recovery. When you go through difficult times like I have, God will remind you of verses like Matt. 11:28–30 that will give you wisdom, endurance, and help you to find rest in Him when your life is in chaos, or you feel like you are falling apart. You don't have to have it all figured out, and you can give up the illusion that you are in control of your destiny. You will never find that soul rest until you make Jesus the Lord of your life.

Stop believing the lie that you do not have enough time to memorize Scripture or that you are not good at it. Most people are not good at memorization. Start by choosing two or three verses from the Bible to memorize this month that will help you with your current situation so that you will have resources to draw from and savings in the bank when hard times come, and then you will experience soul rest.

Ways to Experience Scripture throughout Your Day

1. Take silent walks in nature; bring one of your Scripture memory cards.
2. Listen to Scripture.
3. Read Scripture slowly aloud (ex. Lectio Divina).

4. Sing songs, versess, psalms, or worship songs; this can also be a great way to memorize Scripture.
5. Write Scripture memory cards or create a Scripture memory journal with pages dedicated to particular topics.
6. Pray Scripture from the Bible or from your Scripture memory journal.
7. Revisit a few Scriptures that you are trying to memorize for the week twice a day.
8. Memorize Scripture with your family, a friend, or small group.

Seven Pathways Scripture Memorization Method

Living in the information age, we seldom need to memorize anything. Phone numbers, email addresses, driving directions, important dates—all of this information and much more is at our fingertips constantly by means of a cell phone, tablet, or computer. That means memorization does not come easily or naturally to most people.

Memorizing anything is really just a matter of purposeful repetition. When you repeat—or remind yourself of—something frequently enough, your brain will store that information for easy recall. All you need is a simple practice or formula for placing that information into your mind. Here is the method I have developed for Bible memorization. It's quite simple, and it works. Try it, and you'll see how easy it can be to put God's Word into your heart.

1. *Silence*: After a period of silence, ask God to help you understand, digest, learn, and apply this Scripture or passage.
2. *Read* the Scripture or passage that you desire to memorize out loud a few times.

3. *Meditate*: Focus your thoughts; ponder, think, and reflect on the Scripture.
4. *Create* a Scripture memory system. Write Scripture down on a note card or in a Scripture memory journal.
5. *Meditate* on a Scripture and what it means for you.
6. *Rehearse*: Go over in your mind or speak aloud a Scripture verse or passage. Memorize it in phrases or sentences. Once you can recite the phrase or sentence from memory several times, then add an additional phrase until you have memorized the verse, group of verses, or chapter. Then mark it completed and follow the same steps to memorize another verse.
7. *Pray* that God will apply what you have meditated on to your life and will give you discipline to follow His leading.
8. *Application*: Think of ways to apply the verse or passage and look for ways to apply it to your daily life.
9. *Review*: Incorporate this verse in your prayers, and/or ask a friend to memorize it with you, and check on each other once a week for accountability and to share your verses.
10. *Revisit* this process two to three times over a few days until you have the Scripture or passage memorized. (Note: I would recommend trying to memorize one to three verses a week to start.)

Scripture Memory Card System Tips

1. If you have a card system, mark the card completed, write the completion date on it, and put it in a "completed" file.
2. Every month, leave the last couple of days available to review the verses that you have memorized that month.

Meditation App

Check out *sevenpathways.com* for our biblical meditation resources. We offer biblical meditations on a variety of topics, such as anger, anxiety, loneliness, joy, forgiveness, and more, in your choice of four different voices along with beautiful, original art as your meditation backdrop.

How to Meditate on Scripture

1. Find a quiet place.
2. Pick a verse or group of verses that you want to understand more deeply.
3. Focus
   a. Read the verse or verses in the context of the entire chapter to gain clarity of its meaning.
   b. Read the verse or verses in a different translation.
3. Dig: If you have a study Bible, read any notes about that verse or verses, and then
   a. Ask God to help you understand, memorize, and apply it to your life.
   b. Read it aloud.
   c. Quietly focus on and pay attention to each word.
4. Personalize: Ask yourself, What does this verse or verses mean to me?
5. Practice
   a. Write down the verse on a note card, journal, or your phone.
   b. Review it at lunch, while exercising, during a work break, or between carpooling your children.
   c. Review it before you go to bed, when you wake up, when you are in the shower, or while you are getting ready in the morning.

d. Pray and look for ways to apply the verse.
e. Share it with someone.

Two Examples of Meditations

Biblical meditation, like each of the Seven Pathways, allows a great deal of room for individual expression. Your practice of this pathway may look different from mine, though they will have some common elements. To aid you in developing your own practice, here are two examples of meditative practices from our Seven Pathways meditations library, which can be found on our website at www.sevenpathways.com. There, you will find more topical meditations to meet your needs. I invite you to join us and try them for yourself. Remember that you don't have to perfectly reproduce them in order to enter into meditation. Think of them simply as a helpful guide to get you started.

Anxiety Meditation

When I feel anxious, my thoughts can feel like they are running a race or like they are on replay in my mind. Although I hope to gain more control of those thoughts with each replay, unfortunately, the replay fuels those anxious thoughts and leaves me feeling emotionally exhausted.

First, let's slow down our thoughts. Sit in a comfortable place and close your eyes; breathe in and out slowly ten times with your palms open. If you have a blanket close by, drape it over your shoulders, covering your body. If you don't have a blanket, imagine a soft blanket draped over you. Imagine the soft touch of the blanket against your skin slowing and calming your anxious thoughts.

The Bible speaks of the Lord covering us with His love. Psalm 91 uses the image of God's arms being like the wings of a bird covering us with His feathers. Just as a bird loves on her babies by covering them with her wings, God covers His children with love. Anytime your thoughts start running away, think of calming them by covering them with God's love. As they are covered with His love, those thoughts are brought home.

Here are some exercises to invite God to calm down your thoughts and allow Him to cover them.

- Reaching your arms forward, imagine your hands covering those thoughts, as you clasp your hands together with one hand in a fist and the other hand around it.
- Open your hands with palms up as you release these anxious thoughts to God, and ask God to slow down your thoughts.
- With your palms up, imagine God's hands covering or clasping your hands. Your thoughts are now covered and in God's hands. This means that your thoughts are safe and have entered the Lord's care. He can help you process them. Even if you have done or said something bad, or someone has said something bad about you, God can bring those thoughts safely home to Himself so that they stop replaying in your mind.

No matter how far those thoughts have run away, God always welcomes them home. You can return to these exercises to calm down your anxious thoughts anytime. Your thoughts can find a resting place covered by His love.

Forgiveness Meditation

Often we feel lonely as adults because of the loneliness we may have felt as a child. In order to experience more freedom from loneliness, allow yourself to remember a situation or person who made you feel alone. Our feelings of loneliness can become a voice in our head that says, *You are not enough; you are not worthy of love; your real self is not acceptable.* Forgiveness can set you free from the weight of loneliness and the bondage of unforgiveness.

Stand or find a comfortable chair and feel the floor beneath your feet. If you are a Christian, then, you are grounded in His love (Eph. 3:17). Rest in the strength you have in Him.

Now, we will practice some movements to remind us that we are grounded in His love, and because of this, forgiveness can grow even in muddy waters.

- Looking to the left, imagine the person standing on the left that you need to forgive.
- Look to the right and imagine Jesus on the cross. Now, shift your gaze to the man on the other cross asking Jesus to forgive his sins. Then return your focus to Jesus; His bleeding side, His nail-pierced hands, and His crown of thorns. He suffered the most brutal death so that all people can experience the gift of forgiveness.
- Let this image sink in as you take ten deep breaths and remember that your breath always connects you to God. To experience forgiveness, we must receive it.

Do these movements with me as we practice some more:

- Look to the right where you imagined the cross.
- Take three steps toward the cross.
- Open your arms and extended them to your side and think of what He did for you on the cross.
- Express thanksgiving to God and rest in this forgiveness through one minute spent in silence.
- With the view of the cross on your right, turn to the left, toward the person you need to forgive. Extend your arms high to ask the Lord to help you to forgive.

- Then extend your upper body with an outstretched hand to the left. Speak these words: "Forgive as the Lord forgave you" (Col. 3:13 NIV).
- As you offer forgiveness, imagine that power of forgiveness. His light evaporates the looming clouds of loneliness over your heart.
- Read this verse: "Be kind and compassionate to one another, forgiving each other, just as in Christ God forgave you" (Eph. 4:32). Now, rest here meditating on this verse.

Take a short pause, maybe for ten seconds or so, and then silently read—and receive—this verse: "And when you stand praying, if you hold anything against anyone, forgive them, so that your Father in heaven may forgive you your sins" (Mark 11:25 NIV). Rest here and meditate on this instruction on forgiveness for another minute.

May the muddiness of forgiveness not discourage you or make you feel hopeless. Like the lotus flower blooming in muddy waters, forgiveness blooms even when conditions seem impossible. So let's close with this final movement. We call this the blooming flower pose. Lift your hands to the sky and slowly lower your arms to your side like a flower opens its bud. Open yourself to forgiveness this week.

CONCLUSION

Walking the Pathways

The whole history of Christianity has unfolded by one person who has found a relationship with God and then helped another person find a relationship with God. Think of Jesus' core band, his twelve disciples, who shared with others, with those close to home and also throughout their travels. And then, traversing across the centuries, the voices of many have shared the message of good news. I am now that one helping you find a relationship with God or deepen your relationship with Him. I am just like you, a traveler on the journey to my heavenly home. I may not have traveled the same road as you or had the same difficulties, but I have had difficulties and setbacks in my journey too. I found my way back to a deeper relationship with God through brokenness, pain, and exhaustion, so if I can find my way home in a fog when I could see no clear path, you can too.

Seven Pathways restored a peaceful margin in my days, and now I feel more clearheaded despite still struggling with head pain. I have improved focus and recall and am back in stride with a closer relationship with God. Seven Pathways has been like a spiritual recovery and growth plan for me. I feel like I have my mind back, which had grown foggy from the clutter of our noisy consumer soundscape. Starting my day with thankfulness has brought me joy in spades and is the best medicine for disappointment and helping me persevere through trials. Through practicing thankfulness to God, He has shifted my mindset to start my day with focusing on God's goodness, the blessings in my life, and all the resources that I have as a follower of Jesus such as the presence of God and the Holy Spirit living inside of me.

I think that a lot of people, regardless of how much money they have, walk around consistently dissatisfied with life because there are always people who have more and miss the gift of contentment and appreciation for what they already have. Thanksgiving melts away the attractive lures of consumerism and refocuses our vision on how we can steward our resources rather than acquiring more things. Regularly practicing gratitude as a daily habit has helped discipline me and curb some of my indulgences. It has also given me opportunities to meet the needs of others through my resources—giving away not things that were simply unwanted or unused, but giving of my prized resource.

Silence and confession refuel and cleanse my heart through teaching me to slow down, confess and repent of my sins, and listen to God. And listening to songs that speak the cries of my heart when words are lacking reminds me of God's presence, which is here with me in all circumstances, giving me joy and hope. I tell many that I have sung and prayed my way back to a healthier heart. Prayer has been a lifeline for me to the One who can meet my deepest needs and reorder my priorities. Praying for others has helped me not focus as much on my situation, and it has given me purpose and joy in helping release God's power into the lives of others. Praying Scripture, studying Scripture, and meditating on Scripture has equipped me to handle difficult situations, given me peace and hope, and reminded me of the power and purpose of God's Word to transform me, others, and the people of the world with love.

Seven Pathways will help give you a peaceful margin in your day so that you can get your mind and heart back on God's rhythm and off the chaotic beat of the world. The attractive lure of consumerism leaves you consistently thirsty because it dries out the ground of your heart by never delivering the satisfaction that it promises. Seven Pathways will help the waters of contentment start pumping in your heart and avert your focus from the "shiny" toys to the good things that you already have and to the things that matter most, such as your relationships—with God, His purposes, family and friends, love, and health. The discipline and daily habits designed in our Seven Pathways plan will remove the struggle of trying to figure out how to get close to God by helping you engage in seven spiritual pathways or practices found in Scripture and that have been practiced throughout church history, many even demonstrated by Jesus.

Our Seven Pathways plan represents the right turn toward freedom from guilt and shame, which is only found through a relationship with Jesus. Seven Pathways is one complete and simple plan that walks you back in stride with God's voice, shepherding you to live and thrive from a place of purpose—*His* purpose, bringing life, healing, and peace to your heart and mind.

I know that the Seven Pathways might seem like a lot, so that is why we have created the experience on our website where you can progress at your own pace. Our culture has been training us over the years in the fast and instant, but we all know that good results—whether it be in work or in relationships—require time and investment. So our solution for those who struggle with time is to allow you to build at your own pace. Perhaps you might want to work on only two or three pathways every day for a few weeks, and only then move to four pathways a week for a period of time. And you can keep building until you are engaging in all seven per week.

Imagine how your day could be different if you started your day with five things that you were thankful for, and imagine the feeling of freedom from guilt and shame as you practice confession frequently and get your relationship with God back on track. Imagine how your relationships would be different if you prayed for others and heard the voice of God and His loving, shepherding direction in your life to help guide your life decisions. What if we all started individually, and then gathered in small groups weekly to share and learn together from our Seven Pathways that week? What if we did that for six weeks straight?

Think of how grateful individuals, homes, and churches could transform their communities. What could God do in our lives, churches, homes, and communities if we disciplined ourselves to study and focus on Scripture and allow God's spirit to apply it to our lives?

I invite you today to get back in stride with God by going to www.sevenpathways.com to get started on your Seven Pathways journey through the book of John. Restore peaceful margin in your day and discover more freedom and lasting peace in your life.

Acknowledgments

I thank the Lord for the gift of *Seven Pathways*, which began in 2005 when I felt a need to connect with God through these spiritual practices and to my church, who supported my vision and work by allowing me to teach a class. I had no idea that fifteen years later, God would build out my seven pathways method and use these powerful practices during a very difficult time in my life to help me chart my way back to improved health, give me strength and endurance during a marathon recovery, and deepen my relationship with Him.

Many thanks to Jonathan Merkh the president of Forefront Books for catching the vision of this book and believing in this first-time author. Thank you to the editorial director of Forefront Books, Jennifer Gingerich, whose thoughtful professionalism made the process a joy and who came alongside me to help grow and birth the book through health challenges, diagnosis of a tumor, and surgery. Thank you to Lauren Ward for helping to create a stellar author experience and Landon Dickerson for your work in the editorial process. To the many others at Forefront from designers to editors, we cannot do it without all of you and the extended family of our distributor, Simon & Schuster. Also, to Lawrence W. Wilson my developmental editor, thank you for the encouragement and pushing me more in my writing. This book is a better book because of your insights, Larry, and I can't thank you enough. Thank you Jill M. Smith my copyeditor for your work improving the readability of this work.

I am grateful for the hard work of Emersoft LLC and their talented team led by Marcin Ruman and Pawel Marcniuk and many others to develop the Seven Pathways website. A big thank you to Marcin and Pawel for their leadership skills and client care to make adjustments during my health challenges.

Much gratitude to Brad Ayres of Anthem Republic for your time and talent to provide marketing insights and help with our business strategy and willingness to jump on a call. To the stellar team at Anthem Republic including, Brad Ayres, Jennifer Ayres, Eric Pavol, Hunter Vroman, and many others I am so grateful for your work to establish our communications strategy and social media creation and management. I am thrilled with our direction and believe that your work will help fuel the growth of Seven Pathways.

Many thanks to my talented creative director, Marcus Meazzo of Meazzo Brand Co., who has helped build the Seven Pathways brand from its foundation. I am so thankful for his gifted visual talent and expertise that he continues to pour into Seven Pathways. He is an exceptionally gifted brand developer and a terrific human and trusted friend.

Thank you to my longtime friend, Glenn Lucke and his team at Docent Content Group including James Gordon and

Todd Korpi for the help with specific research for this book. Harper Reed, thank you for helping with the content for some of the meditations especially during my recovery from surgery. My college friend, Jenny Ackerman, thank you for sharing your artistic talent in painting canvases for Seven Pathways.

Colossal thanks to my mom Sandra Hutts who has been a rock in my life. You modeled prayer and listening to the voice of God. In my teens after discussing a question that I had or trying to help me with a problem, you would say, "let's ask God." Though teaching me to pray, I learned that God loves me, speaks to me, and is involved in my life and the world. You have always been willing to let me bounce ideas off you, believed and supported me and Seven Pathways, and used your detailed accounting eye to be my first editor.

And to my nephew, Simon Englert, thank you for being my first scribe to act as my eyes when I had such pain around them that made it hard for me to write before passing off the mantle to Joe when you went back to school. Thank you to my dad for loving me and modeling perseverance. A huge thank you to my step-father, Joe Hutts who transcribed *Seven Pathways* during the early stages of my recovery and has loved me and modeled servant leadership. I so enjoyed the time we spent discussing and wrestling through the chapters of John.

Grateful to all my seminary professors, teachers, mentors, and role models who taught me the ways of Christ, God's Word, loved me, and believed in me. Thank you to Louie Giglio who gave me a vision of God's glory, beauty, and greatness and taught me to worship from the heart at a weekly gathering of students during my years in college at Baylor University. I can still go back to those days like they were yesterday, for they were pivotal in my spiritual life. Thankful for all the years of worshiping at Redeemer Presbyterian Church while living in New York City, the tremendous community of believers, and the wisdom of Tim Keller's teaching who taught me much about communicating the teachings of the Bible in a relevant and meaningful way with historical, theological, and Biblical accuracy and acumen.

Thank you for the prayers of my family, friends, church prayer room, voice over team—David Marell and Janette and Geoff Kragen—and many more prayer warriors and a global prayer network.

Huge thanks to my prayer warrior and close friend, Sheeba Philip who has faithfully lifted me up in prayer and prayed God's Word over me and my circumstances. I have learned so much from you about fighting my battles with God's Word and how to hear God's voice.

And thank you to Dr. James Netterville and the team at Vanderbilt University Medical Center for discovering the cause to my pain for many years, a malignant tumor – acinic cell cancer and for excellent care.

Lastly, I thank my readers for taking the time to read and engage in these seven spiritual pathways, and I pray that you grow closer to God through them and that His love captures your heart and transforms your life.

Notes

1 Gratus animus est una virtus non solum m axima, sed etiam mater virtutum omnium reliquarum, Cicero, Oratio Pro Cnæo Plancio, XXXIII.

2 Emmons Robert A., and Teresa T Kneezel, "Giving Gratitude: Spiritual and Religious Correlates of Gratitude." *Journal of Psychology and Christianity* 24, no. 2 (2005): 140-48.

3 "Thank | Etymology, Origin and Meaning of Thank by Etymonline." https://www.etymonline.com/word/thank.

4 Blue Letter Bible. "H8426 - Tôḏâ - Strong's Hebrew Lexicon (NIV https://www.blueletterbible.org/lexicon/h8426/kjv/wlc/0-1/

5 Blue Letter Bible. "H3034 - Yāḏâ - Strong's Hebrew Lexicon (NIV)." https://www.blueletterbible.org/lexicon/h3034/kjv/wlc/0-1/

6 Mounce, Bill. "Εὐχαριστέω | Billmounce.Com." https://www.billmounce.com/greek-dictionary/eucharisteo.

7 Tello Monique, "A Positive Mindset Can Help Your Heart," Harvard Health Publishing, March 6, 2019, https://www.health.harvard.edu/blog/a-positive-mindset-can-help-your-heart-2019021415999.

8 Jackowka, M., Brown, J., Ronaldson, A., Steptoe, A, (2016), "The impact of a brief gratitude intervention on subjective well-being, biology and sleep." *Journal of Health Psychology*, 21: 2207-2217.

9 Emmons, R. A., & McCullough, M. E. (2003), "Counting blessings versus burdens: An experimental investigation of gratitude and subjective well-being in daily life." *Journal of Personality and Social Psychology*, 84: 377-389.

10 Algoe, S. B., Fredrickson, B. L., & Gable, S. L. (2013). "The social functions of the emotions of gratitude via expression." *Emotion*, 13: 605-609.

11 DeSteno, D., Li, Y., Dickens, L., & Lerner, J.S. (2014) "Gratitude: A tool for reducing economic impatience." *Psychological Science*, 25: 1262-1267.

12 Jayson Georges. *Ministering in Patronage Cultures: Biblical Models and Missional Implications* (Downers Grove: IVP Academic), 88-89.

13 Stephen Witmer, "Gratitude: An Intellectual History," by Peter J. Leithart, *Themelios*, Volume

40, Issue 2. https://www.thegospelcoalition.org/themelios/review/gratitude-an-intellectual-history/

14 E. Randolph Richards and Brandon J O'Brien, *Misreading Scripture with Western Eyes: Removing Cultural Blinders to Better Understand the Bible* (Westmont: InterVarsity Press, 2012), 82-84.

15 Bullock, C. Hassell, *Encountering the Book of Psalms: A Literary and Theological Introduction* (Grand Rapids, MI: Baker Academic, 2005), 162.

16 Kruse, Elliott, Joseph Chancelor, Peter M. Ruberton, and Sonja Lyubomirsky, "An Upward Spiral Between Gratitude and Humility." *Social Psychological and Personality Science* 1, no. 10 (2014), 2. https://doi.org/10.1177/1948550614534700.

17 Terence Eagleton, *Shakespeare and Society: Critical Studies in Elizabethan Drama* (New York: Schocken, 1967), 99-104.

18 Or je tiens, qu'il faut vivre par droict, et par auctorité, non par recompense ny par grâce.

19 Thomas Hobbes, *Leviathan*, Edited by Richard Tuck. Cambridge: Cambridge University Press, 1991. chap.14.

20 David Boonin-Vail, *Thomas Hobbes and the Science of Moral Virtue* (Cambridge: Cambridge University Press, 1994), 185.

21 Helen Thorton, *State of Nature or Eden? Thomas Hobbes and His Contemporaries on the Natural Condition of Human Beings* (Rochester, N.Y., Boydell & Brewer, 2005)

22 John Locke, *First Tract on Government, in Locke: Political Essays*, ed. Mark Goldie (Cambridge Texts in the History of Political Thought; Cambridge: Cambridge University Press, 2006), 7

23 René Descartes, *Passion of the Soul*, 64. www.earlymoderntexts.com/pdf/descpass.pdf. All citations refer to paragraph numbers in Descartes' treatise.

24 Descartes, 153.

25 Jean-Jacque Rosseau, *A Discourse upon the Origin and the Foundation of Inequality among Mankind*. Translated by Charles Elliot. Whitefish, Mont: Kessington, 2004, 35.

26 Rosseau, Discourses, 218.

27 Eugene H. Peterson, *A Long Obedience in the Same Direction Discipleship in an Instant Society*. Commemorative edition. Downers Grove: InterVarsity Press 2019): 185.

28 Peterson, 185–86.

29 C. H. Spurgeon, *The Metropolitan Tabernacle Pulpit Sermons*, 63 vols. (London: Passmore & Alabaster, 1855–1917),* vol. 36, 315, 320, as quoted in https://www.crossway.org/articles/did-you-know-that-charles-spurgeon-struggled-with-depression/.

30 https://www.christianitytoday.com/ct/2021/february-web-only/diana-gruver-companions-darkness-spurgeon-depression.html

31 https://www.christianitytoday.com/ct/2021/february-web-only/diana-gruver-companions-darkness-spurgeon-depression.html

32 Jeffrey J. Meyers, *The Lord's Service: The Grace of Covenant Renewal Worship*. (Moscow, ID: Canon Press, 2003) 87.

33 Crossway Bibles, ed. ESV: Study Bible. (Wheaton, Il: Crossway Bibles, 2008): 344.

34 Crossway Bibles, 345.

35 Eugene H. Peterson, *A Long Obedience in the Same Direction: Discipleship in an Instant Society*. Commemorative edition. (Downers Grove: InterVarsity Press, 2019): 192.

36 Marcel Proust, *Pleasures and Regrets*. Translated by Louise Varèse. (London, UK: Peter Owen, 2000), 136.

37 https://www.blueletterbible.org/lexicon/h3034/kjv/wlc/0-2/#lexResults Strong's H3034

38 https://www.health.harvard.edu/blog/hold-optimism-reap-health-benefits-2017012011003

39 Brennan Manning, *Abba's Child: The Cry of the Heart for Intimate Belonging*, 2015. https://search.ebscohost.com/login.aspx?direct=true&scope=site&db=nlebk&db=nlabk&AN=899227.

40 Kenneth Leech, *True Prayer: An Invitation to Christian Spirituality*. (Harrisburg, PA: Morehouse Pub, 1995), 58.

41 David Owen, "Is Noise Pollution the Next Big Public-Health Crisis?" *The New Yorker*, May 6, 2019. https://bit.ly/3H32jMb.

42 Owen, Ibid.
43 https://www.cardiosmart.org/news/2015/7/traffic-noise-increases-risk-of-stroke-and-death-especially-among-the-elderly
44 Owen, Ibid.
45 Daniel A. Gross, "This Is Your Brain on Silence." *Nautilus*, July 31, 2014. https://bit.ly/3nYR8wg.
46 https://www.mayoclinic.org/healthy-lifestyle/stress-management/in-depth/stress/art-20046037
47 Erling Kagge, *Silence: In the Age of Noise*. (New York, NY: Penguin Books, 2018), 65.
48 Gross, "This Is Your Brain on Silence."
49 Charles Stone, "8 Benefits of Silence and Solitude." OutreachMagazine.Com (blog), July 26, 2018.
50 Richard Foster, *Celebration of Discipline: The Path to Spiritual Growth*. 20th anniversary ed., 3rd ed., rev. Ed. (San Francisco: Harper San Francisco, 1998), 98.
51 Nouwen, *Reaching Out: The Three Movements of the Spiritual Life*. (Garden City, NY: Doubleday, 1975), 13.
52 Nouwen, 15.
53 Dietrich Bonhoeffer and David McI Gracie, *Meditating on the Word*. 2nd ed. (Cambridge, Mass: Cowley Publications, 2000), 50.
54 Nouwen, 18.
55 Nouwen, 25.
56 Yelena Moroz Alpert,"Shh...How a Little Silence Can Go a Long Way For Kids' Mental Health." *National Geographic* (blog), September 10, 2021. https://on.natgeo.com/3KHunqq.
57 Atalanta Beaumont, "10 Reasons Why Silence Really Is Golden," April 21, 2017. https://www.psychologytoday.com/us/blog/handy-hints-humans/201704/10-reasons-why-silence-really-is-golden.
58 Timothy D. Wilson, David A. Reinhard, Erin C. Westgate, Daniel T. Gilbert, Nicole Ellerbeck, Cheryl Hahn, Casey L. Brown, and Adi Shaked, "Just Think: The Challenges of the Disengaged Mind." *Science* 345, no. 6192 (July 4, 2014): 75–77. https://doi.org/10.1126/science.1250830.
59 Lennox Morrison, "The Subtle Power of Uncomfortable Silences" BBC. WorkLife (blog), July 18, 2017. https://www.bbc.com/worklife/article/20170718-the-subtle-power-of-uncomfortable-silences.
60 From *Strong's Concordance* #H7503.
61 Robert Larid Harris, Leason Leonard Archer, and Bruce K. Waltke, *Theological Workbook of the Old Testament* (Chicago: Moody, 1980), 2198.
62 Elad N. Sherf, Michael R. Parke, and Sofya Isaakyan. "Distinguishing Voice and Silence at Work: Unique Relationships with Perceived Impact, Psychological Safety, and Burnout," *Academy of Management Journal* 64, no. 1 (February 18, 2021), https://doi.org/10.5465/amj.2018.1428.
63 Rodney Clapp, "The Theology of Consumption and the Consumption of Theology," in *The Consuming Passion: Christianity and Consumer Culture*, ed. Rodney Clapp (Downers Grove: InterVarstiy, 1998), 188.
64 Augustine of Hippo, Saint, 354-430. *The Confessions of Saint Augustine*. Mount Vernon: Peter Pauper Press, 1940, 1949.
65 Oliver Davies and Denys Turner, *Silence and the Word: Negative Theology and Incarnation* (Cambridge, UK: Cambridge University Press), 2002.
66 Ron Mehl, "What God Whispers in the Night," in *So You Want to Be Like Christ?* by Charles R. Swindoll (Nashville, TN: Thomas Nelson, 2005), 61.
67 Thomas Merton, *Inner Experience* (San Francisco: Harper, 2003), 16.
68 Thomas Merton, *New Seeds of Contemplation* (New York: New Directions, 1949), 33.
69 https://health.clevelandclinic.org/5-great-reasons-you-should-take-a-walk-today/

70 ttps://www.advancedneurotherapy.com/blog/2015/09/10/walking-outside-brai.

71 Henri J. M. Nouwen, *The Return of the Prodigal Son: A Story of Homecoming* (New York: Image, 1995), 3.

72 Nouwen, 8.

73 Nouwen, 10–11.

74 Eugene H. Peterson, *Working the Angles: The Shape of Pastoral Integrity* (Grand Rapids, MI: Eerdmans, 1987), 66.

75 Peterson, 66.

76 Peterson, 67–68.

77 Peterson, 70.

78 Fiona Basile, "What to Expect at an Ignatian Silent Retreat," n.d. https://bit.ly/3sAlCGJ.

79 Mark E. Thibodeaux, SJ, *Reimagining the Ignatian Examen* (Chicago: Loyola Press, 2015), x–xi.

80 Consolation is an experience that causes you to feel fully alive, peaceful, joyful, and close to God.

81 Desolation is an experience that causes you to feel drained, frustrated, irritated, angry, sad, sorrowful, alone, or away from God.

82 Bishop Kallistos Ware, *The Jesus Prayer* (London: The Incorporated Truth Catholic Society, 2014).

83 Some traditions omit "a sinner."

84 Marilynn Larkin, "How Green Is Your Workout?" *The Lancet* 355, no. 9216 (May 13, 2000): 1702.

85 Celu Hamer, "Silent Hiking: Nature As My Guide," n.d. https://www.culturechange.org/NatureMyGuide.htm.

86 Eswaran, Vijay. "Don't Underestimate the Power of Science." *Harvard Business Review*, Health and Behavorial Silence (blog), July 22, 2021, https://bit.ly/3IBo5Ea.

87 Yelena Moroz Alpert, "Shh…How a Little Silence Can Go a Long Way For Kids' Mental Health," *National Geographic* (blog), September 10, 2021, https://on.natgeo.com/3KHunqq.

88 Jonathan Edwards, ed. *The Life and Diary of David Brainard* (Chicago, IL: Moody Publishers)., 34-35.

89 Paul Hiebert, *Transforming Worldviews: An Anthropological Understanding of How People Change* (Grand Rapids, MI: Baker Academic, 2008), 310.

90 E. Randolph Richards and Brandon J O'Brien, *Misreading Scripture with Western Eyes: Removing Cultural Blinders to Better Understand the Bible* (Westmont: InterVarsity Press, 2012), 114–35.

91 Strong's H7725

92 Strong's G3340

93 Hiebert, Transforming Worldviews, 310.

94 From *Strong's Concordance* #3034.

95 Strong's #8426.

96 Hebrew: yadah aon aon ab ma'al (for Lev. 26:40, paraphrased: "If they throw off their iniquity and the iniquity of their forefathers' unfaithfulness to me").

97 https://www.apa.org/news/press/releases/2014/01/truth-guilt

98 For a treatment of these ethical issues, see Richard Foster's *Money, Sex, and Power: The Challenge of the Disciplined Life*.

99 Villacorta, *Tug of War: The Downward Ascent of Power* (Salem, OR: Cascade: 2017), 75.

100 Craig S. Keener, *The IVP Bible Background Commentary: New Testament* (Downers Grove, IL: InterVarsity Press, 1993), 628.

101 From *Strong's Concordance* #3670.

102 Brown, F., Driver, S. R., & Briggs, C. A. (1977), *Enhanced Brown-Driver-Briggs Hebrew and English Lexicon* (Oxford: Clarendon Press), 431.

103 Glenn Packiam. *Blessed Broken Given: How Your Story Becomes Sacred in the Hands of Jesus*. First Edition. (Colorado Springs: Multnomah, 2019), 113–14.

104 Charles Hefling, Charles and Cynthia Shattuck, *The Oxford Guide to the Book of Common Prayer: A Worldwide Survey* (Oxford: Oxford University Press, USA, 2008), 461.http://public.eblib.com/choice/publicfullrecord.aspx?p=430580.

105 Justo L. Gonzalez, *The Early Church to the Dawn of the Reformation*. 1st ed. Vol. 1. The Story of Christianity (San Francisco, CA: Harper & Row, 1984), 63.

106Almost identical language exists in the 1979 *Book of Common Prayer* approved for use in The Episcopal Church.

107 The Anglican Church in North America, *The Book of Common Prayer* (2019). Huntington Beach, CA: Anglican Liturgy Press, 2019), 12.

108 Derek Olsen and David Cobb. *Saint Augustine's Prayer Book* Cincinnati, OH: Forward Movement, 2012): 132.

109 Papavassiliou, Vassilios, ed. *The Ancient Faith Prayer Book*. Chesterton, IN: Ancient Faith Publishing, 2014, 117.

110 The UPCUSA was merged into the PCUSA in 1983.

111 Book of Common Worship, 12.

112 Thomas Hardy, *Under the Greenwood Tree* (London: Penguin Classics, 1998), 7.

113 https://www.hopkinsmedicine.org/health/wellness-and-prevention/keep-your-brain-young-with-music

114 https://www.ox.ac.uk/research/choir-singing-improves-health-happiness-%E2%80%93-and-perfect-icebreaker

115 Salimpoor, V., Benovoy, M., Larcher, K. et al, "Anatomically Distinct Dopamine Release During Anticipation and Experience of Peak Emotion to Music," *Natural Neuroscience* 14 (2011): 257-262.

116 https://www.telegraph.co.uk/news/health/10168914/All-together-now-singing-is-good-for-your-body-and-soul.html

117 Amy Clements-Cortes, "Development and efficacy of music therapy techniques within palliative care, Complementary Theories in Clinical Practices," *Science Direct*, vol. 23, May 2016: 126-129.

118 Blundon, E. G., Gallagher, R. E., & Ward, L. M. "Electrophysiological Evidence of Preserved Hearing at the End of Life," *Scientific Reports* 10, no. 103360 (2020).

119 https://ideas.time.com/2013/08/16/singing-changes-your-brain/; https://www.youtube.com/watch?v=I_HOBr8H9EM;

120 https://www.telegraph.co.uk/news/health/10168914/All-together-now-singing-is-good-for-your-body-and-soul.html

121 https://ideas.time.com/2013/08/16/singing-changes-your-brain/

122 https://ideas.time.com/2013/08/16/singing-changes-your-brain/

123 https://ideas.time.com/2013/08/16/singing-changes-your-brain/

124 https://www.youtube.com/watch?v=I_HOBr8H9EM

125 Peterson, A Long Obedience in the Same Direction, 12.

126 John Calvin, *Commentary on the Book of Psalms*, in Calvin Commentaries, 22 vols. (Grand Rapids: Baker, 2003): 4xxxvii.

127 www.thepsalmsproject.com

128 John H. Walton, Victor H. Matthews, and Mark W. Chavalas, *The IVP Bible Background Commentary: Old Testament* (Downers Grove, IL: InterVarsity Press, 2000), 352.

129 Esau McCaulley, *Reading While Black: African American Biblical Interpretation as an Exercise in Hope* (Downer's Grove, Illinois: IVP Academic, 2020), 55.

130 https://imagejournal.org/article/a-conversation-with-jeremy-begbie/

131 Neal Krause, "Assessing the relationship among prayer expectancies, race, and self-esteem in late life," *Journal for the Scientific Study of Religion*. 2004; 65:35–56 and Cottingham, *The Spiritual Dimension: Religion, Philosophy, and Human Value* (New York: Cambridge University Press, 2005)

132 https://news.gallup.com/poll/393737/belief-god-dips-new-low.aspx

133 https://www.newsweek.com/god-listening-170460

134 https://www.worldreligionnews.com/religion-news/poll-finds-times-crisis-non-believers-turn-prayer/

135 https://catholicherald.co.uk/20-per-cent-of-non-religious-people-pray-poll-finds/

136 https://www.pewresearch.org/religion/religious-landscape-study/frequency-of-prayer/#demographic-information

137 בָּרָא, bārā , Enhanced Brown-Driver-Briggs Hebrew and English Lexicon, Logos Software

138 בָּרָא , bārā, 278a *Theological Workbook of the Old Testament*, Logos Software

139 Ronald B. Allen, *The Majesty of Man: The Dignity of Being Human* (Grand Rapids: Kregel Publications, 2000), 78–79.

140 Brown, F., Driver, S. R., & Briggs, C. A., *Enhanced Brown-Driver-Briggs Hebrew and English Lexicon* (Ox-

ford: Clarendon Press, 1977), 427.

141 Mccomiskey, T. E., 898 יָצַר, *Theological Wordbook of the Old Testament*, electronic ed, eds. R. L. Harris, G. L. Archer Jr., & B. K. Waltke (Chicago: Moody Press, 1999), 396.

142 צֶלֶם,"image" *Enhanced Brown-Driver-Briggs Hebrew and English Lexicon*, Logos Bible Software

143 HALOT, צלם: Logos Bible Software

144 Hamilton, V. P. (1999). 437 דְּמָה. R. L. Harris, G. L. Archer Jr., & B. K. Waltke (Eds.), *Theological Wordbook of the Old Testament* (electronic ed., p. 192). Chicago: Moody Press.

145 Jenni, E., & Westermann, C., *Theological Lexicon of the Old Testament* (Peabody, MA: Hendrickson Publishers, 1997), 340.

146 See John Walton's *The Lost World of Genesis One* and *The Lost World of Adam and Eve* along with Michael S. Heiser's *The Unseen Realm* for more on this.

147 Alexia Salvatierra, *Faith-Rooted Organizing: Mobilizing the Church in Service to the World* (Downers Grove, IL: InterVarsity Press, 2014), 95

148 John Calvin: *Institutes of the Christian Religion*, vol. 1 (Louisville, KY: Westminster, 1960), 43.

149 Hugh Halter. *Righteous Brood: Making the Mission of God a Family Story* (Cody, WY: 100Movements, 2023), 138–139.

150 Ibid, 138–139.

151 Henri Nouwen, *With Open Hands* (Notre Dame: Ave Marie Press, 1972) 85.

152 https://www.fdrlibrary.org/d-day

153 Butler, T. C., *Holman New Testament Commentary*, Luke vol. 3 (Nashville: Broadman & Holman Publishers, 2000), 11.

154 Brennan Manning, *Abba's Child: The Cry of the Heart for Intimate Belonging* (Colorado Springs, CO: NavPress, 2015), 6.

155 J. I. Packer and Carol Nystrom, *Praying: Finding Our Way through Duty to Delight* (Downers Grove, IL: InterVarsity Press, 2009), 157.

156 Timothy Keller, *Prayer* (New York: Penguin, 2018), 18.

157 *The Ancient Faith Prayer Book* (Chesterton, IN: Ancient Faith Publishing, 2014), 125.

158 *The Book of Common Prayer* (ACNA 2019), 665.

159 Claiborne, Shane, Jonathan Wilson-Hartgrove, and Enuma Okoro, *Common Prayer* (Grand Rapids: Zondervan, 2010), 555.

160 https://www.instagram.com/p/CdHh5rqsi86/

161 https://www.pewresearch.org/religion/2019/07/23/what-americans-know-about-religion/

162 https://www.barna.com/research/christians-say-they-do-best-at-relationships-worst-in-bible-knowledge/

163 Keener, The IVP Bible Background Commentary, 554.

164 Timothy Keller, *Counterfeit Gods: The Empty Promises of Money, Sex, and Power, and the Only Hope that Matters* (New York: Penguin Random House, 2009), 37.

165 Keener, 630.

166 Ibid, 728.

167 Horrell, Ch. 2 .

168 Andre Munzinger, *Discerning the Spirits: Theological and Ethical Hermeneutics in Paul*, Society for New Testament Studies 140 (Cambridge, UK: Cambridge University Press), 63–64.

169 "How Accurate Is the Bible? | Ken Boa," August 31, 2016, https://kenboa.org/apologetics/how-accurate-is-the-bible/.

170 Norman L. Geisler and William E. Nix, *A General Introduction to the Bible*, rev. and exp. ed. (Chicago: Moody, 1986), 367.

171 Windle, Bryan. "Top Ten Discoveries in Biblical Archaeology in 2021." *Bible Archaeology Report* (blog), December 28, 2021. https://biblearchaeologyreport.com/2021/12/28/top-ten-discoveries-in-biblical-archaeology-in-2021/

172 https://biblearchaeologyreport.com/2021/12/28/top-ten-discoveries-in-biblical-archaeology-in-2021/

173 Richard Bauckham, *Jesus and the Eyewitnesses: The Gospels as Eyewitness Testimony*, 2nd ed. (Grand Rapids: Eerdmans, 2017), 5.

174 A. N. Sherwin-White, *Roman Society and Roman Law in the New Testament* (Oxford, NY: Oxford University, 1963), 192.

175 ST101, Dr. Scott Horrell, *Bibliology: The Canon of Scripture*

176 John D. Barry and Rebecca Van Noord, "Canon, Timeline of Formation of," in *The Lexham Bible*

Dictionary, ed. John D. Barry et al. (Bellingham, WA: Lexham Press, 2016).

177 Barry and Van Noord, Ibid.

178 Barry and Van Noord, Ibid.

179 Terry Wilder, "How Did We Get the New Testament Canon?" Explore the Bible, LifeWay Christian Resources, May 22, 2014, https://explorethebible.lifeway.com/blog/adults/how-did-we-get-the-new-testament-canon/

180 https://www.centerforbibleengagement.org/research

181 Payne, J. B., 484 הָוָה., *Theological Wordbook of the Old Testament*, electronic ed, eds. R. L. Harris, G. L. Archer Jr., & B. K. Waltke (Chicago: Moody Press, 1999), 210.

182 Kittel, G., Bromiley, G. W., & Friedrich, G. (Eds.). (1964–). *Theological Dictionary of the New Testament* (electronic ed., Vol. 2). Grand Rapids, MI: Eerdmans, 344.

183 Kittel, Ibid.

184 Jenni, E., & Westermann, C., *Theological Lexicon of the Old Testament* (Peabody, MA: Hendrickson Publishers, 1997), 361

185 Dr. Horrell, Ch. 2 Veiled Glory: Trinitarian Evidences in OT.

186 Tertullian, "Adversus Praxean" chap. 5, in *The Ante-Nicene Fathers*, eds. Alexander Roberts and James Donaldson, reprint (Peabody, MA: Hendrickson, 2004), 3:600.

187 https://www.cbsnews.com/news/sanctuary-of-our-lady-of-lourdes-miracles-cures-2022-12-18/

188 Michael O'Carroll, *Trinitas: A Theological Encyclopedia of the Holy Trinity* (Wilmington: Michael Glazier, 1987), 68–70. A second Latin term, circuminsession, emphasizes the abiding reality whereas, circumincession (note the "s" versus the "c" from different roots), stresses "the dyamic circulation of Trinititarian life from each to the others." (69).

189 J. Scott Horrell, "The Trinity and Missio Dei," Ch. 14, Oral Version, Dallas Seminary Missions Conference 2006

190 C. S. Lewis, *Mere Christianity*, revised and amplified edition (New York: Harper Collins, March 2021.

191 Karl Barth, *Church Dogmatics*, vol. II, part 1, (Edinburgh, UK: T&T Clark, 1957), 642

192 Barth, 654.

193 Barth, 647.

194 CHALOT Logos Bible Software

195 L. Koehler, and W. Baumgartner, eds. Hebrew and Aramaic Lexicon of the Old Testament. Translated and edited by M. Richardson. 2 volumes. (Leiden: E. J. Brill, 2001), 457.

196 L. Koehler, and W. Baumgartner, eds. *Hebrew and Aramaic Lexicon of the Old Testament*. Translated and edited by M. Richardson. 2 volumes (Leiden: E. J. Brill, 2001), 457.

197 Barth, Church Dogmatics, vol II, 642.

198 Oswalt, J. N., 943 כָּבֵד., *Theological Wordbook of the Old Testament*, electronic ed, eds. R. L. Harris, G. L. Archer Jr., & B. K. Waltke (Chicago: Moody Press, 1999), 427

199 Brendan Thomas Sammon, The God Who is Beauty: Beauty as a Divine Name in *Thomas Aquinas and Dionysius the Areopagite*, Princeton Theological Monograph Series 206 (2013), 274.

200 Bowling, A., 1071 לֵבָב, *Theological Wordbook of the Old Testament*, electronic ed, eds. R. L. Harris, G. L. Archer Jr., & B. K. Waltke (Chicago: Moody Press, 1999), 466

201 Strong, James and John R. Kohlenberger. *The New Strong's Expanded Exhaustive Concordance of the Bible*. Red letter ed. Nashville, TN: Thomas Nelson, 2001. Strong's 3820.

202 Swanson, J., *Dictionary of Biblical Languages with Semantic Domains: Hebrew (Old Testament)*, electronic ed. (Oak Harbor: Logos Research Systems, 1997).

203 Umberto Eco, *The Aesthetics of Thomas Aquinas* (Cambridge, MA: Harvard University Press, 1988), 93.

204 Timothy Keller, *Every Good Endeavor* (New York: Penguin Random House), 29.

205 Justo L. González, *The Early Church to the Dawn of the Reformation*, 1st ed, vol. 1, of *The Story of Christianity*, San Francisco: Harper & Row, 1984, 88–98.

206 James J. Stamoolis, *Eastern Orthodox Mission Theology Today* (Eugene, OR: Wipf & Stock, 2001).

207 Bryant L. Myers, *Engaging Globalization: The Poor, Christian Mission, and Our Hyperconnected World*, Mission in Global Community (Grand Rapids, MI: Baker Academic, 2017), 120.

208 Myers, 120.

209 Richard P. Margetts, "From Scripture Access to Scripture Engagement" (master's thesis, All Nations, 2013), 113, https://scripture-engagement.org/wp-content/uploads/2020/09/Margetts-R-2013-From-Scripture-Access-to-Scripture-Engagement.pdf

210 Mark Hopkins, "MT500A: Biblical Theology of Mission (Day 2)." Colorado Springs, CO, February 3, 2016.

211 Hopkins, Ibid.
212 https://hendrickscenter.dts.edu.
213 https://voice.dts.edu/free-courses
214 https://www.taylor.edu/center-for-Scripture-engagement/
215 https://bibleengagementproject.com/
216 https://bibleproject.com/explore/how-to-read-the-bible/
217 https://www.nccih.nih.gov/health/meditation-and-mindfulness-what-you-need-to-know
218 Fredrickson, B. L., Cohn, M. A., Coffey, K. A., Pek, J., & Finkel, S. M., "Open Hearts Build Lives: Positive Emotions, Induced through Loving-Kindness Meditation, Build Consequential Personal Resources," *Journal of Personality and Social Psychology* 95, no. 5 (2008): 1045–1062
219 David S. Black, et. Al. "Mindfulness Meditation and Improvement in Sleep Quality and Daytime Impairment Among Older Adults With Sleep Disturbances A Randomized Clinical Trial," *JAMA Internal Medicine* 175.4 (2015): 494–501.
220 Estelle T. Higgins, Richard J. Davidson, William W. Busse, Danika R. Klaus, Gina T. Bednarek, Robin L. Goldman, Jane Sachs, Melissa A. Rosenkranz, "Clinically Relevant Effects of Mindfulness-Based Stress Reduction in Individuals with Asthma," *Brain, Behavior, & Immunity – Health* no. 25 (November 2022).
221 https://ascopubs.org/doi/10.1200/JCO.2015.65.7874
222 https://www.sciencedirect.com/science/article/abs/pii/S0022399909000944?via%3Dihub
223 https://www.annualreviews.org/doi/10.1146/annurev-clinpsy-021815-093423
224 Peter Toon, *Meditating as a Christian* (London: Collins, 1991) 18–19.
225 "Biblical Meditation | Bible.Org."
226 "Biblical Meditation | Bible.Org."
227 Blue Letter Bible. "H1902 - Higāyôn - Strong's Hebrew Lexicon (NIV) https://www.blueletterbible.org/search/search.cfm?Criteria=Higgaion&t=NASB95#s=s_primary_0_1
228 David W. Saxton. *God's Battle Plan for the Mind: The Puritan Practice of Biblical Meditation* (Grand Rapids, Michigan: Reformation Heritage Books, 2015), 26.
229 Blue Letter Bible. "H7878 - Śîaḥ - Strong's Hebrew Lexicon (NIV) https://www.blueletterbible.org/lexicon/h7742/kjv/wlc/0-1/
230 *Our Daily Bread*: "Private: What Is Biblical Meditation?" Our Daily Bread Ministries (blog), April 1, 2019. quoting Harman, Psalms, 99. https://ourdailybread.org/resources/what-is-biblical-meditation/
231 Strong's H1897 or Blue Letter Bible. "H1897 - Hāḡâ - Strong's Hebrew Lexicon (NIV) https://www.blueletterbible.org/lexicon/h1897/kjv/wlc/0-1/
232 Danker, Bauer, and Arndt, *A Greek-English Lexicon of the New Testament and Other Early Christian Literature* (Chicago: University of Chicago Press, 2000), 476.
233 Bill Mounce, "Λογίζομαι | Billmounce.Com." 2019
234 Bill Mounce, "Οἰκοδομή | Billmounce.Com," 2019. https://www.billmounce.com/greek-dictionary/oikodome.
235 Bread, "Private."
236 Ibid.
237 Richard J. Foster, *Celebration of Discipline: The Path to Spiritual Growth*. 20th anniversary ed., 3rd ed., rev. Ed. (San Francisco: Harper San Francisco, 1998), 15.
238 Foster, 15.
239 Foster, 17.
240 Ken Shigematsu, *God in My Everything: How an Ancient Rhythm Helps Busy People Enjoy God* (Grand Rapids, Michigan: Zondervan, 2013), 72–73.
241 Jonathan Edwards, A Divine and Supernatural Light in *Sinners in the Hands of an Angry God and other Writings* (Nashville, Thomas Nelson, 2000), 27–28.
242 Jonathan Edwards, *Works* 19:590. https://www.monergism.com/thethreshold/sdg/edwards/edwards_mandependence.html
243 Denis Janz, *Reformation Reader* (Minneapolis: Fortress Press, 1999), 81.

Appendix

Walk through the Gospel of John with Mary Carmen Englert in *Journey Through the Gospel of John*. This in-depth study uses the Seven Pathways model to help you apply each chapter of John's Gospel to your life. Below is a sample chapter taken from the study of John 3. To join our online experience or to download the digital study, please visit sevenpathways.com.

John 3: New Beginnings

1. Thanksgiving (3 min.)

Think of five things you are thankful for. What's your Five?

____

____

____

2. Silence (3 min.)
Close your eyes and focus on this concept: God is love.

3. Confession (3 min.)
Confession is not for condemnation but reconciliation. Declare to God that you wish to leave old ways behind and be reunited with Him.

4. Song (4–7 min.)
Connect with God through listening to and singing one or both of the following songs wherever you stream music.

> "Amazing Grace" by Andrea Bocelli
> "God so Loved" by We the Kingdom

5. Prayer (7 min.)

On This Day	*Pray for*
Monday	Yourself, immediate family, and one to three nonbelievers
Tuesday	Yourself, immediate family, and extended family
Wednesday	Yourself, your friends, and one to three nonbelievers
Thursday	Yourself, your church, community, leaders, and needs around the world
Friday	Yourself, immediate family, and one to three nonbelievers

Saturday	Yourself, immediate family, and extended family
Sunday	Ask the Lord how He would lead you to pray, and also pray for Christians around the world who are persecuted.

6. Scripture (15–20 min.)
Listen to or read the chapter for today in John 3.

Seeking to understand for himself who Jesus is, Nicodemus engaged Jesus in a private discussion, either not to be seen or to speak to Jesus uninterrupted. Since most of the Pharisees and members of the Sanhedrin, the ruling religious counsel, did not believe Jesus was the Messiah this meeting was politically risky. Like his peers, Nicodemus expected the Messiah to be a military and political leader who would restore Israel's power throughout the world.

Through Jesus' astonishing statement that one cannot understand the things of God without being born again, He is making clear that the requirement for citizenship in God's kingdom was not through physical birth as a Jew or converting to Judaism through various ceremonial requirements such as circumcision and then obeying religious rules but through spiritual birth. Just as no one had anything to do with their physical birth, our spiritual birth must be done for us through the cleansing work of the Spirit of God. As a teacher of Israel and member of the Jewish ruling council, Nicodemus would have been familiar with the Old Testament's future promise of the requirements to be a part of God's family and His kingdom from Ezekiel 36:24-28 concerning the cleansing work of the Spirit within a person. Nicodemus and the religious leaders did not struggle with a lack of understanding of what Jesus was saying, but instead they refused to accept the truth of His eyewitness testimony as God who came to the earth as a man, the Son of Man. In the Greco-Roman culture, eyewitness testimony was widely accepted and validated form of testimony.

Next, Jesus uses a familiar and powerful example from Israel's history to illustrate the fundamental truth of Christianity that salvation and entrance into God's kingdom cannot be achieved by trusting that your good actions will outweigh your bad but through belief in Jesus' death for your sins. Pride in your opinions or assumptions is deadly as it can blind you from the truth and separate you from your forever family in the kingdom of God. Jesus exposes the stumbling block of many religious people: following religious tradition is not the same as following Jesus.

Then John the Baptist squelched a controversy among his disciples by explaining to them his role in employing an analogy of a wedding where he is the friend of the groom and Jesus is the groom. This would have been easy for them to understand because in the Old Testament God often spoke of Israel as His bride. As the friend of the Groom, John's role was only for a season, while God's plan for salvation would be fulfilled through Jesus. Those who believe that Jesus is the Son of God will have eternal life and those who reject Him will face the judgment of God.

The question Nicodemus asked is one that every person must ask: Who is this Jesus? Like Nicodemus sometimes our opinions and assumptions about Jesus become facts to us, and they prevent us from receiving the truth. In today's culture the concept of being born again is often misunderstood and belittled. However, we can only be a part of God's family, enter heaven, and experience God's best plans and purposes for us through a relationship with Jesus. "Born again" means we receive a new nature, and this begins a process of transformation that is progressive in nature as the Holy Spirit gives us new desires, pursuits, and purposes and makes us more like Christ. John Baptist reflected this new nature when he was happy his disciples were following Jesus. Just as John's disciples implied that he should be jealous, sometimes those around us encourage self-focus and divert and distract us from God's ways.

Reflect

1. Who do you think Jesus is?
2. What does "born again" mean to you? Why is this concept hard for people to understand?
3. What is the difference between an intellectual understanding of Jesus and one that transforms your life?
4. How has following Christ been risky for you in your work or social life?

Pray

Lord, I pray for those who look like they are following the ways of Christ but have not yet believed that Jesus is the Son of God and the Savior of the world. Help them to honestly ask the question "who is this Jesus?" Let them experience a life that is transformed. Give us the strength to engage a culture that does not know You. Help us to step out in faith even when it is risky.

7. Scripture Meditation (timeframe open.)
This weeks' scriptures . . .

John 3:16-17

John 3:30

John 4:42

Thought for Today
Focus on the most important question you will ever ask: Who is Jesus?